Revitalizing a Curriculum for School-Age Learners

DAVID HAYES and
JUDY SHARKEY, EDITORS

TESOL Language Curriculum Development Series

KATHLEEN GRAVES, Series Editor

 TESOL Teachers of English to Speakers of Other Languages, Inc.

Typeset in Adobe Garamond with Frutiger Display
by Capitol Communication Systems, Inc., Crofton, Maryland USA
Printed by United Graphics, Inc., Mattoon, Illinois USA
Indexed by Pueblo Indexing and Publishing Services, Pueblo West, Colorado USA

Teachers of English to Speakers of Other Languages, Inc.
700 South Washington Street, Suite 200
Alexandria, Virginia 22314 USA
Tel 703-836-0774 • Fax 703-836-6447 • E-mail tesol@tesol.org • http://www.tesol.org/

Publishing Manager: Carol Edwards
Copy Editor: Vanessa Caceres
Additional Reader: Kelly Graham
Cover Design: Capitol Communication Systems, Inc.

ISBN 9781931185486
Library of Congress Control No. 2008924843

Contents

Series Editor's Preface

The aim of TESOL's Language Curriculum Development Series is to provide real-world examples of how a language curriculum is developed, adapted, or renewed in order to encourage readers to carry out their own curriculum innovation. Curriculum development may not be the sexiest of topics in language teaching, but it is surely one of the most vital: at its core, a curriculum is what happens among learners and teachers in classrooms.

Curriculum as a Dynamic System

In its broadest sense, a curriculum is the nexus of educational decisions, activities, and outcomes in a particular setting. As such, it is affected by explicit and implicit social expectations, educational and institutional policies and norms, teachers' beliefs and understandings, and learners' needs and goals. It is not a set of documents or a textbook, although classroom activities may be guided, governed, or hindered by such documents. Rather, it is a dynamic system. This system can be conceptualized as three interrelated processes: planning, enacting (i.e., teaching and learning), and evaluating, as depicted in the figure on p. vi.

Planning processes include

- analyzing the needs of learners, the expectations of the institution and other stakeholders, and the availability of resources
- deciding on the learning aims or goals and the steps needed to achieve them, and organizing them in a principled way
- translating the aims and steps into materials and activities

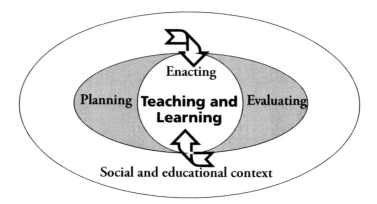

Teaching and learning processes include

- using the materials and doing the activities in the classroom
- adjusting them according to learners' needs, abilities, and interests
- learning with, about, and from each other

Evaluation processes include

- assessing learners' progress toward and achievement of the aims
- adjusting the aims in response to learners' abilities and needs
- gathering information about the effectiveness of the aims, organization, materials, and activities, and using this information in planning and teaching

These processes create a system that is at once stable, rooted in what has gone before, and evolving as it responds to change, to new ideas, and to the people involved. People plan, enact, and evaluate a curriculum.

The Series: Educators Bringing about Change

In these volumes, readers will encounter teachers, curriculum developers, and administrators from all over the world who sought to understand their learners' needs and capacities and respond to them in creative, realistic, and effective ways. The volumes focus on different ways in which curriculum is developed or renewed:

- Volume 1: Developing a new curriculum for school-age learners
- Volume 2: Planning and teaching creatively within a required curriculum for school-age learners
- Volume 3: Revitalizing a curriculum for school-age learners
- Volume 4: Developing a new course for adult learners
- Volume 5: Developing a new curriculum for adult learners
- Volume 6: Planning and teaching creatively within a required curriculum for adult learners
- Volume 7: Revitalizing an established program for adult learners

The boundaries between a program and a curriculum are blurred, as are the boundaries between a curriculum and a course. *Curriculum* is used in its broadest sense to mean planning, teaching, and evaluating a course of study (e.g., a grade two curriculum or a university writing curriculum). A *course* is a stand-alone or a specific offering within a curriculum, such as a computer literacy course for intermediate students. A *program* is all of the courses or courses of study offered in a particular institution or department, for example, the high school ESL program.

The overarching theme of these volumes is how educators bring about change. Change is rarely straightforward or simple. It requires creative thinking, collaboration, problematizing, negotiation, and reflection. It involves trial and error, setbacks and breakthroughs, and occasional tearing out of hair. It takes time. The contributors to these volumes invite you into their educational context and describe how it affects their work. They introduce you to their learners—school-age children or adults—and explain the motivation for the curriculum change. They describe what they did, how they evaluated it, and what they learned from it. They allow you to see what is, at its heart, a creative human process. In so doing, they guide the way for you as a reader to set out on the path of your own curriculum innovation and learning.

This Volume

Curriculum revitalization is a complex, multilayered, dynamic process. In this volume, teachers, teacher educators, and administrators in Canada, Chile, China, Japan, Poland, Thailand, the United Arab Emirates, and the United States describe their experiences revitalizing an existing curriculum for English language learners in primary and secondary schools. The revitalization efforts took place at the classroom, school, province/state, and national levels in response to a variety of needs, including changes initiated by the state or institution, threats to an existing program, and individual dissatisfaction with the current approach to teaching English. Collaboration with colleagues, students, parents, university mentors, or administrators resulted in professional growth for all concerned. The contributors describe their successes and challenges, the role that other stakeholders played, the obstacles they faced, and the resources they developed. In the introductory chapter, the editors explore ways in which curriculum revitalization is a form of *generative* professional development in which educators generate new practices and insights in a supportive setting, or *regenerative* professional development in which educators assert their agency and voice in curricular settings that may be disempowering or restrictive. Taken together, the chapters in this volume provide an inspiring guide for readers who wish to undertake their own curriculum revitalization.

Dedication

This series is dedicated to Marilyn Kupetz, a gifted editor, a generous mentor, and a discerning colleague. The quality of TESOL publications, including this series, is due in no small part to her vision, attention to detail, and care.

Kathleen Graves

Volume Editors' Dedication

To Carolyn

Judy Sharkey

สำหรับเจเจและต้อย ลูกและภรรยาที่รัก

รัก

เดวิด

Introduction
Revitalizing a Curriculum for School-Age Learners: A Multidirectional, Re/generative Dynamic

1

DAVID HAYES AND JUDY SHARKEY

> *revitalize:* To impart new life or vigor.
> *vitalize:* 1. To endow with life; animate. 2. To make more lively or vigorous.
> *vitality:* 1. The capacity to live, grow or develop. 2. Physical or intellectual vigor; energy. 3. The characteristic, principle or force that distinguishes living things from nonliving things. 4. Power to survive.
> *vigor:* 1. Physical or mental strength, energy or force. 2. Strong feeling; enthusiasm or intensity. Latin: vigor, from vigere, to be lively.
>
> *American Heritage Dictionary of the English Language* (1992)

This volume brings together the experiences of a diverse group of teachers and teacher educators working in a number of countries around the world: Canada, Chile, China, Japan, Poland, Thailand, the United Arab Emirates, and the United States. Their work captures curriculum processes at multiple levels (classroom, school, district, province, state, national) and involves learners from preprimary through secondary grades (ages 5 through 18 or 19 years old). The motivations to engage in these processes include dissatisfaction with current approaches, materials, or practices; changing student demographics; and responses to educational policies affecting English language education.

In all of the authors' contexts, English is taught as either a second or a foreign language. Although English as a second language (ESL) and English as a foreign language (EFL) embrace very different teaching and learning contexts, they also convey that what connects the chapters is the teaching of this language to students whose first language is not English. In a spirit of inclusiveness, it may be preferable to use a more all-encompassing term—English as a subsequent language—to unite all of the contexts and to expand the meaning of the acronym ESL. All of the authors, while writing from differing socioeducational, geographic, and economic contexts, describe how they attempted to breathe new life into, or *revitalize*, an established English language curriculum. Each chapter also reveals the commitment these teachers and teacher educators have to the power of education to transform the lives of their students. Equally exciting are the ways in which authors assert ownership of their own professional development and legitimize the role of teacher knowledge in the second language (L2) education knowledge base.

In the series preface, Graves emphasizes "curriculum as a dynamic system." With this phrase she is, of course, referring to all of the curriculum endeavours in this multivolume series, that is, developing a new curriculum and planning and teaching within an established curriculum. For this volume, it seems particularly apt to reiterate the dynamic nature of a curriculum because by revitalization the authors herein recognize that their curricula have become static, outdated, lifeless, or have slipped into the misconceived notion of curriculum as a text or document. The authors of this volume reclaim the concept of curriculum as dynamic, and in the process they themselves are revitalized. For example, as Cade in chapter 9 watches her students' rise to the challenge of a more academically rigorous curriculum level, she uses their success as a renewable source of energy for her planning and teaching processes. Indeed, a sense of vigor, liveliness, enthusiasm, and animation characterizes all the work captured in this volume.

The Multiplicity of Curriculum Revitalization

Curriculum revitalization is a complex and challenging enterprise. The sheer diversity of revitalization that takes place across the world ranges from system-wide to classroom-level activity, involves multiple stakeholders, takes multiple forms, and is facilitated through multiple vehicles. The stimulus for revitalization may be the classroom teacher who feels his or her curriculum is outmoded or inappropriate for the needs of learners in some way. For example, in China, Zhang (chapter 13) observes firsthand the disconnection between the official curriculum and the opportunities for English language use in his students' everyday lives. To redress this issue, he works through a focus on real-world tasks while conforming to the practical necessity of keeping pace with the official curriculum. Faced with similar constraints of "outdated textbooks, overcrowded classes, and lack of exposure to the language" in Polish secondary schools, Krajka (chapter 12) responds by incorporating Internet-based teaching into his regular classes.

Educators working within governmental ministries may also see inadequacies in a curriculum but feel that large-scale curriculum renewal is not the way forward or not appropriate at a particular time in the lifecycle of a national curriculum. Instead, they respond by revitalizing one element of it, as we can see in an experience in the United Arab Emirates, where Clarke and Gallagher (chapter 2) report on attempts to stimulate revitalization through changing textbooks without changing the curriculum itself.

Defining or redefining a school's identity or mission can also be the impetus for curriculum revitalization. Pressman and Ariza (chapter 7) describe how the district decision to designate their elementary school as a magnet school for the International Baccalaureate Primary Years Programme affected their school's curriculum, focusing here on the second grade. In a similar vein, Johnson and Webster (chapter 5) describe how they used cross-curricular integration to enable the staff at a charter school for English language learners in Canada to enact the school's mission to better serve their students.

Curriculum revitalization clearly can take many different forms. In Thailand, Todd, Keyuravong, and Suthidara (chapter 3) document the effects of the use of self-access centres on the revitalization of learning in secondary schools. In chapter 11, the authors show how revitalization in Chile is stimulated through participation in a ministry programme during which a group of teachers traveled to Canada for a teacher development course, giving them an opportunity to reflect on their teaching situations and devise ways to better meet the needs of their students in challenging circumstances. Working under the auspices of a school-wide reform initiative and within the supportive structure of a teacher learning community, Hawkins, Johnson, Jones, and Legler (chapter 8) share three different curriculum inquiries connected by the same goals: to recognize students' families as stakeholders in their children's education and to understand how knowledge of home practices could and should affect classroom practice.

Each chapter in this volume offers a rich description of a particular curriculum challenge; readers naturally will be drawn to those that resonate with their own contexts. For example, ESL educators working in low-incidence areas will appreciate Pierce's (chapter 4) efforts to find ways to work with teachers and administrators across a 40-square-mile (60 kilometres) area. In addition, each chapter also embodies the value of curriculum revitalization as a powerful form of professional development, a topic explored more fully in the next section.

Curriculum Revitalization as Re/generative Professional Development

Curriculum development processes and products serve many purposes, one of which is professional development. In *TESOL Quarterly*'s special 40th anniversary issue, Johnson (2006) argued that TESOL, as a professional learning community and scholarly field, needs to "redraw the boundaries of professional development" so that more professional development activities and opportunities occur in teachers' classrooms and schools:

> *Reclaiming professional development for teachers, by teachers recognizes that they have not only a right to direct their own professional development but also a responsibility to develop professionally throughout their careers. (p. 243)*

Although not the impetus for this volume, clearly a number of the chapters speak directly to Johnson's call, demonstrating the power of teacher-directed professional development that occurs on-site, is sustained over time, and is supported by administrators, colleagues, and university-based teacher educators. Thus, in addition to learning about and from the variety of curriculum challenges addressed by the authors in this volume, readers may also find new forms of professional development to pursue or initiate—whether that is through action research (e.g., Sato & Takahashi in chapter 10), teacher learning communities (e.g., Hawkins et al. in chapter 8), or collaborative classroom research with university-based teacher educators (e.g., Sharkey & Cade in chapter 9).

Curriculum revitalization is professional development that is both generative and regenerative. It is generative when it is inquiry-based and features collaboration among and with colleagues in supportive learning communities that produce new insights, practices, and professional relationships. It is regenerative when it becomes a space where educators reclaim or assert their professional knowledge and voices, particularly in response to mandates they see as questionable or contexts they see as restrictive.

Curriculum Revitalization as Generative: Learning in and Across Communities

Curriculum revitalization is a generative form of professional development when it is guided by questions raised and articulated by educators concerning specific issues in their contexts, and pursuit of these questions entails collaborating with others and presenting their work publicly (e.g., through conference presentations or publications). For example, Johnson, Jones, and Legler, three teachers at an elementary school in Wisconsin, a state in the Midwest region of the United States, wondered how to include the cultural knowledge of their ESL families into their classroom practices in ways that would support their learners' linguistic and academic development. In pursuing their question, they designed inquiries for their individual classrooms but used the structure of a teacher learning community to share their activities, processes, insights, and to ask for feedback. Their endeavours generated collective learning; by sharing their work at a TESOL 2005 presentation and in this volume, they have made a valuable contribution to the knowledge base on school–family relationships.

Although collaboration is integral to generative professional development, educators often need help to establish and foster productive collaborations in their school contexts. Fagan and Benavides (chapter 6) describe how creating a community of collaboration among ESL and non-ESL teachers and administrators at their high school laid the foundation for successful curriculum revitalization. This culture of collaboration, in turn, generated new understanding and appreciation of colleagues' work, paving the way for future collaborations.

Curriculum Revitalization as Regenerative: Teacher Voice and Agency

Curriculum revitalization is a place where the authors in this volume assert their professional voices and identities as legitimate contributors to the language teacher education knowledge base. We draw on Britzman's (1991) definition of professional voice to mean "the individual's struggle to create and fashion meaning, assert standpoints, and negotiate with others. Voice permits participation in a social world" (p. 12). Curriculum revitalization can then be viewed as a form of pedagogical activism set against the ideologically-driven policies and procedures of many centralised education systems in recent times, which all too often serve to *de-skill* teachers (Dadds, 2001) and problematically equate *accountability* (i.e., test scores) with learning (Cochran-Smith, 2004).

The situation described by Day (2000) in the United Kingdom has parallels in many other countries. He notes of government policies: "So far, four outcomes are to be seen: more work for teachers, increased stress levels, fewer attracted into teaching, and a rise in the numbers of students who are alienated by schools" (p. 110). Readers of this volume will find that the experiences described here by Kinnear et al. in particular strike a number of resonant chords, as the authors show how teachers grapple with the problems of a centralised curriculum, overcrowded classrooms, poor facilities, and demotivated students. However, even where conditions seem to be unfavourable, what shines through is the commitment of teachers worldwide to offer fulfilling educational experiences to their students.

For all educators involved in curriculum revitalization, the starting point has to be the current curriculum. No matter how much they may feel it does not meet the needs of their students, it constitutes the framework within which they must operate. Often a curriculum is centrally mandated and written into the educational law of a country, leaving teachers to feel disempowered in relation to meeting the needs of their students. The educational literature is replete with the negative consequences of teachers required to implement a centralised curriculum with minimal support from outside their schools and no pedagogical support from within it. It is hardly surprising that many adopt a "pedagogy for delivery" rather than a "pedagogy for learning" (Dadds, 2001, p. 50). Direct control of the curriculum by educational authorities is not new and in its most recent manifestation in a number of countries—performance-based politicization or the requirement to meet imposed standards and the ranking of schools vis-à-vis their success in meeting these standards, all under the guise of accountability—can be seen as a response to the curriculum autonomy that teachers had begun to exercise in their classrooms (Kelly, 1999).

However, though the stark scenario painted above of disempowered teachers working within the rigidly controlled curriculum frameworks exists in many countries worldwide, there will always be teachers who find—or create—room to revitalize their curriculum, even in the most seemingly unpropitious of circumstances. All of the chapters in this volume show how space can be negotiated, created, or even appropriated by teachers to better serve the needs of their students; and all chapters testify to the value of placing a "pedagogy for learning" at the heart of the curriculum (Dadds, 2001, p. 50). They bear witness to the truth of Fullan's (1991) dictum that: "Educational change depends on what teachers do and think—it's as simple and as complex as that" (p. 117). In the case of the teachers and teacher educators writing in this volume, there can be no doubt that their constant striving to revitalize the curriculum improves the life chances of the students in their classes and schools. To use the phrase *constant striving* recognizes that curriculum revitalization is not a one-off process but is comprised of a continual cycle of improvement, reflection, and renewal.

The quality of reflection demonstrated by the authors in this volume is consistent with Dewey's (1933, 1998) definition of reflective thinking as "active, persistent, and careful consideration of any belief or supposed form of knowledge in light of the grounds that support it and the further conclusions to which it tends" (p. 9). There are two phases in reflective thinking. The first involves a "state of doubt, hesitation, perplexity, mental difficulty, in which thinking originates," and the second involves "an act of searching, hunting, and inquiring" (p. 12). Furthermore, reflective thinking requires the willingness to "endure suspense and to undergo the trouble of searching" (p. 16). There is little doubt that these characteristics can be seen in the experiences of the contributors to this volume, whatever the setting—Wisconsin in the United States (Hawkins, Johnson, Jones, & Legler in chapter 8), Canada (Johnson & Webster in chapter 5), Japan (Sato & Takahashi in chapter 10), Poland (Krajka in chapter 12), and elsewhere. The capacity to reflect is a quality of individuals, unbounded by cultural or institutional settings.

A centralised curriculum can, of course, be very constraining, but centralisation does not *ipso facto* have to mean that the curriculum becomes a straitjacket that provides no freedom of movement for teachers. Even where there is a centralised curriculum at the national level, it is up to teachers at the local level to translate it into classroom practice, and this process often requires revitalization to meet the needs of teachers' particular groups of students. Encouragement and leeway can be given to local-level revitalization by centralised curriculum developers, who themselves recognize that a one-size-fits-all policy may be necessary to ensure uniformity of standards across a country, but that often it cannot meet the particular needs of particular groups of students, something which is best determined by the teacher with his or her local knowledge. As an example, Krajka (chapter 12) writes how in Poland the educational reform programme begun in 1999 meant that teachers became free to modify the curriculum to meet local needs, provided that their changes still fulfilled the formal requirements of the centrally mandated core curriculum and were approved by the Teachers' Board of the particular school.

Further, it is not only the curriculum that is renewed but also those who are engaged in the process. Fagan and Benavides' (chapter 6) report on the efforts of teachers and administrators in one high school in the United States to increase the academic achievement of their English language learners is infused with a sense of renewal for the staff, not just the curriculum. The same is true for Chilean teachers, as Arancibia, Hormazabal, and Soto (three of the authors in chapter 11) explain how their experiences in a Canadian seminar with Kinnear, Hill, and Pigeon-Abolins not only revitalized their curriculum, but also their professional identities. In a similar vein, Zhang (chapter 13) and Krajka (chapter 12) both demonstrate their continuing sense of professional renewal.

The notion of curriculum revitalization as regenerative professional development evokes the important distinction Cochran-Smith (2002) made between inquiry as stance and inquiry as project. The latter is typically a time-bound activity completed as a course or program requirement or it may be participation in a workshop or seminar on action research. In contrast, inquiry as stance emphasizes teacher learning as a lifelong process of posing and pursuing questions pertinent to local contexts. As Cochran-Smith argued, "Taking an inquiry stance means teachers working within inquiry communities to generate local knowledge, envision and theorize their practice, and interpret and interrogate the theory and research of others" (p. 14). If we extend this notion to *curriculum inquiry as stance*, we keep the focus on the living, dynamic nature of curriculum and teacher and student learning which, as the chapters in this volume attest, is where it primarily belongs.

Conclusion

The *TESOL Curriculum Development Series* is an invaluable contribution to the field and to the larger project of validating and legitimating the role of teachers' knowledge in the L2 knowledge base, highlighting "the complex ways in which L2 teachers come to understand their experiences through the multiple discourses . . . and . . . how teachers co-construct and use knowledge that informs their practice" (Johnson, 2006, p. 240). The chapters in this volume represent the first publication for a number of our contributors. We hope that readers are inspired by the ideas, projects, and dedication of these authors not only to reflect on and revitalize the curricula in their own classrooms, but also to see themselves as future authors and to share their experiences in future TESOL publications.

Everyone needs time for reflection, though it can be difficult to find this space in the framework of our busy daily lives. Sometimes it only opens up when we are able to leave the familiar context, transfer to a completely different one, and look at our daily experiences through a new lens. But even when this disengagement from daily realities is not available, the authors in this volume have shown that it is still possible to challenge an existing curriculum and find space to revitalize it. This challenge and revitalization empowers us as professionals. Empowerment should not be thought of necessarily as something grandiose, a challenge to established orders involving their radical reconstruction, but, rather, as "part of our inquiry into what it means to live an educational life and what conditions are educational" (Clandinin & Connelly, 1998, p. 251). This type of inquiry may yet have an impact on the social conditions of TESOL schooling in the contexts from which these chapters were created and may cause others to rethink their own curriculum stories and perhaps, upon reflection, to modify—even to transform—their everyday practices.

Curriculum revitalization entails taking risks. Risk-taking can be energising and affirming, and it can involve rejection and failure as well as acceptance and success. But one thing is certain, in the words of the Chilean proverb cited by Kinnear et al., *"Quien no se arriesga, no cruza el río"*—*"If you don't take a risk, you won't get across the river."* We hope that the risks taken by the authors in this volume, not just in their curriculum revitalization, but also in sharing the process with their worldwide colleagues, will help others across their own rivers.

Revitalizing Curriculum: A United Arab Emirates Perspective

2

MATTHEW CLARKE AND KAY GALLAGHER

Curricular change can assume many forms and can range from a complete revision of curriculum philosophy, aims, syllabi, methodology, textbooks, and resources, to a targeted area of curriculum revitalization involving partial change, such as the fine-tuning of objectives or the introduction of new teaching materials. This chapter discusses an example of the latter, involving the recent initiative of the United Arab Emirates (UAE) Ministry of Education (until 2004, called the Ministry of Education and Youth) to breathe new life into the English language curriculum through the introduction of a new coursebook.

We begin with a brief overview of the contemporary UAE before looking at the role of English. We then consider the current state of school education in this Arabian Gulf society. From these broader considerations, we narrow our focus to outline some of the issues facing English language teaching in UAE schools and the UAE English language curriculum prior to the revitalization attempt. Having set the scene, we move to the main discussion, where we outline the implementation of English language curriculum revitalization in the UAE and examine some of the ensuing tensions surrounding the process as well as some of the successes. We conclude by considering the UAE English language curriculum revitalization experience in the wider context of the challenges that face any curriculum revitalization and offer some recommendations for the future.

As teacher educators with the Higher Colleges of Technology (HCT), we prepare new generations of English language teachers for UAE schools and provide in-service professional development to established English language teachers. Our participation in these activities has allowed us to closely observe this revitalization process. Indeed, as teacher educators, our input was sought, along with that of other UAE Education and English faculties, during the process of selecting a new textbook series in 2000. We have since provided workshops to teachers on working with the new coursebook, both at the request of the Ministry of Education and on our own initiative. Throughout the chapter we refer to comments made to us during these professional development activities or during student teaching supervision sessions by teachers and student teachers who were directly impacted by the revitalization process. We also draw on our own observations in UAE schools, commentary and discussion in the local press, responses of English language school teachers to a survey conducted by the local Abu Dhabi Education Zone, and comments from an online student teacher discussion forum.[1]

The UAE

The past 30 years have witnessed the transformation of the sheikhdoms of the Arabian Gulf into some of the world's wealthiest states, dating from the massive oil boom of the 1970s. Like other oil-rich Gulf States, the UAE has gone through—and continues to experience—startling change, progress, and development in all sectors, as noted by Shihab (2001):

> *The successful implementation of human development policy in the UAE, hand in hand with industrialization, urbanization, and modernization, is one of the rare examples of a country which has successfully used income from its huge natural resources for its long-term development over a very short period. (p. 258)*

The UAE federal government has used oil revenues as an instrument for penetrating and integrating civil society through the development of physical and social infrastructure, including the education system (Kazim, 2000). For example, spending as a percentage of government expenditure has increased in the education sector from 10.4% in 1981 to 16.3% in 1995 (Benjamin, 1999), the level at which it currently remains although, according to one press announcement (Al Deen, 2005), this was set to rise to 37% in 2006. This rapid pace of development is indicative of tremendous energy and ambition, making the UAE a very exciting environment in which to work and live.

---

[1] The student teacher discussion forum is a HCT Web CT site only accessible to staff and students of the HCT.

THE LANGUAGE CONTEXT

Arabic is the official language of the UAE and indeed the only language mentioned in the constitution. Although there is no overt colonial linguistic legacy of English in the UAE, and while it has no official status, English is in effect today the *lingua franca* through which the host of resident nationalities communicate in a country that has only a mere 20% indigenous national citizens and 80% expatriates, the majority of whom are from India, Pakistan, Sri Lanka, and The Philippines. In terms of Kachru's (1997) three-circle model of the status and function of the English language around the world, the UAE at present falls somewhere within the "expanding circle" (p. 12) of countries where English has no special institutionalised status, but where the importance of English as an international language is recognized and where it is taught in government schools as a second language.

In the past 20 years, as efforts to diversify the economy away from its dependence on oil and gas have gathered pace, the UAE's trend towards ever increasing economic expansion has been given a further boost by the increasing saturation of the economy by multinational companies and the growth of consumerism. These trends, along with the surge in tourism, have led to a situation of increasing social and economic power and prestige for English. This in turn has led to concerns for the preservation of Arabic cultural and linguistic traditions in the face of what is represented and perceived as Western influence on, and encroachment into, local culture.

These concerns can be seen in the following comments from one of the new generation of Emirati teachers trained by the HCT in its English language teacher education program:

> *I'm going to study English . . . search and do that and this and then maybe apply it to my country but using Arabic. When the time will come that we're going to use the same strategy, the same implementation, the same ways, to teach Arabic. To enforce our language, when? And then maybe use English for our purpose . . . Now what I want to do is teach my students English so they can tell others that we are good human beings. (Sabah[2])*

This young teacher-in-training wishes to adopt and adapt the best from Western culture, particularly in the realm of pedagogy, but use it for local purposes, including teaching her students English so that they are able to *talk back* to Western culture. Yet the very existence of such comments highlights the fact that global English, far from being the neutral medium

---

[2] Data from student teachers come from interview and focus group transcripts and online discussion boards; pseudonyms have been used here.

of international communication as portrayed by many of its proponents, is rather, in Pennycook's terms (1994, 1995), very much a *worldly* (as opposed to merely a *world*) language, the bearer of particular, and potentially imperialist, cultural values.

Thus, the inexorable spread of the English language has been treated with apprehension in some quarters in the region. For example, in neighbouring Saudi Arabia, the local media reported that the country had "shelved a plan to introduce English language lessons to primary school-children amid fierce criticism of the proposal by the kingdom's powerful religious establishment" (Janardhan, 2002, para. 8). By contrast, the UAE's political rulers have pressed ahead with the development of English language teaching in schools and, unlike in Saudi Arabia, no agitation was evident when the Ministry of Education brought forward the commencement of English language instruction in schools from Grade 4 to Grade 1 in 1992. The following section addresses approaches to education and pedagogy in the UAE.

THE EDUCATION CONTEXT

Along with the spectacular growth of the economy, the UAE has made considerable progress in education. For example, in terms of indicators of levels such as literacy rates, less than 20% of the population was literate prior to independence in 1971, in contrast to rates of 75% for women and 70% for men by 2000 (Kazim, 2000). However, despite these successes, the UAE's education system has been severely criticized by both internal and external sources (external: Loughrey, Hughes, Bax, Magness, & Aziz, 1999; internal: Mograby, 1999; Syed, 2003; Taha-Thomure, 2003). Dr. Abdullah Mograby (1999), head of the Labour and Population Studies Department at the Emirates Centre for Strategic Studies and Research, has listed the following problems in the UAE school system:

- unclear or conflicting missions and goals closely related to problems and discrepancies in study programs and curricula
- inappropriate methods of teaching and learning
- inflexible curricula and programs which lead to high dropout rates and long duration of study (p. 299)

Criticism of the UAE school system has more recently come from the former Minister of Education himself, His Excellency Sheikh Nahayan, who sought to transform K–12 education in the same way he reformed higher education. In a country where the government uses speeches and press releases as the main vehicles to announce new initiatives, a local newspaper recently reported that "Sheikh Nahayan demanded that schools be institutions that encourage students to innovate" (Al Nowais, 2004, para. 3). According to the report, he went on to outline the following demands:

> *We want students to think creatively and not just memorize to pass exams. We want to develop their skills, and we want students to be active partners in the educational process. I am very keen on revolutionising the educational system, and teachers have a huge role in achieving this process. They have to encourage students to learn and make them love the subjects they are teaching. We want to test students differently based on a system that evaluates their skills and not what they have memorised. (para. 4–6)*

To bring about such sweeping changes will require an expanded concept of curriculum, which currently is often equated to use of a coursebook. In their evaluation of English language teaching in UAE schools,[3] Loughrey et al. (1999) noted that although an official curriculum does exist, "Most teachers and many supervisors are not familiar with any other curriculum or syllabus besides the books they use in their teaching" (p. 26). Indeed, although school coursebooks are important cultural tools by which knowledge is developed and mediated in any society, in a context such as the UAE, where the coursebook is the curriculum by default, and where there is but *one* compulsory and centrally approved coursebook for each subject used by *all* children in *all* classrooms across the country, it assumes special significance.

Issues of curriculum are part of a broader set of educational challenges faced by the UAE. As is so often the case in education across the world, school education lags behind the developments that have occurred in other spheres:

> *The public school system in the country requires a complete overhaul. Teaching standards are second rate. The UAE curriculum is outdated and weak . . . In a high-income, developing country where national human resources are limited and scarce and when a major concern for the country's sustainable development is national human development, our government's modest spending for education is baffling and worrisome. (Salama, 2005, para. 3 & 5)*

---

[3] The consultancy group from the University of Surrey, led by Loughrey, was invited to the UAE by the Ministry of Education in 1999. After producing their evaluation report, they were asked to develop a new set of objectives for the UAE English language curriculum, which they did in 2000. Neither the report nor the new curriculum objectives were acted upon or implemented.

As one example of this underresourcing, despite the UAE's image as a dynamic economic environment embracing modern technology, computers are rare in primary classrooms. Those that exist are often for teacher, rather than student, use. Moreover, according to statistics from the late 1990s, although education accounted for approximately 16% of government spending, which compared favourably with other Gulf Cooperation Council countries, it only accounted for 2% of the gross domestic product, which is low in comparison to international standards (Mograby, 1999; examples from other countries cited in Mograby include Canada, 7.6% and the United States, 6.8%). Additionally, only 1% of education spending goes into research and development, compared with 7–8% in Singapore (Mograby, 1999). Investment in school education has not kept pace with the rapid growth and development of the wider economy.

The lack of funding prioritization for school education is reflected in the current lack of systemic professional development or a career structure for teachers. Ninety-nine percent of male English teachers and 70% of female English teachers are expatriates, employed on 1-year renewable contracts. They may not have a teaching qualification, and they are paid up to 50% less than their Emirati counterparts (Ministry of Education, personal communication, June 16, 2004).

English Language Teaching in UAE Schools

The challenges faced by the educational system are also evident in the English language curriculum in UAE government schools. English language teaching—and English learning in the region in particular—has been the subject of negative portrayal in the literature. Syed's (2003) overview of the state of English language learning and teaching in the Arabian Gulf region in general, for example, presents a litany of woes: reliance on rote learning and on memorization, poor student motivation, dependence on high-stakes testing, outdated curricula and methodology, underqualified teachers, and underachieving students.

Specifically, reporting on the curriculum area of English in UAE government schools, in a report commissioned by the Ministry of Education, Loughrey et al. (1999) noted that although

the English language holds a privileged position within both the society and the education system of the UAE . . . [nevertheless,] when a representative sample of students were given a range of internationally benchmarked examinations they achieved very low grades . . . systemic underperformance stems from the interaction of critical weaknesses within the area of curriculum and textbooks, examinations, pedagogy, management, and resources. (p. 3)

A variety of reasons, including the significant underfunding and inflexible curriculum culture noted earlier as well as the requirement for teachers to have a teaching qualification with a minimum practicum component (Loughrey et al., 1999), partially explain this low achievement. Additionally, organized teacher professional development provision is scarce, and there is no career advancement structure for teachers that might encourage independent professional development, other than promotion to a principal or supervisor (inspector) position.

Prerevitalization: The *English for the Emirates* Series

The *English for the Emirates* series, first published in 1992, was developed by a local team of academics and education officials. It was used exclusively in all English language classrooms at primary and secondary level in the UAE until its recent and phased replacement by the international series, *New Parade*. Despite reservations about the textbook being equated to the curriculum, any standard, centrally mandated coursebook has the advantage of providing teachers with a systematically preplanned curriculum. Such a coursebook therefore helps standardize instruction, insofar as all students are exposed to the same target language. Furthermore, it helps provide not only a model of accurate language in a situation where teachers' own command of the target language may require support, but it also provides a source of varied activities for teachers whose repertoire may be limited by their training.

It is important to emphasise that the pedagogical and linguistic underpinnings of the *English for the Emirates* series were, in fact, commendable. This is evident in the "Introduction to the Course" contained in the teachers' book wherein it is stated, *inter alia*, that

> *Our first aim is to provide pupils with a solid grounding in the use of the English language for everyday communication . . . It is a balanced course that combines the insights of the communicative approach with the explicit teaching of functions and structures. It is eclectic . . . but with a bias towards techniques that have proved successful locally. (UAE Ministry of Education & Youth, 1998, p. 2)*

Later it is noted that, "As far as possible, pupils use language meaningfully in authentic situations, rather than simply memorising it" (p. 3). However, these laudable principles were not evident in our observations of the actual implementation of the coursebook in the classroom during school visits and teaching practice observations. There are several possible reasons for this. First, we observed no evidence of the teacher's book actually present in the hands of teachers. Furthermore, the teachers we spoke to were not aware of the series' underlying principles, suggesting that there had been inadequate professional development offered to them when the *English for the Emirates* series was originally introduced in 1992. Second, the accompanying range of materials for teachers for the coursebook, as described in the *English Language Document for Basic and Secondary Education* produced by the UAE Ministry of Education and Youth in 1994, were not present in the many classrooms that we visited. It seemed that the stated intention of supplying a Teacher's Pack containing wall charts and flashcards, a teacher's book, and audio and video cassettes for *English for the Emirates* had not been realised. Nor had the teachers that we observed created the so-called *magic bags* of objects and models of objects that the curriculum document required them to provide from their own resources (UAE Ministry of Education and Youth, 1994, pp. 40–44). Third, the highlighting and decontextualisation of isolated lexical items in the pupils' books mitigated against the principles of meaningful use of language in authentic situations that the series' authors espoused.

Although the *English for the Emirates* textbook series had a number of far-reaching aims, including a communicative orientation and a view of the teacher as a mediating adult, these pedagogical ambitions were unfortunately undermined by shortcomings in the series. Critically, there was no specific statement of language objectives for each lesson or unit beyond itemizing vocabulary, and these items were not always selected to facilitate the forming of semantic schemata (e.g., *use, wonderful, large,* and *agree,* in Unit 2, Lesson 6 of Grade 6). Additionally, the *English for the Emirates* coursebooks provided little cognitive challenge for learners. The new generation of Emirati teachers and student teachers trained by the HCT were openly critical of the former coursebook. "Some of the lessons don't make sense," one student teacher complained during a teaching practice placement. "Sometimes you'll find that the topic's one thing, and then the lesson will just jump to something else. It's not well sequenced. Students learn some new vocabulary in second or third grade, but then you find that it's introduced as new vocabulary again in Grade 4" (Haifa). Another complained that it's "a very simple book that contains no challenge; it focuses on memorising words only and has nothing to do with trying to improve skills" (Halima).

The Process of Revitalizing the UAE English Language Curriculum

In November 2000, the UAE Ministry of Education convened a team to review commercially available English language textbooks as potential replacements for the domestically produced *English for the Emirates* series. The Ministry requested the involvement of representatives from institutes of higher education in the Emirates, including the United Arab Emirates University; Zayed University; and our own institution, the HCT, as part of this review process. Although teachers from the Ministry of Education were not involved in the review and selection process, zone supervisors from the UAE Ministry of Education's Inspectorate represented the UAE classroom perspective.

To facilitate the coursebook evaluation process, the Ministry of Education provided a selection sheet with criteria in different categories against which to evaluate each series. The evaluation criteria included a number of relevant factors such as

- quality and brightness of the illustrations
- layout (ideally, generous with uncluttered pages)
- introduction of new language in small chunks
- inclusion of developmentally appropriate songs, games, and stories
- presence of culturally appropriate content and illustrations
- provision of a student workbook

However, important criteria for language coursebook selection that were not considered included, for example,

- provision of opportunities for real language use
- capacity for flexibility and responsiveness to learners' needs
- integrated revision of key language
- inclusion of authentic materials, such as audio tapes with a variety of accents
- balance of activities across the four language skills areas
- integration of assessment with curriculum content (for more complete criteria for coursebook evaluation, see Halliwell, 1992, pp. 114–15; and Richards, 2001, pp. 256–59)

After 2 weeks of reviewing samples from a range of publishers, the group reviewing books for the elementary years were unanimously in favour of the Longman *New Parade* series (Herrera & Zanatta, 2001), which was developed by a diverse team of experienced international language teachers and teacher educators. The reasons for this selection included

- the series' clear thematic focus
- the developmental appropriateness of its themes and the suggested teaching activities
- its integration of language teaching with other curriculum areas
- its emphasis on multiple intelligences
- its focus on communicative functions
- its provision of suggestions for learning strategies
- its flexibility in terms of sequence and selection of classroom activities

The series also included pupils' books; workbooks; supplementary resources such as stories and tapes; and a comprehensive teacher's book that explained the philosophy underpinning the series, provided a rationale for particular activities, and offered suggestions as to how to implement particular units in the classroom. It thus promised to provide a much fuller resource for effective language learning and teaching in schools than afforded by the former textbook. Table 1 provides a summary comparison between the two textbook series.

Given the perceived gap between the *New Parade* series and *English for the Emirates*, it was clear to the reviewers that the UAE Ministry of Education would need to provide comprehensive professional development to teachers for them to successfully implement the new textbooks. The publishers offered some professional development for teachers as part of the purchase deal, but this was inadequate in light of the significant differences between the new and old textbooks. Certainly, the reviewers, many of whom were UAE-based language teacher educators, had no involvement in identifying, organizing, or delivering any professional development; in fact, contact with the Ministry of Education regarding the *New Parade* series ceased upon delivery of their initial reports.

Table 1. Pedagogical and Linguistic Assumptions Apparent in *English for the Emirates* and *New Parade*

English for the Emirates	*New Parade*
Individual disconnected lessons	Thematic units of connected lessons
Lexis as discrete items of language	Lexis as connected chunks of language
Scope and sequence not discernible	Discernible scope and sequence
Language objectives not discernible	Discernible language objectives
Low cognitive challenge for learners	Higher cognitive challenge for learners
Language as something to be memorized	Language as something to be used
Culturally relevant	Not culturally relevant

Overall, it is important to note that *New Parade* was the first international textbook ever to be introduced in the government school system, which had until then only used local Ministry of Education-produced textbooks for all subjects at *all* levels of primary and secondary education. This was a groundbreaking development for the Ministry of Education. See Figure 1 for a sample page from *New Parade*.

IMPLEMENTING THE REVITALIZATION

When it came to the implementation of *New Parade*, the Ministry ran a pilot in two of the seven Emirates in 2001 before introducing the new series across the country the following year. Feedback from the initial pilot was mixed, with concerns focused on the cultural inappropriateness of some of the material, the perceived lack of structure within the thematic units, and the lack of time to adequately cover the material. The latter concern reflects the wider classroom culture in the UAE, where all teachers are expected to cover the same material over a given period. Despite these concerns, the implementation went ahead, and the series was introduced for Grade 1 in the first year of nationwide implementation, for Grades 1

Figure 1. Sample Page From *New Parade*

and 2 the following year, and so on. After working with the pilot program for 4 years, we are in a reasonably strong position to evaluate the impact of the attempted revitalization of the UAE English language curriculum through the introduction of the *New Parade* series. Although challenges remain, there have been some significant improvements brought about by the revitalization.

CURRICULAR RESISTANCE

Designers of educational change often focus on the product and ignore the process of change (Fullan, 2001). As a result, those who are required to implement change are unprepared for, and consequently resistant to, new approaches. Another factor impeding meaningful change is the failure to fully recognize its complexity and the consequent tendency to adopt a piecemeal approach to reform and revitalization (e.g., addressing curriculum but not assessment). We now discuss these issues in relation to the UAE's English curriculum revitalization initiative.

Curricular Resistance: Product Over Process

In introducing the *New Parade* series, the Ministry of Education conformed to the tendency noted by Fullan (2001) to underestimate the time and effort needed for meaningful preparation and implementation of curricular change. If change is to be successful, teachers need to change their beliefs and take some degree of ownership of the change. Such ownership can be facilitated through strategic processes including an initial needs analysis to assess teachers' current beliefs; extended dialogues on how the change will impact learning objectives, teaching methods, and assessment practices; and an evaluation process to ensure that ongoing issues and concerns are identified and addressed. This all takes time. Merely introducing the product of innovation or revitalization—in this case the new textbook series—is insufficient. In contrast, in preparation for the introduction of *New Parade*, the teachers had been provided with only two orientation workshops on the series; understandably, they felt that this had been somewhat inadequate, given the very different approach to and assumptions about language teaching embodied in *New Parade* (see Table 1). As teacher educators closely involved in preservice and in-service teacher education in the UAE, an insightful comment from one teacher confirmed our perceptions of the inadequacy of the piecemeal approach to the introduction of the international textbook series: "The problem is not with the textbook itself, but with the way the textbook is implemented. In the absence of an adequate vision and implementation [plan], any textbook will produce the same learning outcome." The teacher was surveyed by Abu Dhabi Education Zone in 2005.

The teachers also complained in their feedback on the introduction of the new series that the teacher's guide and accompanying audiovisual aids were not made available to them and that the language level of the new series was beyond the ability levels of pupils. Overall, however, the cultural inappropriateness of the new series was the most commonly raised issue: "It doesn't contribute to the development of students' sense of identity . . . or to their knowledge and understanding of their spiritual, moral, social, and cultural heritage" was one teacher's comment, and another noted that there is "almost nothing about UAE local culture and daily life."

All of the pedagogical and linguistic assumptions underpinning *New Parade* (see Table 1) were new concepts for the teachers. This issue led many schools to approach the HCT for professional development to assist them to prepare for and deliver the new curriculum. Thus, for example, although the series encourages teachers to plan and think in terms of the broad thematic unit implemented over a number of weeks, many teachers that we have worked with viewed the individual daily lesson as the core unit. This means that rather than taking the time to engage students in developmentally appropriate activities related to the theme—such as making a model of a house in the thematic unit "At Home" to provide a meaningful context for new vocabulary—teachers focus primarily on getting through a set amount of the textbook in each lesson. Thus, the recommendations of Loughrey et al. (1999) to "allow for realistic time to be devoted to practice and assimilation" and to "increase exposure to authentic language use," as well as "the provision of greater opportunities for student self-learning" (p. 60), remain unfulfilled.

Overall, the lack of adequate professional development to prepare teachers for working with the *New Parade* series has diminished the potential impact of the revitalization. Because teachers have not had access to the curricular assumptions of *New Parade* and how they differ from those in *English for the Emirates*, the majority continue to teach from *New Parade* using the same approaches and activities they employed when working with *English for the Emirates*.

Curricular Resistance: The Need to Align Curriculum and Assessment

The English Language Teaching in the UAE: Evaluation Report (Loughrey et al., 1999), referred to previously and written prior to the supplanting of the local series by *New Parade*, critiqued assessment practices in schools as exercising a profoundly negative backwash effect on the learning and teaching of English:

> *It actually discourages the acquisition of the English language skills that are needed by students in order either to study at tertiary level or to*

take up employment where English is required . . . The impact of tests was huge and damaging. Teachers and pupils are pressurized into a test mentality in which language practice and assimilation are sacrificed for memorization. (p. 52)

Unfortunately, since the introduction of *New Parade,* there has been little evidence of an associated change in the *memorize-then-test* approach to assessment. The system has yet to make the paradigm shift from a "testing and examination culture to an assessment culture" (Gipps, 1994, p. 1). The assessment of language learning in schools remains based, as indeed it is in many other countries around the world, on summative teacher-devised or ministry-devised unit tests and quizzes that depend on memorisation of language by learners; language that is then produced in isolation for the purposes of the test—in other words, assessment *of* learning rather than assessment *for* learning (Black, Harrison, Lee, Marshall, & Wiliam, 2003). More formative approaches to assessment (e.g., teacher-maintained running records, teacher observations, teacher checklists, student writing portfolios) that are embedded in day-to-day learning and teaching have not been seen in the classrooms we have visited. In addition, the assessment of speaking skills remains underdeveloped, and we have seen no criteria by which speaking is assessed. Although the question of assessment in schools is not itself directly related to the change of textbook, the value of embedding assessment in day-to-day learning and teaching has yet to be recognized. This deficit is indicative of the view in which the curriculum is equated merely to the textbook and where assessment is disconnected from learning and teaching. To change such perceptions would, of course, necessitate large-scale professional development.

Such tendencies are by no means unique to the UAE. In the United States, for example, Tharp and Gallimore (1988, p. 14) commented despairingly on the predominance of "the recitation script" characterized by surface learning and the dominance of an assessment culture of quizzes and tests. This is indeed unfortunate, for assessment is increasingly recognized as a powerful tool to promote effective learning (Black et al., 2003; Black & Wiliam, 1998; Wiggins, 1998), but to be effective it must be integrated within the curriculum and not divorced from it as a disconnected summative activity.

CURRICULAR REVITALIZATION

There also have been a number of positive outcomes flowing from the UAE Ministry of Education's initiative to revitalize the English language curriculum through the introduction of the *New Parade* series. One of the improvements we discuss is a consequence of the pedagogical scope and structure of the new curriculum series. The other resulted from a parallel development in UAE education in the form of the preparation of a new generation of student teachers for whom the introduction of the new series was a timely bonus.

Curricular Revitalization: Lexical Range

One discernible improvement in students' English language learning that can be attributed to the new international series is the exposure it affords young learners to a much wider range of lexis than before. As Cameron (2001, p. 90) points out, children's worlds today are bigger than ever before because of the cognitive stimulation they get from interaction with multimedia such as television, the Internet, and computer games. This is as true for children in the UAE today as it is for children all over the developed world—therefore, children may well be able to absorb a much more extensive repertoire of lexical input than coursebooks have traditionally expected of them. The surge in the range of vocabulary input afforded by the new coursebook becomes clear when one compares a vocabulary-focused lesson that was observed by the authors some years ago in a third-grade English language classroom, with a vocabulary-focused lesson observed more recently in a Grade 2 classroom.

The lesson we observed some 5 years ago, based on the old *English for the Emirates* textbook, focused on four disconnected and decontextualised lexical items that were highlighted at the top of the page: *right, left, up,* and *tail*. This lesson was typical of a tendency that had been previously observed in many other English language classrooms at that time, that is, to overteach a few isolated lexical items, limiting students to a narrow range of individual words, and teaching these words over and over again, long after students knew them. The limited lexical range of the *English for the Emirates* series fostered this approach. By contrast, the lesson that was observed some 4 years later based on *New Parade* showed a greatly expanded range of lexis and lexical collocations being successfully acquired in a Grade 2 classroom, where young learners were observed confidently using meaningful chunks of language for real communication such as "slices of tomatoes" and "a carton of yoghurt" (see Figure 1). Of all developments in applied linguistics during the past few decades, the new insights into the central role of vocabulary in language learning and teaching have been among the most invigorating (Cameron, 2001; Lewis, 1993, 1997, 2000; Nation, 1990; Sinclair, 1991).

Curricular Revitalization: A New Generation of Teachers

One group of key stakeholders who welcomed the introduction of the *New Parade* series to replace *English for the Emirates* were the student teachers with whom we work and who represent the future of English language teaching in the UAE. This new generation rejects a classroom culture that is dominated by the textbook, adhering instead to a learner-centered approach. This is exemplified in their practice, where student teachers and graduates have implemented a theme-based approach built around topics that provide meaningful integration across a series of lessons, as well as in comments from student teachers who advocate a student-centered rather than a textbook-centered curriculum: "I strongly believe that we must begin teaching where learners are" (Azza). Another student listed a number of perceived shortcomings of English teaching in UAE schools, which began with the dominance of the textbook: "Relying heavily on the coursebook as only the syllabus to be used and ignoring the students' needs and interests and without adapting. No flexibility is given to the teachers. No time is provided to expand on things" (Manal). By adopting a thematic approach to their teaching, the new generation of teachers is able to link language with content and activities and to recycle key language items over an extended period of time, using a variety of learning activities linked to a common theme.[4] The *New Parade* series is intended to support this theme-based approach. The new generation of teachers' preference for learner-centered approaches and rejection of traditional, teacher-centered or textbook-centered approaches is part of the discursive construction of the *new* UAE teacher (Clarke, 2006).

Cultural Issues

We touched earlier on the issue of language and culture and the complex local attitudes towards global English. In this context, it is worth noting that there were some ripples of sociocultural tension in UAE schools upon the arrival in classrooms of the new international textbook, which was feared by some to be a Trojan horse for foreign cultural influences. Despite the inclusion of cultural appropriateness of content as a textbook selection criterion by the Ministry of Education, questions were raised about the cultural appropriateness of the *New Parade* series. Questions were raised in the local press as to whether a foreign curriculum, in conflict with the country's culture and heritage, was being imposed; while school teachers were said to object to the series on the grounds that the new book used foreign names and images, whereas the old book contained Arabic names and pictures of teachers wearing national dress. Furthermore, critics noted that instead of reinforcing local values, such as showing youngsters accompanying the

---

[4] Examples of curricular themes used by the student teachers include The Ship of the Desert (a reference to the camel), a theme exploring the UAE desert environment, and traditions of the local Bedouin culture through a series of linked language learning activities and lessons.

elderly to the mosque, the children in the new textbook are seen playing and singing.

However, an anonymous official in the Ministry of Education refuted these allegations and was quoted in the same article as responding that it is not possible to teach an English language course containing Arabic names and customs only because "language and culture are inseparable." The new international series was also warmly welcomed by the new generation of Emirati teachers of English in schools, who much preferred *New Parade* for the pedagogical and linguistic strengths noted earlier. Nevertheless, they were also very keen that the content be made more relevant to the local culture:

> *It is clear that there is a big gap between the culture of the characters in* New Parade *and the culture of the students. All of this means that the Ministry of Education had to think carefully before deciding on a suitable coursebook for [English as a foreign language] students. It could adapt the way* New Parade *is taught and then design the coursebook so that it would be appropriate for students in the UAE. (Nashita)*

Unfortunately, the predominant one-size-fits-all approach in global English language textbook publishing entails the exclusion of the local (Gray, 2002) although, of course, it is always possible to complement the coursebook with more culturally attuned supplementary resources. Although the publishers have recently produced a version of *New Parade* entitled *UAE Parade,* the content, characters, and illustrations remain the same as the international books, with the putative element of localisation confined only to the window dressing of the front cover title. Yet there are examples of countries such as Spain and Italy with a sufficiently large market, commissioning textbooks with a "glocal" (global + local: Robertson, 1995, p. 28) flavour that recognize global and local pressures and priorities; alternatively, publishers can produce coursebook series that agglomerate countries in a region to viably provide a more culturally sensitive product (Gray, 2002). The consequent issues are compounded by the lack of provision of supplementary classroom materials that might enable teachers to infuse the international series with local culture. Interestingly, the Ministry of Education chose the U.S. English version of the series rather than the United Kingdom version, mirroring a shift in other spheres away from the former dominance of the United Kingdom in the region and perhaps echoing arguments that globalisation fundamentally means Americanisation (Bourdieu, as cited in Phillipson, 2004, p. 79).

Overall, the issues we have encountered in the preceding discussion of various aspects of curricular revitalization in the UAE reflect the many and complex challenges of revitalization in any context. To shed further light on the experience of curricular revitalization in the UAE, we briefly discuss some of these challenges.

The Challenges of Revitalization

One commentator has noted that the curriculum process can be described as something that "combines *given* knowledge and societal conditions with the anticipation of future societal states in general and future forms of education in particular" (Rosenmund, 2000, p. 600, emphasis in original). Curriculum revitalization thus requires dialogue with key stakeholders to achieve at least some degree of consensus and commitment to a vision of the future, as well as to the implications of this vision for current practice. Ideally, curriculum revitalization needs to involve all key stakeholders—students, teachers, parents, principals, teacher education providers, and other education officials—in the cyclical stages of planning, implementation, continuation, and evaluation, but rarely is this ideal scenario enacted in practice (Fullan, 2001). As we have seen, both the range of stakeholders involved and the extent of the revitalization process were limited in the introduction of the *New Parade* series into UAE schools. Building the perspectives of such key stakeholders into a more extended and enriched revision cycle would be one way the UAE Ministry of Education could improve the likely success of any future curriculum change.

Instead, as is so often the case elsewhere, the revitalization in this instance was planned without realisation of the need for an overall vision and consultation with all key stakeholders. This resulted in a situation where objectively and subjectively, the revitalisation had quite different and even incompatible meanings; for curriculum developers, *New Parade* represented an attempt to introduce more up-to-date pedagogical approaches into English language teaching in UAE schools whereas for many teachers, it was seen as just another textbook to be incorporated within existing teaching approaches.

Such disparate perceptions may result in an attempted revitalization being ignored, or worse, undermined by those intended to implement them; we saw this with the teachers who continued to teach with *New Parade* in the same way they had always taught with *English for the Emirates*. However, curricular revitalization may also change attitudes and practices in unintended ways as we saw with the new generation of student teachers, and this may influence the eventual outcome of the innovation; in this case, the student teachers' positive response may help embed the revitalization. The implication of all this, as previously noted, is that prior to initiation and implementation of any innovation, there needs to be extensive consultation and dialogue among stakeholders to clarify visions, consolidate perceptions, and achieve consensus on the rationale for, and processes of, change. Indeed, we can note that the success of the attempted revitalization of the UAE English language curriculum would have been greater had the following factors been fully addressed:

- recognition of the multiplicity of factors involved in effective curriculum revitalization
- involvement of key stakeholders, particularly teachers, to identify the problems underlying the need for revitalization and in the selection of new curricular materials to revitalize the curriculum
- wide communication of the purposes and processes of curriculum revitalization
- provision of adequate professional development to assist teachers in understanding the curriculum revitalization

This array of factors echoes Fullan's remark that "solving today's educational problem is complex; it *is* rocket science" (2001, p. 101, emphasis in original). It is also consonant with our observations of the *English Language Teaching in the UAE: Evaluation Report*: "Poor levels of student achievement do not seem to stem from any single overriding cause" (Loughrey et al., 1999, pp. 3 & 38). The aforementioned factors, and in particular, engaging teachers in dialogue and providing them with needs-based professional development, offer a roadmap for the UAE Ministry of Education in the coming years to enhance the benefits already gained from the revitalization of the English language curriculum through the introduction of the new textbook series.

Conclusion

In this chapter, we have described how, in response to recognized inadequacies in English language teaching in schools, the UAE Ministry of Education attempted to revitalize the curriculum through the replacement of the indigenously produced *English for the Emirates* series with the international *New Parade* series without changing the official curriculum itself. We noted how this curriculum revitalization attempt focused on only one of the complex array of factors comprising curriculum, that is, the textbook, omitting key aspects such as a needs analysis, assessment practices, teaching methods, learning objectives, or an evaluation process. We also noted how key stakeholders, that is, the teachers, were not consulted in this revitalization process and how they were not provided with the crucial professional development that would have enabled them to effectively revitalize the curriculum through the new textbook series.

As we have seen, the consequences of this revitalization process have been mixed. There has been some predictable resistance and confusion on the part of the teachers in UAE schools but also some improvements in classroom practice, for example, in the area of vocabulary teaching. We also have seen how the parallel development of a new generation of teachers, whose training aligns with the assumptions of the new textbook series, has been a fortuitous benefit that the Ministry of Education probably did not anticipate in planning the revitalization of the UAE English language curriculum.

The overall lessons from the UAE experience are not revolutionary; rather, they are resonant of the challenges of innovation and change in language education all over the world (Rea-Dickens & Germaine, 1998). To achieve maximum impact, curriculum revitalization needs to be conceptualized in terms of a full cycle from needs evaluation to implementation and evaluation; it needs to incorporate a broad notion of curriculum including teaching materials, teaching methods, classroom materials, and assessment, all of which need to be meaningful and relevant to the lives of learners; and, most critically, it needs to involve all key stakeholders, particularly teachers, at all these stages and in relation to each of these aspects. Addressing this complex and challenging set of issues more comprehensively would enable the UAE Ministry of Education to build on the positive step taken by the introduction of *New Parade* and to realize fully the revitalisation of English language teaching in the UAE.

In this chapter, we have described a groundbreaking introduction into the Emirati state school system—the use of an international coursebook. Since then, the pace of curricular change in the K–12 state school system has gathered momentum, and international educators from Anglophone countries, including Canada, Australia, the United States, and the United Kingdom are now managing and teaching in state schools, where they are introducing a whole range of international curricular materials and coursebooks. Our chapter has examined a critical early initiative in this wave of revitalisation and identifies some of the challenges current and future curricular changes are likely to face.

High Hopes for Self-Access Learning at Two Secondary Schools in Thailand

3

RICHARD WATSON TODD, SONTHIDA KEYURAVONG,
AND KULLAKAN SUTHIDARA

In this chapter, we examine how the establishment of self-access centers at two secondary schools in Thailand has affected classroom teaching and the curriculum. Self-access is an approach to language learning that usually involves the establishment of a self-access center, or a place where "students can select and work on tasks on their own and obtain feedback on their performance" (Sheerin, 1991, p. 143). To do this, a suitable location and appropriate facilities must be allocated, learning materials appropriate for independent learning should be provided along with relevant equipment such as computers, systems to manage and organize the center need to be set up, teachers must be trained, and students need to learn how to maximize the use of self-access centers' resources (Gardner & Miller, 1999; Rost, 2002).

The Motivation for Change

A self-access center can provide an effective and individualized way to supplement classroom learning. More importantly, the availability of self-access learning can actually change classroom teaching practice, especially in terms of a more autonomy-focused teaching philosophy and a greater focus on skills and strategies in the classroom (Moore & Reinders, 2003). The introduction of self-access learning into a school can, therefore, have a revitalizing effect on classroom teaching and the curriculum within that school.

The provision of self-access learning facilities in schools in Thailand follows general legislation governing education. In 1999, the National Education Act was promulgated. Amid the legislation about educational administration, the Act contains sections that provide progressive guidelines for developing the curriculum. For example, Section 24 of the National Education Act concerns the nature of the learning process and requires educational institutions to "provide substance and arrange activities in line with the learners' interests and aptitudes, bearing in mind individual differences" and "enable individuals to learn at all times and in all places," alongside other laudable goals (Office of the National Education Commission, 1999, p. 11). Education in Thailand, therefore, has a solid foundation for progressive learning-oriented practice, and the law provides a clear motivation for schools and teachers to follow this kind of learning.

There is, however, a yawning gap between the ideals of the National Education Act and the reality of teaching and learning, particularly in secondary schools. For several years now, the Ministry of Education has pushed for secondary education to be more learner-centered, with few signs of success. Reliance on ineffectual top-down strategies to manage change and general educational inertia have meant that, in most schools, lecturing still dominates, memorizing and rote learning are still rewarded with good grades, and English lessons are still conducted primarily in Thai (Watson Todd, 2001). In those few schools that have switched to a learner-centered curriculum, the practice often falls short of the ideal, with students complaining that teachers do not understand a learner-centered approach and that they simply assign students long reports to write outside of class (Bunnag, 2000). If any real change toward a learner-centered approach is to occur, it is apparent that more than hopeful directives are needed.

Although very few schools could be considered successful in their efforts to implement learner-centered education, some key Ministry of Education initiatives suggest a more promising future (Wiriyachitra, 2002). Of particular relevance to this chapter is a new Basic Education Curriculum based on standards (in contrast to the previous model that just dictated which textbooks should be used in classrooms). This new curriculum allows teachers far more freedom in their teaching than previously and, for English language teaching, states that learners should be encouraged to "engage in self-directed learning" (Ministry of Education [Bangkok], 2001, p. 2). Although promising, these initiatives still rely on hopeful top-down directives for change.

The stress on self-directed learning in the curriculum, however, has led to one major concrete initiative that holds real promise to change English education in Thailand. As part of a World Bank-funded project to improve secondary education in Thailand, self-access centers, called Student English

Access Rooms (SEARs), were established at 80 schools throughout the country. For these schools, there is a hope that these centers can be a catalyst for a move toward learner-centeredness and lead to a much-needed revitalization of English teaching and learning. In this chapter, we examine how the SEARs project was implemented at two schools and the effects of the SEARs on English teaching and learning to see if this project can fulfill its promise of revitalizing English education at secondary schools in Thailand.

Within the SEARs project, rooms for the self-access centers were assigned at each school, furniture was provided, extensive teacher training was given at three points in the project, and self-access materials were provided (for full details of the project, see Watson Todd, 2005). The materials for the SEARs, in both paper-based and electronic formats, consisted of published materials appropriate for self-access use and materials specifically designed for secondary self-access contexts in Thailand. The SEARs opened in June 2004 and had been in operation for more than a year when we began to investigate their impact on classroom teaching.

All three authors of this chapter have been involved in the SEARs project, albeit not in the role of secondary school teachers who implement self-access learning. The first author (Watson Todd) acted as a consultant throughout the project and thus was involved in many of the decisions concerning teacher training, resources for SEARs, and project monitoring. The second author (Keyuravong) was one of the principal designers of the project's self-access materials. The third author (Suthidara) conducted an initial evaluation of the effectiveness of the self-access support systems in SEARs.

Although the initial evaluation of the self-access support systems showed that the organization of the SEARs had little effect on students, we also were interested in the long-term effects of the SEARs. When the Ministry of Education apparently decided to end support for the project following a government decision to stop accepting World Bank funding, we were worried that all the good work and effort put into the SEARs would go to waste. Given the potential promise of the SEARs, we were concerned that, without Ministry of Education support, schools and teachers would be unable to continue to develop their SEARs, and that the centers would undergo a steady deterioration and have little or no wider impact on the curriculum and teaching and learning in the school. However, there was a chance that the SEARs could fulfill their potential to revitalize the curriculum and lead to a genuine shift toward learner-centeredness. From our initial involvement in the project, then, we were interested in following up on the SEARs to examine how they were implemented and their wider impact.

This chapter examines the effects on the curriculum and classroom teaching of additional learning facilities in the form of a self-access center.

With pressure from government legislation and Ministry of Education directives to develop more learner-centered teaching, with more freedom for teachers to implement changes due to the standards-based Basic Education Curriculum, and with the potential impacts of a self-access center on classroom teaching and learning, the situation in the two schools examined is one ripe for curriculum revitalization and teaching development.

Curricular Context

The two schools analyzed in this study are both provincial secondary schools in the central plains of Thailand. They were selected because they are easily accessible and represent typical provincial secondary schools in this area of Thailand. Both are government-funded and cater to children within the province. The Pakklang School has 650 students in the last 3 years of secondary education for whom the SEAR is provided (equivalent to U.S. Grades 10–12); Nakhao School is larger, with 1,320 students (pseudonyms have been used for the school names). Similarly, the English language departments are also different, with 10 Thai and 2 native-English-speaking (NES) teachers at the Pakklang School and 16 Thai and 4 NES teachers at the Nakhao School. In both schools, the Thai teachers were fully responsible for the SEARs because a high turnover of NES teachers meant that they could only play a minor role in the departments.

The curricula at both schools are fairly traditional. English courses, offered 3 hours per week in the timetable, follow a coursebook chosen to meet the Ministry of Education standards. Generally, the Thai teachers simply teach the coursebook for 2 hours a week, focusing largely on grammar and vocabulary, with the third hour taught by a NES teacher to cover speaking skills. Evaluation is conducted through a mix of continuous assessment based on homework and traditional multiple-choice examinations.

One key difference between the two schools, however, is that Nakhao School already had set up a self-access center about 4 years before the SEARs project, when two teachers from the school were sent to the United Kingdom for training in self-access. On their return, one was assigned to set up a self-access center, in addition to her normal teaching workload. She was expected to provide books and worksheets for the students, but only a few students were permitted to use this self-access center. With a general lack of materials and restricted use, the center was not a success and had almost no effect on the teaching and learning of English at the school. When the SEAR was established, the limited materials and equipment from this previous self-access center were incorporated into the SEAR.

The principals at both schools were sympathetic toward and supportive of the SEARs project, so there were no problems in assigning rooms, setting them up, or obtaining other staff members' cooperation. In both schools, after an initial period of all staff working together to set up the SEAR, two teachers took primary responsibility for its operation.

The SEARs at both schools have similar resources. Both were provided with tables, chairs, and shelves, and both received around 150 published books and 12 sets of computer software. Both schools also received 192 sets of materials specifically designed for Thai secondary self-access, each set covering 1 hour of use. In addition, each SEAR contains multiple copies of self-access support materials such as generic worksheets and learner contracts (examples of these can be found at http://arts.kmutt.ac.th/SEARs /Workshop.htm). Because of procurement problems, the computers and other equipment expected never arrived. In both schools, however, the school directors ensured that some computers were allocated to the SEAR, five in the case of Pakklang School but only two workable computers in the case of Nakhao School. A difference between the two SEARs is that although the SEAR at the Nakhao School consists of one large room, two rooms at the Pakklang School are used for the SEAR, one of which also acts as a classroom. Table 1 summarizes the situations in the two schools.

From Table 1, we can see that, with the exception of computers, the

Table 1. SEARs Context at Two Schools

Factor	Nakhao School	Pakklang School
Students	1,320 students in Grades M4–M6 (U.S. Grades 10–12)	650 students in Grades M4–M6
Staff	20 English teachers: 16 Thai and 4 native speakers	12 English teachers: 10 Thai and 2 native speakers
English curriculum	Based on coursebook	Based on coursebook
English language instruction	3 hours per week (2 for grammar and vocabulary; 1 for oral skills)	3 hours per week (2 for grammar and vocabulary; 1 for oral skills)
Self-access experience	Previous largely unsuccessful self-access center	No previous experience with self-access
SEAR staff	Two teachers responsible	Two teachers responsible
SEAR resources	• 150 published books • 192 sets of specifically designed materials • 12 sets of computer software • 2 computers	• 150 published books • 192 sets of specifically designed materials • 12 sets of computer software • 5 computers
SEAR rooms	One large room	Two rooms

resources provided at the two schools are similar. However, with twice the number of students at Nakhao School, these resources are spread more thinly, meaning that a lower proportion of the student population can access the SEAR at the same time. Furthermore, the rather unsuccessful previous experience with self-access learning at Nakhao School could mean that the teachers there had lower expectations of the potential benefits of the SEAR.

To investigate the effects of the establishment and use of the SEAR on the English language curriculum at the two schools, we sought four main sources of data: two document-based and two interview-based. For documents, any documentation available regarding the SEARs project was examined. These included questionnaires regarding the challenges and successes in the set up and operation of the SEAR, records of interviews with the teachers responsible for the SEAR in the first semester of its use, and written observations of how students used the SEAR. These documents were collected by the Ministry of Education committee responsible for implementing the SEARs project, and their prime purpose was to monitor its implementation and to identify areas where schools could benefit from further support. The second type of documentation, which was collected specifically for the present study, was the handout used by teachers in class to introduce their students to the SEAR and to train students to use the SEAR.

Interviews initially were conducted in August 2005 with the teachers responsible for the SEAR at each school. In both cases, two separate interviews were conducted, each lasting around an hour, the second being a follow-up with the same interviewees. Teachers were interviewed in pairs due to time constraints and because the teachers stated that they felt more comfortable if they were interviewed together. At Pakklang School, the head of the SEAR (Siriluck; all names are pseudonyms at the request of the interviewees) and another teacher responsible for assisting in the SEAR (Pranee) were interviewed. Similarly, at Nakhao School, the head of the SEAR (Praphai) and another involved teacher (Somjit) were interviewed. The topics covered in these interviews were

- background knowledge of self-access learning
- ways to prepare students to use the SEAR
- how the SEAR is used
- how the English curriculum at the school is organized
- effects of the SEAR on teaching and assessment
- attitudes toward the SEAR

The second type of interview, also conducted in August 2005, was a group interview with students. Three groups of five students at Pakklang

School and two groups of five students at Nakhao School were interviewed as groups. Each interview lasted around 45 minutes. The topics covered in the interviews were

- frequency of SEAR use
- reasons for using the SEAR
- evaluation of the SEAR work and evaluation criteria used on English courses students are studying
- support for SEAR use
- relationship between the SEAR and the classroom
- differences in learning English before the SEAR was established and the present

In our reliance on interviews as the prime source of data in this study, we tried to avoid the problems of biasing the interviewees' responses—both subconscious biases evinced through supralinguistic and kinesic signals and more general biases deriving from interviewer–interviewee power differences (Brown, 2001). For the teacher interviews, the authors who conducted the interviews held similar social positions to the interviewees, allowing a relatively symmetrical interviewer–interviewee relationship. In addition, the interviewees' first language—Thai—was used in all interviews, and care was taken to retain an interested and nonjudgmental atmosphere during the interviews.

The documents collected and the data from the interviews were analyzed to examine how the establishment and use of the SEAR at each school had affected the curriculum in terms of

- how English learning was conducted
- how students were evaluated
- how attitudes had changed

For the interviewee data, interviewee utterances were recursively categorized following the topics of the interviews given previously, which allowed the categorization of the vast majority of the interview data. The quotations from teachers and students that follow in this chapter are fairly loose translations from the interviews in which we try to represent the meanings that the interviewees were trying to convey. Loose translations are used for clarity because the actual interview data contain frequent repetitions, false starts, redundancies, and references to knowledge about the school and Thailand shared with the interviewers. Table 2 summarizes the sources of data and how they are used in this study.

Table 2. Data Source and Uses

Data Source	Date of Data Collection	Uses in the Present Study
Ministry of Education project data (e.g., questionnaires, records of interviews, observations)	March–September 2004	Background information concerning the set up of the SEAR and its initial operation
Documents for training students how to use the SEAR	August 2005	Demonstration of how students learn to use the SEAR
Interviews with teachers	August 2005	• Background information concerning the number of students who used the SEAR and methods to encourage students to use the SEAR • Findings concerning the effects of the SEAR on teaching and attitudes toward the SEAR
Interviews with students	August 2005	• Background information concerning methods to encourage students to use the SEAR • Findings about attitudes toward the SEAR

Process of Integrating the SEAR Into the Curriculum

The first half of 2004 was devoted to setting up the SEARs. With rooms, furniture, and materials ready, a small group of teachers at both schools started work. Although there were some constraints on the amount of time allotted to set up the centers, especially at Pakklang School, the SEARs were ready for students in May 2004, the start of the academic year. At that point, the Ministry of Education documentation revealed that teachers at both schools were worried about setting up appropriate administrative systems (e.g., user registration, materials classification) and encouraging students to use the SEARs.

In the first semester from May to September 2004, as part of the overall SEARs project, the implementation of self-access learning at both schools was monitored and documented by the Ministry of Education. From this documentation, at Pakklang School, the teachers reported that they were particularly pleased with the effectiveness of the user registration system they had set up and were proud of the extent to which the students were using the SEAR. At Nakhao School, there was a similar feeling of achievement because of heavy student use of the SEAR; the system for classifying materials was noticeably effective. It was apparent that the teachers at both schools had successfully managed to deal with the issues that had worried them during the set up of the centers. However, with the SEARs in operation for a couple of months, a new worry had arisen at both schools, namely, how to integrate the SEARs with classroom teaching. The teachers were concerned that the SEARs did not play any major role in the curriculum but were just a separate, isolated add-on to English teaching with little relationship to the classroom. This was a concern common at many of the 80 schools with SEARs throughout Thailand. Because of this, in December 2004 a workshop specifically addressing this issue was organized by the Ministry of Education and run by one of the authors (Watson Todd).

In collecting the data for the present study in August 2005, we hoped that the teachers would have had time to work on issues such as integrating the SEARs into classroom teaching so that we would be able to see the full effects of the SEARs on the curriculum. However, the limited physical size of the SEARs and the extent to which all teachers were involved in running them mean that the SEAR at an individual school is fully utilized by only a proportion of students.

In the following discussion, we focus on how the SEARs are used at the two schools and the effects of the SEARs on those teachers and students who are most familiar with them.

PAKKLANG SCHOOL

At the Pakklang School, the SEAR is intended for the students in the 3 years of upper secondary school termed M4–M6 (equivalent to U.S. Grades 10–12). For the M4 students, because it is the first time they will use the SEAR extensively, there is a need for learner training to introduce them to the SEAR and how to use it effectively. This typically takes 2 hours of classroom time and involves the teacher bringing sample worksheets into the classroom to show how the students can learn English from the SEAR, giving students a tour of the SEAR (using the task sheet shown in Figure 1) and explaining regulations, introducing how to make study plans (using the handout shown in Figure 2) and keep records of learning, and demonstrating briefly how to use the computer programs available. After this, the students take a placement test (available at http://arts.kmutt.ac.th/sears/Placement_test.htm) to identify the aspects of English on which they need to focus.[1]

---

[1] The main widely available resource for SEARs is the SEARs Web site, available at: http://arts.kmutt.ac.th/sears/. This site is designed to provide support for teachers and includes materials for learner training and supporting student self-study, a placement test, and a discussion forum. Within the first year, the Web site was visited more than 1,500 times by teachers from the 80 schools with SEARs.

Figure 1. Task Sheet for Introducing the Students to the SEAR at Pakklang School

Orientation Quiz

Name _____ Class _____ No. _____

1. How many corners are there in the SEAR? What are they?

   _____

2. How many different newspapers are there in the newspaper corner? What are they?

   _____

3. Write the name of an English dictionary in the dictionary corner.

   _____

4. If you want to improve your speaking, which corner will you go to?

   _____

5. The first thing you should do when you visit the SEAR is

   _____

6. How many TVs and VCD players are there in the SEAR?

   _____

7. Write the name of one game you can find in the SEAR.

   _____

8. Write the name of a graded reader from the reading corner.

   _____

9. What does KMUTT stand for?

   _____

10. Write down one motto from the notice board.

    _____

11. What do we call the students who help in the SEAR?

    _____

12. What colour is the reading skill in the KMUTT materials?

    _____

13. How many levels are there in the KMUTT materials?

    _____

14. If you don't understand about the use of the past perfect tense, which corner should you go to? On which page can you find help about the past perfect?

    _____

15. Which corner do you like most?

    _____

16. What does CALL stand for?

    _____

17. Which program do we use to practice English through CALL?

    _____

**Figure 2. Handout for Making a
Study Plan Used at Pakklang School**

Self-Study Plan

Date _____

Name _____ Class _____ No. _____

Number of hours a week I will spend on self-study

_____

The best time of the day/week for me to study is

_____

The number of weeks this plan covers is

_____

In my study I need to

_____
_____

The thing(s) I need to improve most is/are

_____
_____

My self-study timetable

Week no.	Number of hours	Activities planned

To encourage the students in M4 and M5 to use the SEAR, they are assigned some work, and 20% of the marks for their English course are allocated for the completion of a SEAR portfolio. For M4 students, the teacher asks them to read at least one graded reader, to complete at least 10 computer-based lessons and 10 worksheets, and to listen to at least five listening tapes. For M5 students, there is more freedom in that they are simply asked to do at least 60 activities in the SEAR per semester. M6 students are not assigned work in the SEAR, but many visit because they enjoy using the facilities and find them helpful. For all of these students, their teachers also may occasionally recommend specific worksheets or activities in the SEAR as follow-up to what they learn in their lessons. The M1–M3 students of lower secondary school are not required to use the SEAR but are encouraged to watch videos and listen to music there to become familiar with the SEAR.

From these requirements and encouragement, most M4 and M5 students use the SEAR for 2–3 hours per week (in addition to their 3 hours of classroom English). Based on attendance records, on average, 70% of M4 students and 55% of M5 students use the SEAR every week. Although there are no records of the use of the SEAR by M6 students, in the interviews, the teachers stated that many of them use the SEAR at least once a week. Finally, a significant minority (roughly 40%) of lower secondary school students visit the SEAR occasionally.

NAKHAO SCHOOL

For M4 students at Nakhao School, the situation is similar to that in Pakklang School. At the beginning of the year, students are trained in how to use the SEAR (using a task sheet similar to that in Figure 1 to familiarize the students with the SEAR and the study plan shown in Figure 3) and are then assigned to complete a SEAR portfolio each semester. However, when compared with the Pakklang School, teachers exert a substantial amount of control over students' learning in the SEAR in two main ways. First, the teachers sometimes take the whole class to the SEAR so that the students' use of materials can be closely monitored. Second, the teacher may assign specific work to be completed in the SEAR. For example, where the classroom learning focuses on the vocabulary of the home, the teacher may require the students to find further related vocabulary items in the SEAR and present these items in the next lesson; or, the teacher may ask the students to watch a particular movie related to the content of the lesson (using the generic worksheet shown in Figure 4). The teachers say that they exert such control over the students because they are worried that if the students do not focus on the content of the English course, they will fail the exam. In contrast to the control over the M4 students' SEAR use, neither M5 nor M6 students at Nakhao School are assigned to use the SEAR, although occasionally teachers take SEAR materials into the classroom to help their teaching. Nevertheless, a number of these students either visit the SEAR to study every week or borrow materials from the SEAR to study by themselves. From the attendance records, around 12% of M5 students and 17% of M6

Figure 3. Handout for Making a Study Plan and Keeping Records of SEAR Use at Nakhao School

Learner Profile for

Name _____

Surname _____

Class _____ No. _____

To learners

The contents of this profile are all about you. The purpose of the profile is to give an accurate picture of what you are able to do well and what you need to improve. You can add whatever you like to this profile.

Section 1: What you are able to do well

Instructions: Please tick (✓) the items that you are able to do well.

Language focus	What I can do well
Listening	
Speaking	
Reading	
Writing	
Grammar	
Vocabulary	
Pronunciation	
Other (please list)	

Section 2: Needs analysis: What you need to improve

Instructions: Please tick (✓) the items that you need to improve.

Language focus	What I need to improve
Listening	
Speaking	
Reading	
Writing	
Grammar	
Vocabulary	
Pronunciation	
Other	

Section 3: Your study plan

Instructions: Fill in the blanks by choosing 3 items from section 2 that you want to learn first.

3.1 _____

3.2 _____

3.3 _____

Figure 4. Generic Worksheet Used When Students Watch Movies in the SEAR at Nakhao School

Date _____

Name _____ Class _____ No. _____

Instructions: Put a tick (✔) in the boxes, and fill in the spaces provided.

1. Name of the movie

   _____

2. Type of movie
   - ☐ Historical ☐ Drama ☐ Horror
   - ☐ Action ☐ Musical ☐ Detective
   - ☐ Adventure ☐ Romance ☐ Other _____

3. Main characters

   _____

   _____

4. Main points in the story

   _____

   _____

   _____

5. New words I have learnt

New word	Meaning

6. Interesting sentences/expressions I have learnt

   _____

   _____

   _____

7. New information or knowledge I have learnt

   _____

   _____

students use the SEAR at least once a week. Around 10% of lower secondary students visit the SEAR occasionally.

The different levels of usage of the two SEARs are summarized in Table 3. Although the percentage of students using the SEAR is higher at Pakklang School, the actual numbers of users are similar because there are more students at Nakhao School.

Table 3. Use of SEARs at Two Schools

	Nakhao School	Pakklang School
SEAR use with M4 students	• SEAR portfolio with specified tasks • 100% of students use the SEAR (during class time)	• 20% of assessment from SEAR use • SEAR portfolio with some restrictions • 70% of students use the SEAR every week
SEAR use with M5 students	• No SEAR assignments • 12% of students use the SEAR every week	• 20% of assessment from SEAR use • SEAR portfolio with freedom of choice • 55% of students use the SEAR every week
SEAR use with M6 students	• No SEAR assignments • 17% of students use the SEAR every week	• No SEAR assignments • Many students use the SEAR every week
SEAR use with M1–M3 students	• 10% of students use the SEAR occasionally	• 40% of students use the SEAR occasionally

From these descriptions, it is apparent that, after initial learner training, the SEARs are used in four different ways with different levels of teacher control. Starting with the most teacher control, these ways are

1. an assigned SEAR portfolio where work to do is specified and/or monitored by the teacher (M4 students at Nakhao School)
2. an assigned SEAR portfolio with some restrictions on student choice (e.g., M4 students at Pakklang School)
3. an assigned SEAR portfolio where there is freedom of choice for students (e.g., M5 students at Pakklang School)
4. voluntary use of the SEAR (e.g., M1–M3 and M6 students at Pakklang School; M5 and M6 students at Nakhao School)

The Effects of the SEARs on Teaching, Teachers, and Students

The curricula at both schools are based on very broad objectives, such as "ask for and give basic personal information," which in turn are based on 2001 Ministry of Education standards (e.g., Section 1 on page 6 states that students should be able to "use simple language to ask for and give information about people and things"). From these objectives, the English department chooses a coursebook appropriate to each level of students. The teaching and learning process is closely controlled by this coursebook, with the content of both teaching and examinations matching the content of the coursebook. Furthermore, the restrictions on the number of students who can use the SEAR mean that, although some teachers can encourage their students to use the SEAR to its fullest extent, others cannot, and the students of this latter group of teachers must rely primarily on classroom learning. To ensure that different groups of students studying the same course meet the same objectives and are evaluated in similar ways, priority is given to classroom learning and the coursebook. The constraints of meeting the standards-based course objectives, following the coursebook, and preparing students for examinations mean that, within the English curriculum, there appears to be little leeway for the SEARs to lead to change or development.

For Nakhao School, these constraints appear to have limited the potential impact of the SEAR on the curriculum. Rather than enabling the curriculum to develop, the SEAR has become just one more resource that can be used to reach existing objectives. In the words of Somjit, the teacher helping with the SEAR,

> I think that the objectives of the curriculum haven't changed. We simply use the SEAR as a place for extra learning activities. Previously, one objective of the curriculum was to have the students learn outside the classroom as well as within it. This objective is still in the curriculum, but the method of reaching the objective has changed from assigning extensive reading of newspapers or short stories to making use of the SEAR.

Furthermore, although the teachers agree that the SEAR is potentially useful, they have no immediate intentions of further integrating the SEAR with the curriculum more, although they would like to do so. As Somjit said,

> I think the concept of the SEAR is good, but it's not easy to put this into practice. We need a lot more training if we are going to improve the implementation of the SEAR. We don't have any plans to integrate the SEAR and the curriculum yet. To do this, we need a lot more time, and we need personnel to work in the SEAR regularly.

However, a general lack of time, confidence, and applicable training suggests that any plans to develop the SEAR are unlikely to become a reality, as Somjit also states,

> I do not have time to contribute to the SEAR. There are so many things to do already. I have plans to do a lot of things, but they do not mate-

rialize simply because I do not have time . . . I have no confidence in developing self-access materials. When we attended the training organized by the British Council [before the SEARs were set up], there was no hands-on experience.

In addition to their concerns about a lack of applicable training and time, the teachers at Nakhao School who use the SEAR extensively are also worried about the constraints of the English courses. Compared with those teachers who do not utilize the SEAR in their teaching, SEAR teachers are worried that if they ask their students to use the SEAR a lot, they may not be able to cover all of the required content of the coursebook in class, that the students' classroom learning will be adversely affected, and thus the students will not be fully prepared for the examination, which is based on the content of the coursebook. For Nakhao School, therefore, it appears that the constraints existing in the school context have meant that the SEAR is not exploited to its full potential, and its impact on the curriculum has been limited.

Nevertheless, even with the constraints and the limited use of the SEAR, some of the students at Nakhao School, as we have seen, are willing to use the SEAR to learn even when their teacher does not assign them to do so. In fact, students voluntarily using the SEAR highlight their freedom of choice in contrast to the control exercised when the teacher assigned work in the SEAR. As students stated in a group interview,

We like the SEAR because it has many resources available, and we can choose what to study ourselves . . . I especially like the song corner . . . It's not difficult to use the SEAR, but it's more suitable for proficient and hard-working students because we have to study by ourselves . . . We need to both learn in class and find something for our own interest.

The students at Pakklang School have an even greater willingness to use the SEAR and wider ranging reasons for doing so, as shown in the following quotation from one student explaining how most of the students work in the SEAR:

At first, when the SEAR was set up, we were forced to use it by our teachers, but later we became more willing to come and use it by ourselves . . . Originally when we used the SEAR, we would always watch TV, but later we moved on to do other things in the SEAR...Now we often use the SEAR at lunchtimes or when we have free time, because we feel happy using it and it's fun . . . I like the computer programs such as Discovery where we can practice listening, speaking, and reading, and we can record ourselves . . . If we don't understand something in the classroom, we can come to the SEAR to find something extra to read

*such as grammar, vocabulary, and short stories . . . The knowledge that
we get from the SEAR and the classroom is different. From the SEAR
we get more general knowledge, but in the classroom we get more specific
knowledge.*

In fact, from the group interviews, the students at Pakklang School
showed a greater depth of awareness concerning the purposes and uses of the
SEAR and more positive attitudes than the students from Nakhao School.
These differences may be due to the extent to which the SEAR at Pakklang
School has influenced the curriculum.

Although, as with Nakhao School, the existing formal objectives of the
English curriculum at Pakklang School have remained intact, the teachers
have felt the need to add an extra objective. As Pranee, the teacher helping with the SEAR, said, "We have inserted the idea into the objectives of
the courses that students should engage in extensive self-study. We use the
SEAR in this way, although it's now just a pilot program."

If the students' self-study proves effective (which seems likely given the
students' responses to learning through the SEAR), the teachers will consider offering a new optional course based very heavily on SEAR use, which
would clearly imply a new direction for the curriculum at Pakklang School.
As yet, there are no solid plans concerning this course, and it is unclear how
likely it is that this hope will be realized in practice.

In addition to the extra course objective, at Pakklang School the SEAR
has also had an impact on teaching. As well as devoting time to learner
training in the classroom, the existence of the SEAR also has led the teachers
most closely involved with the SEAR to adapt the ways they extend learning
beyond the classroom. According to Siriluck, the SEAR head,

*The teaching methodology has changed because of the SEAR. The nature
of the SEAR has made this change inevitable. Previously, we taught the
lesson in the classroom and finished teaching within that period. Except
for assigning homework to students, we didn't extend the class learning
outside of the classroom, and there was no real structure to the homework we assigned. Now, from only teaching in the classroom, we can
give the students assignments to do in the SEAR to follow up on their
learning, and the students now have a choice of what to do for their
assignments . . . Another change is when the students have problems or
difficulties with their learning in the classroom. Previously I would just
give the answer to the student in the classroom. Now, we assign the students to go and look for the answer in the SEAR, especially for grammar
and pronunciation . . . Students have a new resource for learning, they
are more responsible for their own learning, and they have more options
available to them for learning.*

In turn, these changes in dealing with students' problems and extending learning beyond the classroom have affected teachers' and students' attitudes at Pakklang School. As Siriluck said,

The students' perceptions about language learning have changed so that they like English more. For example, in class, students were always quite shy about speaking out, especially for pronouncing words, but with the CALL [computer-assisted language learning] program, they aren't shy. Instead of being embarrassed in front of their peers in class, they can repeat and practice pronunciation on their own with the computer, and this helps to create self-confidence.

Thus the teachers see that the SEAR has brought many benefits to the school. As Siriluck added,

The SEAR is really good and useful. It helps reduce our teaching load, students don't feel bored with learning English or get tired of listening to the teacher all the time, and it offers something different so that our work and teaching are more interesting than before.

Overall, the reactions of both students and teachers to the SEARs are positive, and the extensive use of the SEARs by students, especially the voluntary use, highlights the potential value of the SEARs as an extra resource for English language learning. However, the students and teachers at Pakklang School seem to have taken to self-access learning more than at Nakhao School, with students at Pakklang School demonstrating a greater willingness and responsibility for learning through the SEAR, especially as shown by the proportions of students using the SEAR voluntarily. Teachers appear committed to implementing self-access learning and are not overly concerned about constraints. Fortunately, our initial worries that the SEARs would become degraded and redundant have not been realized. Rather, the SEARs, especially at Pakklang School, have provided an extra dimension to English education and have great potential for further revitalizing the curricula in the future.

Issues Underlying the Impact of the SEARs

Although the experience at the two schools *suggests* that the SEARs are valuable additions to the English language curricula, *proving* this is not possible. Self-access centers are incredibly complex entities, and the number and range of factors potentially influencing their effectiveness make any evaluation of self-access learning difficult at best (Gardner, 1999). Nevertheless, some patterns emerge from the interview data that have implications for other situations in which teachers and principals may consider revitalizing the English curriculum through the implementation of self-access learning.

The most noticeable finding in this study concerns the students' willingness and desire to use the SEARs, even when not required to do so by the teacher. This independent learning suggests that the students have become, at least to some extent, autonomous in their learning. At Pakklang School, this autonomous behavior is very apparent as the students, perhaps because of the teachers' initial encouragement, use the SEAR to attempt to solve their learning problems by themselves.

Such autonomous learning behavior among Thai students contrasts with previous studies in two main ways. Firstly, a previous investigation of self-access learning in Thailand (Rujiketgumjorn, 2000) suggested that independent learning is a point of particular difficulty for Thai students and that extensive support and assistance for self-access learning is needed. In this study, however, the initial support provided was not extensive, and assistance in using the SEAR is minimal (e.g., there is no counseling service available to provide guidance in self-directed learning). Despite these limitations, the students' independent use of the SEARs highlighted in the present study suggests that with the provision of sufficient appropriate resources, Thai students are not only able, but also willing, to engage in autonomous learning.

The second contrast with previous studies concerns the importance of learner training for effective self-access learning. In the literature, the aspect of self-access learning most frequently identified as crucial to success is learner training (Miller, 2000; Yeung & Hyland, 1999), leading to suggestions for long-term learner training courses (Ellis & Sinclair, 1989). In the present study, however, the learner training provided could probably be described as perfunctory, yet the students actively engage in self-access learning (although we do not know the extent of the effectiveness of their learning). Instead of identifying learner training as the key issue that influences self-access learning, perhaps we should examine the differences between Pakklang School and Nakhao School (which both provided similar training) to see how these may have influenced the impact of the SEAR.

From the interviews, it appears that the SEAR at Nakhao School is viewed as just an extra resource for English language learning and has had little impact on the curriculum in general. At Pakklang School, on the other hand, there is evidence that the SEAR has had a greater impact on the curriculum, with the addition of an objective concerning self-study and changes in the teaching methodology and on the students, especially in terms of their attitudes toward English and learning in general.

At Nakhao School, although the teachers are dedicated and generally view the SEAR positively, they do not seem to have truly accepted the idea of self-access learning because their implementation of the SEAR involves high initial levels of control over how the students engage in self-study. They are also worried about the constraints associated with self-access, perhaps to a greater extent than they are enthusiastic about the extra learning opportunities it creates. Together with a certain lack of confidence as evinced by their expressed need for further training, it appears that the teachers at Nakhao School, despite their positive attitudes, have neither a sense of ownership over the SEAR nor positive beliefs in their own ability to implement effective learning through the SEAR.

The teachers at Pakklang School, on the other hand, are much more committed to both the principles of self-access learning and the SEAR itself. In integrating the SEAR into the curriculum, students are given control over their learning, and, instead of assigning work for students to do in the SEAR, the teachers encourage the students to find their own answers and solutions. The teachers at Pakklang School have also started to develop additional materials for the SEAR, including paper-based self-access worksheets, CALL materials to review classroom learning, and a set of materials concerning careers to cover a student need that was not otherwise addressed. Such involvement in developing the SEAR is likely to lead to a greater sense of ownership among the teachers, which, together with their commitment to self-access learning, may be the key factor behind the greater impact of the SEAR at Pakklang School.

The experience at Pakklang School leads us to conclude that when teachers accept and commit to self-access learning, the provision of sufficient and appropriate self-access facilities can have a positive impact on revitalizing a curriculum. This impact may not be directly observable at the surface level of the curriculum in terms of altered objectives and classroom materials. Rather, the impact may be deeper and more pervasive in the long-term through beneficial changes to teaching methodology, ways in which students approach learning, and the attitudes of both teachers and students.

Conclusion

To conclude, we would like to state our personal reactions and learning from conducting this research into the SEARs.

Watson Todd: From the evidence we collected, my initial fears that the potential benefits of the SEARs would be lost without further Ministry of Education support have not been realized. Rather, it appears that so long as teachers are dedicated, Ministry of Education support is not always necessary and may even be detrimental. The dedication and devotion of the teachers and the voluntary use of the SEARs by large numbers of students provide a welcome change to the usual media reports of doom and gloom in Thai secondary education. Students can be motivated to learn by themselves, teachers can implement beneficial projects (although further support and training appear necessary if the SEARs are to continue to develop), and self-access learning is appropriate for Thai students. Overall, I see the SEARs as a ray of hope for Thai education.

Keyuravong: Conducting this research has enriched my knowledge about self-access learning in two aspects—the students' ideas about self-access learning and the sustainability of self-access centers. My previous research studies and interest have centered on the self-access center itself, teachers' preparation, and the operation of self-access, but these studies have not focused on students. With this research, I had a chance to look closer at the students and learn about their thoughts, likes, dislikes, and needs, and I realized that more work needs to be done in this aspect. Another point is the sustainability of self-access. During the interviews at both schools, I noticed the teachers' enthusiasm in making the SEAR work for their students. They worked on the systems for students' use, allocation of marks, and materials development. However, there were no realistic long-term plans for the sustainability of the SEARs; when students had worked through all the materials, they felt bored. This aspect should be considered when preparing teachers to run a self-access center.

Suthidara: Based on the findings, it appears to me that the beliefs and attitudes of the teachers involved in running the SEAR are the most important factor in determining whether self-access learning is successful or not. Teachers with positive attitudes toward self-access learning are likely to devote more time and effort to the SEAR. Their positive attitudes are likely to rub off on students who, consequently, may be more willing to use the SEAR.

Weaving Meaning Into the ESOL Curriculum Using Thematic Matrices

4

JANET L. PIERCE

This chapter describes how incorporating thematic matrices into a K–12 English to speakers of other languages (ESOL) curriculum benefits ESOL classroom instruction. It is based on my experience using the matrices to help teachers new to ESOL develop a curriculum. I describe how the matrices have helped my planning and teaching and provide examples of completed matrices as well as sample classroom activities and student products.

Motivating Factors

As the only full-time certified ESOL teacher in a suburban school district in the United States, I was used to juggling a variety of teaching and administrative responsibilities as I worked with 20 to 25 K–12 nonnative-English-speaking (NNES) students scattered among five different buildings. In 2003, however, my school district decided that to meet the state's time requirements for instruction for all NNES students and to provide enough teaching time for other contracted teachers, it would assign six other current teachers to teach one ESOL class each. One of my new responsibilities was to supervise these teachers, who had little, if any, training in teaching NNES students. Given this daunting challenge, I needed to find something that would help the teachers understand how to use the ESOL curriculum and that aligned state literacy standards with the *ESL Standards for Pre-K–12 Students* (TESOL, 1997) but that did not depend on a specific textbook series to teach NNES students. Thematic matrices seemed to be the answer.

In 2004, the state prohibited noncertified ESOL teachers from teaching ESOL classes. I again became the lone ESOL teacher. However, I continued to use the matrices to guide my curriculum.

The Curricular Context

COMMUNITY DEMOGRAPHICS

Two rural communities and one suburban small town make up the 40-square-mile Franklin Regional School District, which lies 19 miles outside the city of Pittsburgh, Pennsylvania. The more than 22,000 people in the district include farmers, middle-class working families, and, more recently, upwardly mobile professionals who moved to the communities to purchase more land and pay lower taxes.

The school district campus is composed of a senior high building for 1,200 students in Grades 9–12, a middle school for 980 students in Grades 6–8, and two elementary buildings for K–5, one with 250 students and the other with 680 students. All schools are within a half mile of each other. Another elementary school with 700 students is 2½ miles away. There are 1–7 NNES students in each building.

The school district has a small ESOL population, ranging from 10 NNES students in 1991, 27 in 1998, to 21 at present. Students have spoken Arabic, Czech, Finnish, French, German, Hindi, Icelandic, Iraqi, Japanese, Korean, Lithuanian, Mandarin Chinese, Polish, Portuguese, Puerto Rican Spanish, Romanian, Russian, Swedish, and Urdu, with 7–9 of the languages represented in any school year. Although the district has a growing population and new homes are developing in each area, the number of NNES students has remained constant since I began teaching in the district in 1991.

Although the needs of individual students vary, in general the Franklin Regional ESOL Program meets the needs of two types of students. First are the transient NNES students. These include students whose parents come to the district to work and will return to their countries when their assignment with a company has ended and a few exchange students who need more ESOL instruction. The second type includes immigrants and refugees who will graduate from the local school system and be integrated into U.S. culture and life. At the secondary level there is an ESOL student group that serves as a peer and support group as each student integrates into the U.S. culture.

ASSESSMENT AND PLACEMENT PROCEDURES

All new NNES students are interviewed and given the *IDEA English Proficiency Test* (IPT) (*IDEA Proficiency Tests*, 1993). The IPT is a standardized test composed of a grammatically graded interview, picture and conversation stimuli for speaking, and writing and reading excerpts that test vocabulary knowledge, skills use, and literacy applications. Students' IPT scores determine the amount and type of standards-based ESOL instruction they will receive. Our state recommendations for daily instruction are from 2 to 3 hours for NNES students; 2 hours for beginners, 1–1½ hours for intermediate students, and 1 hour for advanced students (Pennsylvania Department of Education, 22 Pa. Code §4.26, 2005).

INSTRUCTIONAL ORGANIZATION

The ESOL instructional grade clusters include Grades K–2, 3–5, 6–8, and 9–12. Instructional time depends on the student's English proficiency and grade level. Fourth- to 12th-grade students may have from one 45-minute ESOL class up to three 45-minute ESOL classes daily. Kindergarten to third-grade students may have one 45-minute class or two 45-minute classes daily. I use a master schedule, which includes time spent traveling between buildings and classes, so that I can teach six classes (three elementary-level, three secondary-level) a day. The students in Grades 6–12 have ESOL as a regular class, and students in Grades K–5 are pulled out of their English or language arts and reading block for ESOL instruction. This is according to Pennsylvania ESOL regulations (22 Pa. Code §4.26, Pennsylvania Department of Education, 2005).

Designing Thematic Matrices

Before 2003, I traveled to four of the five school buildings a day; carried materials in the trunk of my car; and taught in libraries, closets, storage rooms, and boiler rooms. My new responsibility of helping six teachers design lesson plans for their ESOL classes was the challenge that forced me to rethink the ESOL curriculum. I found a colleague, reading specialist Elaine Gribar, who was willing to help. She had taught NNES students at the elementary level and was 1 of the 6 teachers who would have an ESOL class. Together, we decided to look at common threads of information or themes that could be found throughout our district's content-area curricula (e.g., science, social studies, language arts). We found we could make the ESOL curriculum easier to understand and use through the use of thematic matrices.

A thematic matrix is a template with monthly themes. The matrix is used to guide planning, assist in material development, and provide instructional choices for teachers. We chose a thematic approach for several reasons: Themes help integrate content and language, provide coherence for learners and teachers, provide flexibility in planning for teachers, and allow teachers to meet the needs of students at different levels. As such, the thematic matrix offers a logical progression of skills to be taught in a given curriculum. In addition to skills, thematic matrices include a comprehensive framework of motivating and relevant topics and concepts as well as a variety of activities. The topics and concepts tie into regular classroom content areas. Matrices also allow flexibility in choosing material; for example, ESOL teachers can pick and choose from the activities that teach language functions to NNES students at different proficiency levels.

The use of themes helps students focus on meaningful content, not only on linguistic structures. Sociologist Ken Hyland (2003) stressed the importance of using themes to organize a series of lessons into a unit of work: "Unit themes are best seen as real-life activities or situations in which people do specific things through writing [and language use] rather than [just] grammatical structures, functions or text-types" (p. 77). Concrete topics relate to learners' previous experiences and everyday life. Topics such as Our School and Home Environment are simple concepts that deal with the "most urgent needs of learners" (Hyland, 2003, p. 79). From there, the themes move to more complex, advanced topics and activities such as Native Americans of the Northwest, allowing NNES students to expand their knowledge from classroom vocabulary to encompass vocabulary and understanding of other cultures, in this case the geography, climate, and history of the United States and the expansion and impact of colonization. Each theme has different amounts of information, tasks, and concepts for different grades and proficiency levels. I will expand on this later.

Organizing lessons around themes provides an "overall coherence to the course for students and [it] is crucial in devising materials and activities" (Hyland, 2003, p. 79). For new teachers unfamiliar with the ESOL curriculum, creating lesson plans and materials in accordance with the curriculum is complex and daunting. Add traveling to the school to the mix, and the task may seem overwhelming. Thematic matrices guide this process and make it easier for teachers to understand the curriculum because they offer ideas around which to organize activities. These activities can vary from year to year but still support and teach the same theme.

Another reason we chose to use thematic matrices as an organizing tool was that we needed to find ways to provide language instruction that would spiral English and content-area language concepts for NNES students who take ESOL for several years. By finding themes similar to the regular content areas, we sought to provide the NNES students with a foundation of vocabulary and concepts they could apply to their content area classes. This process of topic selection within the themes adds variety each year while strengthening the ESOL curriculum and NNES students' understanding and use of the school district curriculum. This flexibility is important. Teachers in the Franklin Regional School District have flexibility in the types of materials they use to implement their curriculum while meeting Pennsylvania state standards.

We wrote the ESOL curriculum to be in line with state standards and incorporated the same type of flexibility that the district curriculum offers. The matrices provide choices to make it easier for teachers to teach English using areas of their strengths and to provide multiple pathways to learning for NNES students. Because the ESOL curriculum allows teachers to provide different materials to teach concepts in different ways, the curriculum can differentiate instruction for NNES students in multilevel and multi-grade clusters in lesson plans that use the standards set forth by the state and TESOL (Pennsylvania Department of Education, 2005; TESOL, 1997).

As we examined the learning materials, stages of language acquisition, and how NNES students become accustomed to a new world, we decided to create three sequential organizers to outline our themes. These organizers correspond to the amounts of time students spend in school, from the beginning to the end of the year. The sequential organizing concepts are called New Beginnings, Expanding Horizons, and Applications. From this basic structure we organized topics, which we could vary to teach similar concepts and language functions each year. Thus, although necessity might require us to revisit some sequential organizers as new students enter the school district, there is still flexibility within the themes and topics. The themes, chosen to support a district's curriculum common strands or themes, may change as the district's themes and students' needs change.

UNDERSTANDING THE PROCESS

The matrices are flexible because each year, teachers can choose different topics that reinforce ideas within each theme. Thus, the theme is the overarching concept. Topics are the vehicles to explain and present ideas and language to NNES students based on their individual proficiency level and grade requirements. The themes are organized to engage NNES students in "meaningful activities that focus on areas of inquiry rather than a specific skill" (Diaz-Rico & Leed, 2002, p. 134). As the students become accustomed to their new English-speaking world and classroom expectations, they can grow and use language beyond the first part of the New Beginnings sequential organizing theme (i.e., Proficiency Assessment; Getting to Know You/Conversation, and Survival Skills). Because their needs are expanding, students move on to learn how to live in two cultures—their native-language-speaking culture and the English-speaking school world. An example of this is teaching a unit on Living in Two Worlds. For this unit, each year NNES students would learn about a group of immigrants or Native Americans who experience the dichotomy of living in two cultures. In this way, they learn language functions through the vocabulary and use them in reading and conversation as they discuss what they are learning. Figure 1 shows the first section of the matrix for TESOL (1997) Goal 1, Standards 1–3.

For the theme Life in the United States/New Places/Immigrants/Living in Two Cultures, NNES students examine science and history concepts and geographical features of the land of the country in which they currently live and the land of their native country; they also read literature from both cultures. Some of the literature selections I use include the following:

- *The Native Nations of North America Series: Nations of the Northwest Coast* (Kalman & Smithyman, 2004)
- *Crossing Borders: Stories of Immigrants* (Lang, 2005)
- *We Are Americans—Voices of the Immigrant Experience* (Hoobler & Hoobler, 2003)
- *Discover American Indian Ways* (Soeder, 1998)
- *Contact USA: A Reading and Vocabulary Textbook* (Abraham & Mackey, 1997)
- *Through Indian Eyes: The Untold Stories of Native American Peoples* (Walker, Maynak, & Cassidy, 1995)

All activities in the lessons become the vehicle to teach the following language functions:

- grammar forms of the verb *to be* in the present, past, and future tense with vocabulary associated with history and time concepts of today, yesterday, and tomorrow
- numbers and math pertaining to dates and events

Figure 1. Sequential Organizer for TESOL Goal 1, Standards 1–3

Sequential Organizer 1: New Beginnings
Themes: Proficiency Assessment; Getting to Know You/Conversation and Survival Skills; Back to School; Alphabet/Numbers/Colors; Environmental Print; Life in the United States/New Places/Immigrants/Living in Two Cultures; Holidays and Seasons.

- vocabulary pertaining to clothing and activities associated with the climate, customs, and culture of the people being studied
- geographic vocabulary related to place
- vocabulary related to civilizations in a specific time period associated with specific climatic conditions as well as social and political aspects

When I teach ESOL, I tie my classes into content-area topics for several reasons. First, content-area activity gives students opportunities to ask questions and seek answers to content-area issues in which they are interested and to which they can relate. Second, content-area activities involve not only teacher–student interaction but also student-to-student interaction as well; this helps NNES students connect concepts to issues and significant ideas (Diaz-Rico & Leed, 2002; Freeman & Freeman, 1998). Through content-area activities in the ESOL classroom, NNES students are prepared for academic vocabulary in regular content-area classrooms as they continue to learn English (Ferris & Hedgecock, 2005). This creates an interactive classroom that allows for continuous concept development as well as vocabulary and language structure expansion in several contexts that students perceive as real and academic. The activities also allow differentiation of instruction within a class that takes into consideration each student's age and English proficiency. This flexibility is important to teachers with students of many ages and many cultures who have different levels of English proficiency. Allowing for variations in themes through different topic, activity, and materials choice lets the teacher spiral instruction from year to year for NNES students who are in the ESOL program for 2 or more years. For instance, using the theme Living in Two Cultures, each year I can teach the geography and history of the United States as I teach about different Native American or immigrant groups. Thus, I provide students with chances to revisit geography, climate, and history vocabulary as they learn about new people who live in two cultures, as they do. Allowing for the variations in topics within themes is another way for districts with a small ESOL population to effectively meet the instructional needs of the few NNES students at all grade and English proficiency levels.

Applying the Matrices to Instruction

Once the matrices were written, the new teachers found that using them helped simplify the task of differentiating instruction to meet the need of NNES students to learn language as they use language. It helped teachers organize and develop their own materials to teach concepts and standards through different activities to NNES students at all grades and levels of English proficiency. In one case, a family and consumer science teacher of elementary-age NNES students was able to focus on the themes of health and nutrition to teach the names of nutrition objects and simple present-tense verbs and actions. Using familiar materials she was knowledgeable about and had on hand, the teacher was able to teach concepts and language skills. In another building, a teacher helped two boys improve their writing skills. By examining the themes, the teacher found worksheets and literature the boys could read and write about and then use in different genres of writing such as poems, recipes, and writing fiction and nonfiction endings to stories. This helped the students become more proficient English language writers.

Let's look closer at the themes as they fit into the Franklin Regional School District's ESOL curriculum's three sequential organizers: New Beginnings, Expanding Horizons, and Applications. New Beginnings covers the first 6 weeks of school and deals with issues that can challenge students who are new to the country, school, and school year. This sequential organizer has themes that progress as the students' world widens through the use of their second language (L2), English. The example shown in Figure 2 is for TESOL (1997) Goal 1, Standards 1–3, for Grades 6–8.

Expanding Horizons, the second sequential organizer of the matrices, covers the next 12 weeks. It deals with issues that occur as students expand their knowledge of English and their environment. The third organizer, Applications, covers the last 18 weeks of school. It pertains to how students apply what they are learning to their basic interpersonal communication and content-area academic English skills.

Although I show specific time periods for each sequential organizer, the time period can be extended or shortened. In addition, the ideas can be revisited throughout the year and adapted as needed. We examined activities in these periods of instruction and compared them with the activities and themes of content-area teachers at each grade level used during the school year. We found common themes that revolve around concepts in history, science, math, and health. Literacy, art, music, math, and drama are used to accomplish the activities in each theme. These activities are incorporated into the curriculum theme and time frame, with time available to assess students in the program. Figure 3 shows the themes in each sequential organizer in the Franklin Regional School District. The themes give teachers structure when they think about specific activities in lesson plans, which is a topic covered in the next section.

A sample of the Franklin Regional School District ESOL curriculum is shown in Figure 4. The organization of the thematic matrices is superimposed into the curriculum template to show how the topics and activities relate to the themes and sequential organizers with standards, goals, and assessments. The proficiency levels are noted, as are the modalities of listen-

Figure 2. Sequential Organizer for TESOL Goal I, Standards 1–3, for Grades 6–8

Goal 1, Standard 1, Sequential Organizer 1: New Beginnings

(Key for proficiency levels: B = Beginning; I = Intermediate; A = Advanced)

Themes: Proficiency Assessment; Getting to Know You/Conversation and Survival Skills; Back to School; Alphabet/Numbers/Colors; Environmental Print; Life in the United States/New Places/Immigrants/Living in Two Cultures; Holidays and Seasons.

Life in the United States/Immigration/New Places/Living in Two Cultures, activities:
1. Role play telephone conversations and other social situations at school, in the cafeteria, and in the hallway with picture cards and modeling (B, I) or with or without modeling (I, A).
2. Orally point out and then label items in the house, school, and community; identify and talk about them with overhead visuals and pictures as needed (B, I, A).
3. Talk about culture shock and moving to and living in the United States (B, I, A).
4. Discuss and describe lifestyles for specific culture groups in the United States (B, I, A).

Goal 1, Standard 2, Sequential Organizer 1: New Beginnings

Themes: Getting to Know You/Survival Skills; Life in the United States/Immigration/New Places/Living in Two Cultures.

Life in the United States/Immigration/New Places/Living in Two Cultures, activities:
1. Read stories from people in the culture to be studied (I, A).
2. Make posters, art, outlines, and charts showing the action and plot in the stories (B, I, A).

Goal 1, Standard 3, Sequential Organizer 1: New Beginnings

Themes: Getting to Know You/Survival Skills; Life in the United States/Immigration/New Places/Living in Two Cultures.

Life in the United States/Immigration/Native Americans/Living in Two Cultures, activities:
1. Create pictionaries to remember new vocabulary (B, I).
2. List key concepts on word walls and webs (I, A).
3. Play charades to act out feelings in newcomer situations (B, I, A).
4. Go to the Media Center to explore resources; label items in groups (B) or not in groups (I, A).
5. Use the verb chart to organize action verbs in the present tense and to discuss action in the new place (B, I, A).
6. Create timelines to show the action in the stories students read (B, I, A).

Figure 3. Themes in Each Sequential Organizer

Sequential Organizer 1: New Beginnings
Themes: Proficiency Assessment; Getting to Know You/Conversation and Survival Skills; Life in the United States/New Places/Immigrants/Living in Two Cultures; Holidays and Seasons; Back to School; Alphabet/Numbers/Colors; Environmental Print

Sequential Organizer 2: Expanding Horizons
Themes: Favorite Things/Colors; Number Words/Parts of the Body/Health Issues; Seasons/Food/ Plants/Harvest or Thanksgiving/Colonists/Explorers; Winter Holidays; Customs Around the World; Environmental Print; Government/Veteran's Day/Racial Issues/Famous Americans; Animals/Habitats

Sequential Organizer 3: Applications
Themes: Presidents; Friendship; Dental Health/Keeping Healthy/Heredity and Other Health Issues; Mammals/Humans and Other Animals; Holidays/Seasons/Weather; Our Community/Sharing Cultures/World Geography/Ecology/Recycling/Arbor Day; Telling Time/Fractions; Independent Reading Project/Skills Review; Newspaper/ Recipe Book; Manners/Money/Economics/Restaurant Skills; Post-assessment of English Proficiency/Summer Plans/Record Keeping

ing, speaking, reading, and writing. The beginning proficiency level includes TESOL entering and beginning levels; the intermediate proficiency level, TESOL developing and expanding levels; and the advanced proficiency level, TESOL bridging level. Grade cluster information for K–2, 3–5, and 9–12 can be developed by using the same themes and sequential organizers and standards, but adapting the activities to be age and grade appropriate. The themes are included under each sequential organizer. For the purposes of this chapter, the curriculum sample in Figure 4 shows sequential organizers 1 and 2 for Goal 1, Standards 1–3 as set forth by the state (Pennsylvania Department of Education, 2005) and TESOL (1997).

From Matrices to Lesson Plans

This section takes the information gathered from the sequential organizers time frame and themes and explains how to plan a lesson for NNES students in Grades 6–8. As stated earlier, the matrices are a guide to help teachers keep on track with the consecutive development of ideas and keep in line with TESOL goals and standards that are developmental and sequential. The matrices are more flexible, however, as they expand the language functions to include relevant and content-area materials, which in turn,

Figure 4. Franklin Regional School District Instructional Planning Organizer

Course English as a Second or Other Language Grades 6-8

Unit of Instruction: Sequential Organizer 1—New Beginnings Instructional Time Allocation: Approximately 6 weeks
Sequential Organizer 2—Expanding Horizons Instructional Time Allocation: Approximately 12 weeks
Sequential Organizer 3—Applications Instructional Time Allocation : Approximately 18 weeks

Statement of Content Standard	Modalities and Process Indicator (M/ PI)— Students will be able to:	Themes with suggested activities to engage student in learning process.	Suggested assessment to verify mastery of standard.
TESOL/ PA ESL Goal 1 – To use English to communicate in social settings **Standard 1** – Students will use English to participate in social interactions. *PDE Standard 1.4 – Types of Writing* *PDE Standard 1.6 – Speaking and Listening*	**TESOL/PA Goal 1 Standard 1 (M/PI):** • Share and request information • Express needs, feelings and ideas • Use nonverbal communication in social settings • Get personal needs met • Engage in conversations • Conduct transactions *1.4a – write narrative pieces* *1.4b – write informational pieces* *1.4c – write persuasive pieces* *1.4d – maintain written records* *1.4e – write personal resume (advanced proficiency only)* *1.6a – listen to others* *1.6b – listen to fiction and nonfiction literature selections* *1.6c – speak using skills appropriate to formal speech situations* *1.6d – contribute to discussions* *1.6e – participate in small and large group activities* *1.6f – use media for learning purposes*	**Key for Proficiency Levels:** **B- Beginning I-Intermediate A-Advanced** **TESOL/PA Goal 1 Standard 1** **Sequential Organizer 1:** **New Beginnings** **THEMES:** • **Life in the USA/ Immigration/New Places/ Living in two Cultures**- activity: 1. role play telephone conversations and other social situations at school, cafeteria, hallway with picture cards and modeling (B, I), with or without modeling (I, A) 2. orally point out then label items in house, school, community identifying and talking about them with overhead visuals and pictures as needed (B, I, A) 3. talk about Culture shock, moving and living in the USA (B, I, A) 4. Discuss /describe life styles for specific culture groups within the USA(B, I, A)	**Key for Proficiency Levels:** **B- Beginning I- Intermediate A- Advanced** **TESOL/PA Goal 1 Standard 1** • Ask peers for their opinions, preferences and desires -I • Write personal essays -A • Make plans for social engagements -I • Shop in a supermarket for specific items -B I • Engage listener's attention verbally or non-verbally-B • Volunteer information and respond to questions about self and family - B I • Elicit information and ask clarification questions -B I • Clarify and restate information as needed -I A • Indicate interests, opinions, or preferences related to class projects-I A • Give and ask for permission B I • Offer and respond to greetings, compliments, invitations, introductions and farewells - B I • Negotiate solutions to problems, interpersonal misunderstandings, and disputes -I A

continued on p. 64

Figure 4 (cont.). Franklin Regional School District Instructional Planning Organizer

Statement of Content Standard	Modalities and Process Indicator (M/ PI)— Students will be able to:	Themes with suggested activities to engage student in learning process.	Suggested assessment to verify mastery of standard.
TESOL/PA ESL Goal 1 Standard 2 – Students will interact in, through, and with spoken and written English for personal expression and enjoyment.	**TESOL/PA Goal 1 Standard 2 (M/PI):** • Describe, read about or participate in a favorite activity • Share social and cultural traditions and values • Express personal needs, feelings, and ideas • Participate in popular culture activities	**TESOL/PA Goal 1 Standard 1** **Sequential Organizer 2:** **Expanding Horizons** **THEME:** **TESOL/PA Goal 1 Standard 1** **Sequential Organizer 3:** **Applications**	**TESOL/PA Goal 1 Standard 2** • Recommend a film or videotape to a friend -I A • Write in a diary or personal journal - B I A • Discuss issues of personal importance or value -I A • Write a poem, short story, play or song -I A • Recommend a game, book or computer program - I
PDE Standard 1.4 – Types of Writing	*1.4a – write narrative pieces* *1.4b – write informational pieces* *1.4c – write persuasive pieces* *1.4d – maintain written records* *1.4e – write personal resume (advanced proficiency only)*	**TESOL/PA Goal 1 Standard 2** **Sequential Organizer 1:** **New Beginnings** **THEMES:** • **Life in the USA/ Immigration/New Places/ Living in two Cultures**- activity: 1. Read stories from people in the specific culture to be studied (I, A) 2. Make posters, art, outlines, charts showing the action and plot in the stories (B, I, A)	• Listen to, read, watch, and respond to plays, films, stories, books, songs, poems, computer programs and magazines -I A • Recount events of interest - B I • Ask information questions for person reasons - I • Make requests for personal reasons -I
PDE Standard 1.6 – Speaking and Listening	*1.6a – listen to others* *1.6b – listen to fiction and nonfiction literature selections* *1.6c – speak using skills appropriate to formal speech situations* *1.6d – contribute to discussions* *1.6e – participate in small and large group activities* *1.6f – use media for learning purposes*	**TESOL/PA Goal 1 Standard 2** **Sequential Organizer 2:** **Expanding Horizons** **THEMES:** **Sequential Organizer 3:** **Applications**	

continued on p. 65

Figure 4 (cont.). Franklin Regional School District Instructional Planning Organizer

Statement of Content Standard	Modalities and Process Indicator (M/ PI)— Students will be able to:	Themes with suggested activities to engage student in learning process.	Suggested assessment to verify mastery of standard.
TESOL/PA ESL Goal 1 Standard 3 – Students will use learning strategies to extend their communicative competences	**TESOL/PA Goal 1 Standard 3 (M/PI):** • Test language hypotheses • Listen to and imitate how others use English • Explore alternative ways of saying things • Focus attention selectively • Seek support and feedback from others • Compare nonverbal and verbal cues • Self-monitor and self-evaluate language development • Use the primary language to ask for clarification • Learn and use language "chunks" • Select different media to help understand language • Practice new language • Use context to construct meaning	**TESOL/PA Goal 1 Standard 3** **Sequential Organizer 1:** **New Beginnings** **THEMES:** • **Life in the USA/Immigration/Native Americans/Living in two Cultures**-activity: 1. create pictionaries to remember new vocabulary (B,I) 2. list key concepts on word walls, webs (I,A) 3. play charades to act out feelings in newcomer situations (B,I,A) 4. go to the media center to explore resources, labeling items (B, in groups, I, A) 5. use the verb chart to organize action verbs in the present tense (B,I, A) to discuss action in the new place 6. Create timelines to show the action in the stories students read (B, I, A)	**TESOL/PA Goal 1 Standard 3** • Use a dictionary to validate choice of language -B I A • Ask a classmate whether a particular word or phrase is correct - B I A • Use a computer spell checker to verify spelling -B I A • Use written sources to discover or check information -I A • Keep individual notes for language learning -B I A • Test appropriate use of new vocabulary, phrases and structures -B I A • Ask someone the meaning of a word -B I A • Understand verbal directions by comparing them with nonverbal cues (e.g., folding paper into eighths, lining up) - B • Tell someone in the native language that a direction given in English was not understood -B • Recite poems or songs aloud - B I A • Associate realia or diagrams with written labels to learn vocabulary or to construct meaning - B I A
PDE Standard 1.4 – Types of Writing	*1.4a – write narrative pieces* *1.4b – write informational pieces* *1.4c – write persuasive pieces* *1.4d – maintain written records* *1.4e – write personal resume (advanced proficiency only)* *1.6a – listen to others* *1.6b – listen to fiction and nonfiction literature selections* *1.6c – speak using skills appropriate to formal speech situations* *1.6d – contribute to discussions* *1.6e – participate in small and large group activities* *1.6f – use media for learning purposes*	**TESOL/PA Goal 1 Standard 2** **Sequential Organizer 2:** **Expanding Horizons** **THEMES:** **Sequential Organizer 3:** **Applications**	

allows individual teachers to find the most suitable methods and materials to present the information to their NNES students. It becomes easier to differentiate a lesson because ideas and materials are more accessible. Therefore, teachers have more time to meet the diverse needs of NNES students in multicultural, multigrade, and multilevel proficiency classes.

For example, consider the theme Life in the United States/Immigration/ New Places/Living in Two Cultures in the Instructional Planning Organizer (see Figure 4). One year, you could use the literature of various immigrant groups and in another other year, of Native Americans from different parts of the United States. In the 2006 school year, my NNES students in Grades K–12 focused on the Native Americans of the Northwest, reading *Alaskan Igloo Tales* by Edward Keithahn (1988) and *The Native Nations of North America Series: Nations of the Northwest Coast* by Kalman and Smithyman (2004). The goal was to open a window to another world and another way of thinking and seeing while using English. As the students began to understand concepts about the U.S. culture (e.g., how Native Americans live in two worlds), they compared and contrasted differences between their lives and those of the Native Americans. As they read the stories, students learned weather, geography, and history vocabulary that described where the various Northwest coast tribes live and their past and present way of life. The literature served as a starting point for students to explore the culture and answer questions.

For example, NNES students with different levels of proficiency can use the book *Discover American Indian Ways* (Soeder, 1998). The book features a present-day Cherokee family, the Youngs, who travel from their Seattle, Washington, home to the state of Tennessee, where their grandmother lives. Along the way, they visit friends from other tribes and enjoy learning their customs. A NNES student at the Beginning English proficiency level could learn key words for pictures from the stories and construct simple sentences to describe the characters and story plot. A NNES student at the Intermediate English proficiency level could search for more information in other books or on the Internet to expand on what he or she learned from the Young family. A NNES student at the Advanced level could read additional sources and write more extensive summaries of the findings of the Young's trip, for example, by looking at the motivations of the parents in planning the trip and contrasting their travels to those of his or her family. All three students could create a picture using clip art, magazines, or their own drawings or make a project to show what they have learned.

Posters and brochures of the states or areas in which the immigrants or Native Americans live help NNES students use language to show what they are learning. One year, using English to state facts and opinions, my students made posters and brochures as a culminating activity to show what they had learned about a specific group of people in a specific place. A NNES student with Beginning English proficiency labeled and constructed simple sentences around the key ideas he needed to know about his state and its inhabitants. A fifth-grade NNES student at the Intermediate English proficiency level used his multiple opportunities in ESOL class to learn about early explorers and settlers in the United States. He focused on Pennsylvania and used the Internet to determine the key facts about the state, which he then organized and printed in a brochure. Older NNES students in Grades 7–12 researched a state of their choice and made a brochure to present to the class. Samples of their work are presented in Appendix A. For this project, each NNES student worked at his or her own pace and used words and pictures to illustrate the key historical and geographical concepts. The project taught English while helping each NNES student relate to the real world and learn new information about the United States. Less proficient students were able to produce information when they worked in groups or with more capable students. With practice, each NNES student was able to present his or her brochure and explain the key facts to others in the class (see the unit plan in Figure 2 for details).

The sequential organizer within the district's curriculum for the theme Life in the United States/Immigration/New Places/Living in Two Cultures provides a time-frame approximation that stipulates NNES students will learn about Life in the United States and Living in Two Cultures from September to November. Goals 1.2, 1.3, 2.1, 2.2, 2.3, and 3.1 for New Beginnings as set forth by the state (Pennsylvania Department of Education, 2005) and TESOL (1997) as shown in Life in the United States/Immigration/New Places/Living in Two Cultures list several activities that can be used for lesson planning (Figure 5). All activities use English to teach the language at various levels; therefore, the activities can be adapted from year to year to cover different immigrant groups or Native American tribes or specific places and different focuses. The matrix activities also indicate what is appropriate for each English proficiency level. This helps teachers decide what type of activity to use to teach science content-area English to NNES students who are at the Beginning, Intermediate, or Advanced English proficiency level. In multilevel classes, the teacher can provide many activities within a lesson to meet the varied requirements while still focusing on vocabulary needs.

The Sample Unit Plan for Life in the United States/Immigration/New Places/Living in Two Cultures, as shown in Figure 6, has several activities to meet the varied needs of students in a 45-minute ESOL class.

In subsequent lessons, students can role play visits to specific states (Figure 6). They could make a timeline or another brochure that compares the state they live in now to their native country; they could write

Figure 5. Life in the United States/Immigration/
New Places/Living in Two Cultures

1.2 Life in the United States/Immigration/New Places/Living in Two Cultures,
activity:
1. Talk about and explain newly acquired concepts to each other with pictures
   mostly as context (B) or in writing/projects (I, A).

1.3 Life in the United States/Immigration/New Places/Living in Two Cultures,
activity:
1. Talk about and explain newly acquired concepts to another, then explain how
   this builds on previous knowledge (I, A).

2.1 Life in the United States/Immigration/New Places/Living in Two Cultures,
activities:
1. Discuss the names of groups of people and where they are found, looking
   at pictures and matching the name to pictures (B, I, A) and matching
   characteristics and other information of the people with their name (I, A).
2. Use literature selections for reading and grammar discussions, supplying
   context for students (B, I, A).
3. Summarize key concepts with pictures and labels (B), with simple sentences (I)
   or with more elaboration in paragraphs (A).
4. Role play a person's role in that particular culture or an animal of the area after
   watching a video or reading a story/information about the cultural group (B,
   I, A), present to the class or a small group (B) a poster, brochure, or diorama
   naming the habitat, the people and their lifestyle, types of animals, weather
   conditions, and plant life found in the region (using the labels put on the
   shoebox diorama (A), adding a little bit more information (I), or with more
   elaboration (A).

2.2 Life in the United States/Immigration/New Places/Living in Two Cultures,
activities:
1. Discuss names of people and animals and where they are found, looking
   at pictures and matching the name to pictures (B, I, A) and matching
   characteristics and other information of the people and culture to their name
   (I, A).
2. Summarize key concepts with pictures and labels (B), with simple sentences (I),
   or with more elaboration in paragraphs (A).
3. Answer questions about the reading materials in writing with phrases (B),
   simple sentences (I), or with more elaborations (A).
4. Use *National Geographic* and the Internet to gather information about the
   groups of people and their cultures as group work (B), with a partner (I), or
   independently (A).
5. Brainstorm on how to use the reading materials to create a poster, brochure, or
   diorama (B, I, A).

continued on p. 69

Revitalizing a Curriculum for School-Age Learners

**Figure 5 (cont.). Life in the United States/Immigration/
New Places/Living in Two Cultures**

6. Make a poster, brochure, or diorama of a specific culture, including pictures
   or models of people, animals, plants, and weather conditions in the poster,
   brochure, or diorama and label the parts (B); label and write a small report in
   simple sentences (I) or in paragraph form (A).
7. Follow oral and written directions to make a historical timeline with picture
   cues (B) or with a partner (I, A).
8. Look at the *Grand Canyon: A Trail through Time* by Vieira (1997).

2.3 Life in the United States/Immigration/New Places/Living in Two Cultures,
activities:
1. Summarize key concepts from classroom discussions or readings with pictures
   (B, I) or with or without pictures (A)
2. Use literature selections for reading and grammar discussions, supplying
   context for students (B, I, A).
3. Role play a person doing something specific to the culture after watching a
   video or reading a story/information about the immigrants or Native American
   in a group of people (B, I, A) or working in a group (B).
4. Working independently, make a timeline/chart of environmental development
   in a region of the world (I, A).

3.1 Life in the United States/Immigration/New Places/Living in Two Cultures,
activities:
1. Role play giving and answering questions or asking for help in classroom
   situations about different topics, such as the lifestyle of the immigrants or
   Native Americans in different periods of time with scaffolding and picture
   prompts (B) or without the picture prompts (I, A).
2. Use a picture dictionary to validate choice of language and words when
   discussing customs, habitats, health, and issues (B, I) or use a regular dictionary
   or other books and reading materials (A).

a comparison or make a poster to show similarities and differences. One
year, I had students present their brochures to each other and compare and
contrast the respective information and brochure design. Using the different
types of activities, this unit covers broad concepts in the district's K–12 science and social studies curricula. Students are assessed according to a rubric,
which has highlighted the key components each student must meet. Points
are allocated for each section (e.g., brochure must be neat, understandable,
and colorful and must have appropriate information; see Appendix B).
Students know beforehand how the brochure will be graded and are shown
other students' brochures from previous years. The teacher also provides the
materials and layout guidelines.

Conclusion

As I think about how I apply and use these thematic matrices in my district curriculum, I realize that one thread runs through the process: adaptability and change. Instruction is not a smooth, clear path. Every day, ESOL teachers must overcome dips, detours, and roadblocks. Students from different cultures have varied views on instruction and the paths to learning. I remember one boy from Japan who would shut down verbally whenever he had to speak. At the same time, he wrote more reflective journals than his more verbal brother. Providing variation proved the key to helping both boys increase their L2 learning. At the same time, the themes and subsequent activities within the thematic matrices are varied enough that although activities can differ from year to year, they teach the same basic concepts in a spiraling fashion, depending on the progression NNES students make with their L2 learning. It is much easier for teachers to develop additional activities around the themes when they have ideas on which to build. This strategy also allows new NNES students with no English to step into the L2 learning situation because the teacher can integrate past concepts into new activities. This process creates flexibility within the ESOL curriculum so that as they use grade-level concepts to teach English, teachers can also consider their NNES students' interests, cultural differences, and proficiency levels. These factors support incorporating thematic matrices into a K–12 ESOL curriculum because they enhance ESOL instruction.

Using thematic matrices reduces my planning time; thus, I can spend more time being creative and adapting specific tasks for individual student needs. When I finish a unit, such as Native Americans of the Northwest or Discovering the States, I can refresh my mind more easily because the next ideas and concepts are already organized in the curriculum and matrices. I simply need to devise a way to teach the material differently than I did the year before. Teachers in other districts with whom I have shared these concepts report similar feelings. For example, one colleague wrote,

> *As I constantly move from building to building, the thematic matrices help keep me organized as to what type of materials I need at different times in different buildings. This way I know that during a certain time period I will need to get materials to Building A so that I can teach my [English language learners] simple verb tenses as they talk and read and write about their world and community. In Building B I will use other materials to teach similar concepts, but I may need to add the past tense in our discussion and writing. The thematic matrices help me choose materials and topics around which to teach language, in a more organized way. (C. Morgan, personal communication, April 21, 2005)*

Figure 6. Sample Unit Plan for Life in the United States/ Immigration/New Places/Living in Two Cultures

Unit Theme
Life in the United States/Immigration/New Places/Living in Two Cultures
(grades 6–8)

Unit Plan General Objective
Students will learn English words to describe the geography and history of a
people and place and write the information with pictures in a brochure. (Unit title:
Discovering the States)

Specific Objective
Students will be able to name key facts of their state, including the capital and
abbreviation, and describe the geography and climate of the state as well as its
natural resources, historical background, industry, early settlers, government,
Native Americans, and entertainment with simple words and phrases (B), in simple
sentences (I), or in more complex paragraphs (A). (TESOL/PA Goals and Standards:
2.1, 2.2, and 2.3)

Materials
Sample travel brochures, Internet, atlases, construction paper, note paper

Motivation
Ask students whether they have ever been to or seen pictures of the Grand Canyon
or seen the Statue of Liberty. Ask where are they located. Ask what state the students
are living in now? Locate it on a map. Discuss how big "grand" is and what a canyon
is. Look it up on a map and discuss its location in relation to where the students live.
Show students travel brochures and talk about how they learned about the United
States before they moved there. Ask how they acquired the information. Hand out
the rubric and explain how their project will be graded.

Activities
Day 1: Have students look at the pictures and brochures as the teacher or more
proficient students read each page, labeling the key features with Post-it® notes with
specific vocabulary words on them (B, I).
Day 2–5: Have students search for information in books, atlases, and the Internet
and then organize it in a brochure following a sample layout provided by the teacher;
have students do this in a group (B, I) or independently (A).
Day 6–8: Have students print out and write up the information and then proofread
it in groups with the teacher (B) or with each other (I, A) before gluing it on the
brochure paper.

Closure
Day 1. Have students draw pictures (B) or write simple sentences (I) or a paragraph
summary (A) to say what information the brochure has given them.

continued on p. 72

Figure 6 (cont.). Sample Unit Plan for Life in the United States/Immigration/New Places/Living in Two Cultures

Ask students how the title ties into what they have read. Explain they will pick a state to do research on and answer the following key questions: What is the capital and abbreviation? How would you describe the geography and the climate or weather of the state? How would you describe the state's natural resources, historical background, industry, early settlers, government, Native Americans, and entertainment?

Day 2–5: Organize reading and written material and pictures for the brochure, checking with the teacher or others in the group as needed (B, I, A).

Day 6–8: Decide what to speak about and practice speaking.

Assign
Practice orally reading key facts from the brochure to present to the class on days 9 and 10; describe one fact (B), several facts (I), or all facts (A).

Language Function
- Grammar forms of the verb *to be* in the present (B) or past and future tenses (I, A) with vocabulary associated with people, history, and weather and the time concepts of today, yesterday, and tomorrow
- Numbers and dates for important facts and mathematic conversions of Celsius to Fahrenheit (B, I, A)
- Vocabulary about discoveries, natural resources, clothing, and activities associated with weather, history, and entertainment (B, I, A)
- Geographic vocabulary related to civilizations in a specific time period associated with specific climatic conditions of the state (B, I, A)

Evaluation
Were the students able to do the task at their proficiency level for what was required of them? Grade students' projects based on the rubric provided.

Thematic curriculums offer opportunities for NNES students to use language and language learning strategies to create their identity in the new culture (Atkinson, 2002; Block, 2003; Watson-Gegeo, 2004) and negotiate meaning in a new culture (Donato, 2000; Johnson, 2004; Savignon & Sysoyev, 2002) while they are learning a second language. As they begin to understand their new world and the diverse people in the United States, they can begin to see how they can relate to their new world. Thematic matrices help us articulate and enact our beliefs about quality teaching and learning. Borrowing from a well-known writer, I would like to encourage students and ESOL teachers to try the concepts of matrices in their curriculum and know that they will then have the freedom to know:

Oh the places, you'll go! . . . Today is your day. You're off to Great Places! You're off and away! You have brains in your head. You have feet in your shoes . . . you can steer yourself any direction you choose. You're on your own. And you know what you know. And YOU are the [one] who'll decide where to go. You'll look up and down streets. Look 'em over with care. About some you will say, "I don't choose to go there." With your head full of brains and your shoes full of feet, you're too smart to go down any not-so-good street . . . . Out there things can happen and frequently do to people as brainy and footsy as you. And when things start to happen don't worry. Don't stew. Just go right along. You'll start happening [learning] too. Oh! THE PLACES YOU'LL GO! (Geisel as Dr. Seuss, 1990, pp. 1–8)

Appendix A: Sample Product

OUTSIDE OPENED PART OF BROCHURE
BY AN ADVANCED NNES STUDENT IN GRADE 11

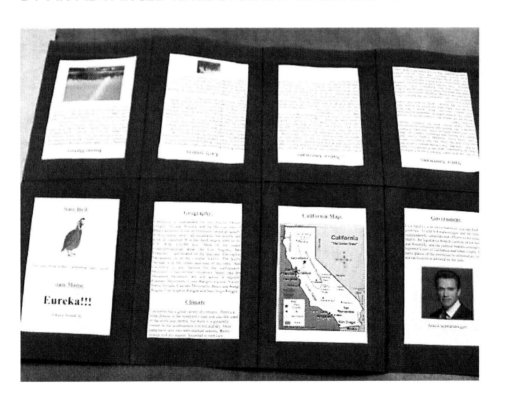

OUTSIDE VIEW OF THE BROCHURE
BY AN INTERMEDIATE NNES STUDENT IN GRADE 7

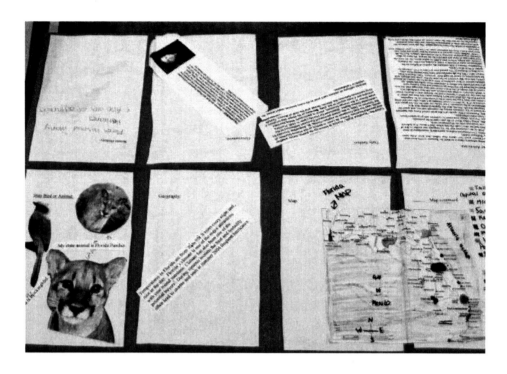

Appendix B: State Travel Brochure Rubric

Name _____

Grade _____ / 125

For sample layouts, see illustrations on the board and copy on the back.

In class, work:

Quiet, on task	5 points per day
On task or quiet	3 points per day
Trying	1 point per day
No effort or work	0 points per day

T   W   TH   F   M   T   W   TH   F

___ ___ ___ ___ ___ ___ ___ ___ ___ = ___ / 45 total

Brochure Grading:

Appearance: _____

Neat, colorful, easy to read, understand, follows directions = 20 points

Project has all elements stated above:	20
Most elements above	17
Some elements above	15
A few elements above	10
Tried	5
No elements	0

YOUR TOTAL   ___/20

Content:

Answer: What is your state's name, abbreviation, location, climate, geography, historical facts such as early settlers, immigrants, Native Americans; industry, natural resources, entertainment, state flag, flower, animals, government, a map of the state with the capital and key cities.

You have:	All	Most	Some	Few	None
• answered all questions	5	4	3	2	0
• organized your information	5	4	3	2	0
• written in YOUR OWN WORDS	5	4	3	2	0
• with your own opinion	5	4	3	2	0
• grammatically correct	5	4	3	2	0
• used elaboration	5	4	3	2	0

• 60 points (5 points for each element stated above for each of the 14 questions maximum)

YOUR TOTAL   _____ / 60   FINAL TOTAL   _____ / 125

Revitalizing Language Learning Through Cross-Curricular Integration

5

CARLA JOHNSON AND SUZANNE WEBSTER

This chapter is based on the work of a struggling elementary/junior high school that had been teetering on the brink of closure. In the late 1990s, a charter school opened in Calgary, Alberta, Canada, that was to cater to the English as a second language (ESL) population. The Alberta government granted permission for this school to open its doors for 5 years, after which the school would be assessed. The school struggled to find success. When 5 years had passed, the government granted the school a conditional license. The whole school needed to improve its results to gain full renewal; the assessors would be back to check on progress in two years. With the threat of the school's closure, the staff embarked on a journey together that would lead to a new approach to curriculum and language learning for the entire school.

The Curricular Context

Calgary is an up-and-coming urban center in Canada. The energy sector is fueling its growth. Both immigrants and native-born Canadians alike are flooding into the city, drawn by the promise of good jobs and a healthy economy. Due to this influx, Calgary's ESL population is growing exponentially; young ESL learners attend public, Catholic, private, and charter schools by the thousands. The number of ESL students in the province has tripled over the past 7 years. There are approximately 40,000 ESL students enrolled in the provincial school system; our own city has accepted close to half of these students as it is the fourth largest immigration population intake center in Canada (*ESL in 2006: 17,613 students and counting*, 2006). An overwhelming number of these learners are in mainstream classrooms and use the mainstream curriculum. There is little consistency in ESL program delivery across the city; from pullout to in-class to sheltered to bilingual support, educators are trying to meet the needs of ESL learners the best way they know how.

Our program is set in a small charter school for school-age learners from Kindergarten to Grade 9. There are nine charter schools in Canada, all of them in the province of Alberta. These schools are publicly funded the same as any other public educational institution, the difference being that charter schools specialize in one particular area to focus on the specific needs of the learning community.

Our learning community is approximately 600 ESL students and 40 teachers. The predominant first language of the students is Arabic; however, there are a number of other languages represented in the student body, such as Somali, Amharic, and Urdu. The charter school is required to teach the mandated provincial curriculum to its students as well as to provide a distinctive language-learning program. Due to the demanding nature of teaching the provincial curriculum and providing a distinctive language-learning program at the same time, an innovative approach to instruction has been devised. A sheltered program is the support method of choice; at every grade level, learners have been placed in classrooms with other learners who demonstrate similar language proficiency. The 40 teachers on staff are required to differentiate their instruction appropriately, according to the language-learning needs in their classroom. Many of them have turned to thematic instruction to address the dual objectives in the school in order to help their students learn the curriculum content through another language.

The teaching staff has varying levels of experience and expertise in teaching ESL. Some have taught English as a foreign language, and many have taken a few courses from the local university, but most expertise has been developed on the job and in the classroom. Efforts in professional development at the school have focused on teaching language through content. Building the professional capacity of the teaching staff has been a priority for the past 5 years; experts from the university were often brought in to deliver workshops and seminars. As the skill levels of the staff rose, many teachers felt they needed more than sporadic workshops to continue to improve; they required an in-house teaching specialist (i.e., a TESL specialist or coordinator) to provide support for classroom teachers through assessment, team planning, and teaching. It is from this perspective that we, the authors, are writing—we became the ESL program coordinators, one of us as the first coordinator at the school followed subsequently by the other as a second coordinator. As ESL program coordinators, we were also able to serve as TESL specialists. As the professional capacity of staff is on the rise, the awareness of the enormity of this challenge increases as well. As usual, the educational clock is ticking; time is always a factor. The charter school must prepare its learners for the public system where they will be expected to compete with their native-English-speaking peers.

Collier (1987) stated that language learners have to receive an average of 1.5 years of content for every 1 year of school to achieve grade-level proficiency. Therefore, second language learners need to learn 50% more information than mainstream learners in the same amount of time so that they can succeed in their academic achievement, given that they need to learn the language needed to understand curriculum in addition to the content. It is a constant race against time, and anything teachers can do to facilitate this process is valuable. Teachers in our charter school have discovered that thematic teaching is an asset when racing against the educational clock, and there is a movement within this group to become even more effective through the cross-curricular integration of core subjects.

Motivation for the Innovation

The idea of cross-curricular integration is not new. Cross-curricular integration is the combination of subject areas that can make learning significant for students by giving them the opportunity to build their own knowledge, undergo learning experiences that are better adjusted to the way they naturally learn, and apply varied study skills in a purposeful way (Johnson & Janisch, 1998; Lipson, Valencia, Wixson, & Peters, 1993; Loughran, 2005; Vogt, 1997). It is common practice in cross-curricular integration to merge content areas under a theme that is inspired by the learners' interests. Cross-curricular thematic teaching facilitates the construction of knowledge and enables students to take ownership of their own learning (Loughran, 2005; Vogt, 1997).

Language instruction through cross-curricular thematic teaching can save language learners a significant amount of time. For instance, a Grade 9 student in the province of Alberta must receive 150 hours of language arts instruction and 100 hours of social studies content. Social studies is an overwhelming subject for language learners in that it contains an enormous amount of academic language and is focused on such complex concepts as quality of life and industrialization. One hundred hours seems like an insufficient amount of time for a student who is struggling to *catch up*.

Considering that the Alberta language arts curriculum is fairly unconstrained and can be easily integrated into and learned through other subject areas, it seems reasonable for a teacher to integrate these two subjects. By doing so, teachers can give language learners 250 hours of exposure to social studies academic lingo, as opposed to 100, and simultaneously attend to the language arts objectives. Language learners have more time to acquire language, expand both oral and literacy skills, and gain knowledge of social studies and language arts concepts through a common theme that is interesting to them.

The benefits of cross-curricular integration for language instruction are not restricted to the time factor. Second language research shows that learners acquire language more efficiently when it is meaningful and authentic for them (Edelsky, Altwerger, & Flores, 1991; Freeman & Freeman, 1992; Haas, 2000; Krashen, 2004; Nunan, 2004). The thematic nature of cross-curricular integration offers a meaningful, connected context in which language is intentionally enriched, reconciling language and content learning for second language learners in mainstream classrooms (Haas, 2004; Johnson & Janisch, 1998; Lipson et al., 1993; Loughran, 2005; Vogt, 1997). In other words, second language instruction benefits from three elements: meaningfulness, authenticity, and intentionality. Cross-curricular integration can provide a forum for all of these components.

A CROSS-CURRICULAR LANGUAGE CLASS IS MEANINGFUL, AUTHENTIC, AND INTENTIONAL

Students learn when something is meaningful to their reality. They construct meaning to fill in gaps in their own conceptual framework (Loughran, 2005). Given that cross-curricular integration frequently relies on thematic teaching, students actively construct their knowledge in the context of the theme, one that is often interesting and motivating to them. One of the themes in the Grade 9 curriculum is Quality of Life. This topic could be abstract; however, students can be easily motivated to examine their own quality of life. This is a natural starting point for the more complex concepts surrounding quality of life for the broader community.

Like cross-curricular thematic teaching, second language acquisition research suggests that people acquire language when engaged in meaningful interactions (Edelsky et al., 1991; Freeman & Freeman, 1992; Krashen, 2004; Nunan, 2004). A focus on meaning allows second language learners to connect content to their own experiences and background knowledge as well as to critically analyze the information in the material (Ahmed, 1994; Cummins, 2001a; Vygotsky, 1978).

According to Vogt (1997), authentic tasks are defined as "ones in which reading and writing serve a function . . .They focus on student choice and ownership [and] extend beyond classroom walls" (p. 1). Authentic, real-world tasks provide meaning to students, who draw upon their background knowledge to solve problems in the classroom. In our Quality of Life unit, for example, the students began the unit with a critical look at their own quality of life. Students were required to assemble an artifact box that represented their lifestyle. Once students had been guided through this process, they were introduced to a television infomercial. Students had to reflect and reassess what quality of life really means and how it is constructed. The infomercial was the real-world, authentic task that students face every time they turn on the television.

Through language, individuals are able to share ideas. The importance of the negotiation for meaning in language learning has been highlighted in many sources as a necessary condition in the mastery of a second language (Cummins, 2001a; Long, 1985; Long & Porter, 1985; Pica, Holliday, Lewis, & Morgenthaler, 1989; Porter, 1986). Effective language learning occurs when language is intentionally spiraled, scaffolded, and recycled in a meaningful, authentic context (Gibbons, 2002; Roessingh, 1999; Roessingh & Johnson, 2004; Roessingh & Kover, 2003). Intentionally incorporating language in themes and lessons requires students to use it, which makes it more difficult to avoid unfamiliar language. Incorporating language structures right into the learning task leaves them no option but to use it. By intentionally combining language in the context of a cross-curricular theme, teachers promote its use as an essential building block to access curriculum content as opposed to something mechanical and uninteresting.

A CROSS-CURRICULAR LANGUAGE CLASS RELIES ON BROAD CONCEPTS EMBEDDED IN THE CURRICULUM

The Alberta Language Arts Program of Study (Alberta Education, 2000a) stated on its home page that concepts learned through their curriculum

> *reflect the essential knowledge, skills and attitudes that . . . students need to be well-prepared for future learning and the world of work; integrate how the study of a subject contributes to student personal growth and development; and ensure that each grade provides a foundation of knowledge for successful learning in subsequent years.*

A curriculum can prepare students for the world around them by helping them reflect on essential questions or broad concepts about the world, such as labels and names, community, identity, quality of life, needs, and wants. Language learners are able to understand broad concepts with instructed support (Roessingh, 1999; Roessingh & Kover, 2003). However, they often lack the academic language needed to understand the particularities of specific curriculum objectives built around these concepts; consequently, the particularities "get in the way" of broad concepts. For example, a concept that is dealt with in Grade 9 social studies is the idea of human needs; all humans have needs that must be met, and acquiring these needs fuels change and development on a global scale. Embedded in this broad concept are specific objectives; for example, students must be able to draw conclusions about technological change and identify its effects on quality of life. Although the idea of technology evolving to meet our needs is an intriguing one that students can understand, this idea is communicated through the use of dense grade-level text. By the time our students sort through the vocabulary and make sense of the details pertaining to how technology revolutionized the automobile industry, for example, the broad concept of how quality of life was improved is buried beneath a pile of notes on new vocabulary definitions.

By combining academic vocabulary, grammar, language functions, and a cross-curricular thematic organization, language is learned within the meaningful context of the theme and serves as a vital tool to access broad concepts. Language learners stand a better chance of success in understanding broad concepts if they are connected, overlapping, and supported by language instruction.

The Process of Adapting

It was recognized that all teachers needed to plan themes and lessons that would provide a meaningful context for language instruction. It was also recognized that all teachers did not have the time, inclination, or expertise to immediately revolutionize and alter their practice. An action research project was developed to bring all teachers up to speed and on board. The Language Through Content movement became the foundation of the teachers' work. Although content served as the vehicle, language became the essential learning. Comprehending the language led to understanding content. A Web tool created by Roessingh (2005) called Learning by Design became the backbone of the project. Learning by Design is a language-focused curriculum framework that provides the components necessary for the creation of thematic units that connect language and content, with an emphasis on language. Learning by Design requires that the teachers make pedagogical decisions around (a) what is intentional learning and what is incidental learning, (b) how the language component will assist in the learning of content, and (c) how the presentation of content will intentionally support the language component. In addition, the framework relies on the use of learning strategies, an important element for language learners who need to overcome their language shortfall.

The project began with all teachers on staff benefiting from intensive support in their planning as they learned to use the Web tool. Through this tool, the foundational ideas of authenticity, meaningfulness, and intentionality were applied. Teacher leaders were established in the first year of the project. Six teachers who volunteered were provided with 2 days of school-supported leave from their classrooms to engage in team learning and planning with the ESL coordinator. In the following year, these six teachers along with the coordinator took on teams of their own to guide through the planning process. As the capacity of the staff increased, so did the level of discourse. Staff teams now discussed how they could better support their learners through the curriculum. These discussions led to an extension of the existing action research project. The project moved from its foundations of teaching language through content to teaching language through cross-curricular integration.

Once again, a similar process was begun. A small group of volunteer teachers were given intensive support through school-supported leave so that they could become in-house specialists, capable of leading their own team of teachers in the future. The larger staff body took part in after-school workshops and planning sessions where they developed thematic materials as grade-level teams. This intensive work resulted in language being intentionally planned. The cross-curricular work facilitated this process. The connection between overlapping broad concepts—normally separated by the boundaries of subject areas—provides a rich, more connected context for language development. Language is more effectively spiraled, scaffolded, and recycled when a cross-curricular theme becomes the focus.

Artifacts: The Cross-Curricular Unit

The Humanities unit, a product of one of the staff teams in the fourth year of the project, integrates Grade 9 social studies and language arts around the theme of Quality of Life. This is only one example from the collection of over 150 units produced by the staff team over the course of the project. The purpose of this unit is to teach the academic language necessary for the acquisition of social studies content as well as to practice literacy skills from a language arts perspective. The language arts learning outcomes allow for the development of academic language.

The curriculum-planning tool Learning by Design helped us keep track of our pedagogical choices and served as both a guide and resource through the many complex decisions involved in teaching language through cross-curricular integration. The following are the steps we took in developing our Quality of Life unit.

DESIGN CUBE

1. Identify the broad concepts and rationale for social studies as written in the curriculum.
2. Reorganize the social studies content as laid out in the curriculum to enable increased scaffolding, spiraling, and recycling.
3. Merge the language arts curriculum with social studies. (We started again by identifying the broad, general language arts outcomes.)
4. Identify grammar, vocabulary, language functions, and learning strategies embedded in the concepts and outcomes to ensure that every objective or outcome is integrated within the context of the theme. These are either written explicitly in the curriculum or will be necessary scaffolds to reach the curriculum objectives.

DEVELOPMENT CUBE

5. Develop a lesson sequence to assess prior knowledge, build background knowledge, bolster language skills, integrate new content, and assess learning.

MATERIALS CUBE

6. Develop tasks to follow the lesson sequence and provide scaffolding for learning. Return to the Development Cube.
7. Identify appropriate assessments.

Our tasks are related to and relevant for our students' reality: teenagers and their perceptions of quality of life, technology (or lack thereof), and how technology affects one's quality of life. Our context provides the meaningfulness needed to make this unit interesting and motivating, which ultimately facilitates the learning of language in context. The materials were taken from real-world sources, making the tasks authentic. These materials were modified to fit our students' language proficiency levels. Grammar and language functions are directly taught to students but drawn from the context of the tasks.

Figures 1 and 2 show the steps we took in developing our Quality of Life Unit. Appendixes A–D provide samples of the materials developed or modified for the humanities unit. This unit was delivered to a Grade 9, low intermediate class of 22 students over the course of a month. The class had daily instruction for 50 minutes each period. The unit was implemented for language arts during the course of each day. For more detailed information and a guide through the process, please refer to www.learningbydesign .ucalgary.ca.

Conclusion

TEACHER REFLECTIONS

Overall, the Humanities unit (shown in Figures 1 and 2 as well as Appendixes A–D) was well received by the students. They were engaged and interested in the material. The learners were able to identify reading strategies in this unit and successfully transfer these strategies to other subject areas. They became conversant with the target vocabulary and language structures. One of the learning strategy goals was elaboration; this was very successful, as the students became candid in regards to lifestyles in their countries of origin. An offshoot of this was a stronger student–teacher bond because students were sharing personal information about themselves that was seen as valuable to their learning. The cooperation learning strategy seemed to teach itself, as students were genuinely interested in their classmates' life stories and opinions. In retrospect, this unit had significant transference as there is a strong sense of community in the class that was not there before.

Figure 1. Sample Curriculum Products:
Grade 9 Humanities Unit

Project Information

LEARNING BY DESIGN

Curriculum Unit designed by:	Suzanne Webster & Carla Johnson
Date:	October 15, 2005
Theme title:	Grade 9 Humanities — Quality of Life

Student Profile of Target group:

Age:	Division Three (ages 12–14)
Proficiency:	General Proficiency

Rationale:	To help students understand technological change and its effect on the quality of life within a mixed economy in order to make informed choices about economic growth

continued on p. 86

Figure 1 (cont.). Sample Curriculum Products:
Grade 9 Humanities Unit

DESIGN CUBE

Strategies:

Chamot and O'Malley[1]:	☐ Advance organization
	☐ Previewing the main ideas and concepts of the material to be learned, often by skimming the text for the organizing principle.
	☐ Inferencing
	☐ Using information in the text to guess meanings of new items, predict outcomes, or complete missing parts.
	☐ Cooperation
	☐ Working together with peers to solve a problem, pool information, check a learning task, or get feedback on oral or written performance.
	☐ Elaboration
	☐ Relating new information to prior knowledge, relating different parts of new information to each other, or making meaningful personal associations with the new information. Dividing language into meaningful chunks

Language:

Vocabulary:	☐ Lifestyle, change, choices, opinion—related vocabulary
Forms:	☐ Present simple tense vs. past
	☐ Parts of speech
Functions:	☐ Expressing belief
	☐ Opinion
	☐ Expressing agreement and disagreement

Concepts:

Concepts:	☐ Individual
	☐ Community
	☐ Choices
	☐ Change

continued on p. 87

[1] Chamot, A. U. & O'Malley J. M. (1994). *The CALLA handbook: How to implement the cognitive academic language learning approach.* Reading, MA: Addison-Wesley.

Figure 1 (cont.). Sample Curriculum Products: Grade 9 Humanities Unit

Content Specific Concepts:	Social Studies (Alberta Program of Study):
	• Quality of life, lifestyles (physical, economic, spiritual, social etc.)
	• Identify and define topic
	• Acquire information to find answers
	• Differentiate between main and related ideas
	• Identify and evaluate relationship among the purposes, messages and intended audience of visual communications
	• Make notes that outline the main idea and related ideas while listening and observing
	• Compare information about a topic from 2 or more sources
	• Draw conclusions about technological change and its effect on quality of life
	• Categorize information to develop concepts
	• Make generalizations by stating relationships among concepts
	• Write point of view in a position paper
	• Develop increased facility in communicating with others
	• Observe the courtesies of group discussion, contributing to the group and group processes
	• Accept that change is a common feature of life
	• Awareness that technology raises many ethical issues
	• Appreciation that social issues are complex
	Language Arts (Alberta Program of Study):
	1.1. (discover and explore)
	1.2. (clarify and extend)
	2.1. (use strategies and cues)
	2.2. (respond to texts)
	2.3. (understand forms, elements and techniques)
	2.4. (create original texts)
	3.1. (plan and focus)
	3.2. (select and process)
	3.3. (organize, record and evaluate)
	3.4. (share and review)
	4.1. (enhance and improve)
	4.2. (attend to conventions)
	4.3. (present and share)
	5.1. (respect others and strengthen community)
	5.2. (work within a group)

continued on p. 88

**Figure 1 (cont.). Sample Curriculum Products:
Grade 9 Humanities Unit**

MATERIALS CUBE

Realia:	• Artifact box • Artifacts
Text:	"American Teens Say Quality of Life and Relationships Are Important" — article "Embrace" — poem "All This Technical Wizardry" — poem "Once Upon A Time" — short story from Alberta authorized resource
Audio-visual:	• Infomercial • Graphic Organizers

DEVELOPMENT CUBE

Lessons:	1. Lifestyle survey (cooperative learning/getting to know you and your priorities) 2. What is quality of life for you? (Introduction to article, artifact box) 3. Teenagers and Quality of Life (reading strategies, graphic organizer, grammar instruction) 4. Infomercial (video, graphic organizer, jigsaw, grammar recycle) 5. "Embrace" & "Technophobe" (concepts, vocabulary, figurative language, grammar recycle) 6. Back to the artifact box (reflection on quality of life, application of new concept, vocabulary and grammar recycle) 7. Position paper (graphic organizer — brainstorming) 8. Language of opinion (functions to express opinion in an essay) 9. Writing and editing 10. Response to core literature (writing assessment in response to "Once Upon A Time")

continued on p. 89

Figure 1 (cont.). Sample Curriculum Products: Grade 9 Humanities Unit

Tasks:	Survey Article — vocabulary prep work (contextual guessing game), contextual guessing within the article, reading strategies, graphic organizer artifact box — representing concepts with realia, vocabulary recycle infomercial — graphic organizer jigsaw poems — contextual guessing, introduction to literature circles (guided discussion to access imagery and metaphor) form and function worksheets scaffolded writing response to literature
Assessment:	Vocabulary (worksheets, use of vocabulary in writing tasks) graphic organizer writing (position paper/response to literature)

Linguistic impact was evident as well. The final exam elicited a reading response, and all students were able to answer this portion of the test using the format of the opinion essay they had worked on in class during the unit.

The Humanities unit was so successful that we shared it with another colleague on another school board. In this school, the same outcomes were observed; both students and teacher reported that they enjoyed the work. The teacher and students were so engaged with the unit that it seemed to take on a life of its own. This new teacher contributed additional materials she developed for the unit that she felt would help to scaffold some of the concepts. This material has been added to the collection to be used by other practitioners in the future.

THE PROCESS OF EVALUATING OUR REVITALIZATION

The assessment of our project has been easily facilitated by the nature of our school context. As a learning community, we strongly believe that the value of curriculum revitalization is in the improved results that the process of said revitalization can produce. If we as practitioners improve how we deliver the curriculum, this should result in measurable improved student learning. As such, we rigorously measure student progress. As a charter school, we are held to meticulous assessment standards by the education branch of our provincial government, Alberta Education. Standardized content exams are set by the province for all of its learners, ESL students included. It is through these exams we are able to measure our progress against learners in the rest of the province. These standardized tests provide a statistical measuring stick we use to track our progress through the years. However, these exams are

Figure 2. Grade 9 Humanities Unit Overview

Learning by Design Language/Cross-Curricular Theme	Social Studies Objectives (From Alberta Curriculum)	Language Arts Outcomes (From Alberta Curriculum)	Language (Vocabulary, Grammar, Functions, Strategies)
Quality of Life	*Topic C — Canada: Responding to Change* **General objectives:** • Quality of life is affected by changes in technology. • Technology has affected our way of life and will continue to influence our future. **Specific objectives:** • Identify and define topic • Acquire information to find answers • Differentiate between main and related ideas • Identify and evaluate relationship among the purposes, messages and intended audience of visual communications • Make notes that outline the main idea and related ideas while listening and observing • Compare information about a topic from 2 or more sources • Draw conclusions about technological change and its effect on quality of life • Categorize information to develop concepts • Make generalizations by stating relationships among concepts • Write point of view in a position paper • Develop increased facility in communicating with others • Observe the courtesies of group discussion, contributing to the group and group processes • Accept that change is a common feature of life • Awareness that technology raises many ethical issues • Appreciation that social issues are complex	*Alberta Language Arts Outcomes* 1.1. Discover and explore 1.2. Clarify and extend 2.1. Use strategies and cues 2.2. Respond to texts 2.3. Understand forms, elements and techniques 2.4. Create original texts 3.1. Plan and focus 3.2. Select and process 3.3. Organize, record and evaluate 3.4. Share and review 4.1. Enhance and improve 4.2. Attend to conventions 4.3. Present and share 5.1. Respect others and strengthen community 5.2. Work within a group	**Vocabulary:** • lifestyle, change, choices, opinion (related vocabulary) **Forms:** • present simple tense vs. past • parts of speech • comparative language **Language Functions:** • expressing belief • opinion • comparing (quality) • expressing agreement and disagreement **Learning Strategies:** • advance organization • inferencing • cooperation • elaboration • dividing language into meaningful chunks

Note that the unit overview is not part of the usual process; it is only a visual aid to demonstrate how the objectives in the curricula overlap.

only a small piece of the assessment puzzle. Our charter school maintains detailed portfolios for every student in the school. These portfolios contain information on student educational history as well as a record on standardized reading measures, writing samples, phonics and spelling exams, and oral language proficiency and vocabulary knowledge assessments. These portfolios have been in use since the inception of the school in 1996. With the advent of each new initiative, we are able to easily track the program effects and our progress through analysis of our portfolios in regards to student progress.

Since the inception of this new program of curricular revitalization, the school has been selected by the province on numerous occasions to present its exemplary work and progress to other school boards, and it has been recognized by the Fraser Institute, an independent public policy organization that focuses competitive markets through statistical analysis, as one of the "fastest improving schools" in the province. The school was granted a 5-year renewal based on two factors: the rapid improvement of student results in standardized assessments set by the province and the quality of programming that had been developed through the project. Five years is the maximum duration a charter can be granted in the jurisdiction. This means the school will come up for renewal again; provided the work continues, another 5 years will be granted.

Standardized test results alone demonstrate the impact of the work done in the classrooms. At the school level, portfolios are used to inform our work. Reading scores have increased at a more rapid rate since the inception of this program, language that has been explicitly addressed shows up in student writing samples, and the writing samples also demonstrate more cross-curricular connections. In addition to student progress measures, the staff agreed to implement progress measures that help them examine their own practice. The teachers developed a checklist of ESL teaching strategies that included providing for cooperative learning opportunities, modifying materials, direct grammar instruction, and vocabulary recycling. The checklist, published in the teachers' daily planner, was used in a number of different ways. It provided a focus for team teaching, team planning, and teachers observing other teachers in action, and as a tool for teachers to use to reflect on their practice. In addition to the checklist, reflective, anecdotal comments on each professional learning opportunity were expected of the staff team. These reflections were shared with the coordinator to provide insights as to the next steps in future professional development.

A school-wide undertaking such as this one does come with its share of challenges. Resistance to change is always a challenge. Moreover, a change that requires teachers to adjust their practice and how they approach their learners all within a new program structure (e.g., the sheltered model) can be overwhelming, to say the least. However, school-based administrative support was integral in moving through this resistance. A lesson learned early on was the importance of keeping administration informed. Many hours were spent with various levels of administration from teacher coordinators to curriculum leaders to principals to superintendents. If ever this step was overlooked, progress would be invariably slowed until the situation had been remedied and administration at all levels were informed and made a part of plans.

The six teachers who were provided with release time took ownership of the program early in the process. These teachers became the bearers of good news. We recognize the need to start small. By the time the second year of the program commenced, word of the program, its philosophies, and the tools (e.g., Learning by Design) had spread. The staff as a whole was ready to move forward. With so many teachers wanting to learn, time became an issue. Additional funding was gained through the province to provide every teacher in the school with 3 release days to learn and to plan as a team. These days were used to plan units, learn current ESL pedagogy, and adapt materials for students who needed language and content. At the programmatic level, another challenge has emerged. How does the coordinator provide ongoing support for those teachers who are now team leaders themselves in addition to new teachers on staff and everyone in between? Although this can be addressed through small team meetings, this challenge still presents itself at whole-school professional development days. We have tried to address this challenge through intensive training early in the year for teachers new to our program before they are integrated into other staff teams. We look to our teacher leaders for further insight on how this issue can be addressed in the coming years.

Appendix A: Modified Materials for Lesson 3 in the Development Cube

Modification: Text re-written

Strategies: Previewing the main ideas and concepts of the material to be learned, often by skimming the text for the organizing principle, inferencing, using information in the text to guess meanings of new items, predict outcomes, or complete missing parts, relating new information to prior knowledge, relating different parts of new information to each other, or making meaningful personal associations with the new information.

Language: Vocabulary, present simple tense vs. past, opinion

Concepts: Individual, community, choices, additional subject area objectives

American Teens Say Quality of Life and Relationships Are Important

NEW YORK, February 3, 2003

Teenmark surveyed teenagers about their life *goals*. Most of them say quality of life and relationships with family and friends are more important than being famous or going into business.

Teenmark is an American company that surveys teenagers every year. In 2002, the Teenmark surveyed American teens on how they feel about money. The teenagers were realistic about their *finances*. Seventy-one percent of the teens said they choose how to spend their money. Twelve percent of them think credit cards are great. Sixty percent said credit cards are dangerous because you spend more than you have.

Teenmark mailed the surveys to the teenagers between April of 2001 and July of 2002. Four thousand six hundred young people between 12 and 19 years old *responded* to the survey.

The number one goal for American teenagers is enjoying life. Eighty-two percent said good relationships with friends is important. College and good relations with parents also *ranked* high. Eight-two percent of the teenagers said these things were important. Seventy-two percent agreed that having children was a goal. Only 17% agreed that going into business was a future goal.

Table 1. What are your life goals?

	% Agree	% Agree (Boys)	% Agree (Girls)
Enjoy life	**86**	**82**	**89**
Good relationships with friends	82	78	87
Go to college	82	79	86
Good relationships with family	82	78	86
Buy a house	81	78	84
Have a good job	80	78	82
Get married	78	73	83
Make lots of money	73	74	72
Have children	72	68	76
Travel	65	62	68

continued on p. 94

Table 1 (cont). What are your life goals?

	% Agree	% Agree *(Boys)*	% Agree *(Girls)*
Give back to community	41	37	45
Retire early	32	36	27
Be famous	29	29	28
Go into the arts	17	15	20
Go into business	17	20	13

Source: Mediamark Research Inc. (MRI) 2002 Teenmark Study

Stress

Teenagers today do not feel relaxed. Most of them say they live with *significant* stress in their lives. More than half of American teenagers said they feel stressed out all the time or sometimes. Schoolwork is the number one cause for stress. Seventy-one percent of teenage girls think that schoolwork is a cause for *tension.*

Table 2. How often do you feel stressed out?

	% Agree	% Agree *(Boys)*	% Agree *(Girls)*
All the time/sometimes	51	43	58
Almost never	41	45	36
Never	2	3	1
Why do you get stressed?			
A lot of school work	66	61	71
Not enough sleep	50	41	59
Not enough money	42	40	46
Not enough time	40	34	47
Relationships with your parents	37	31	44
Relationships with your friends	37	28	47
Too many responsibilities	35	31	39
Relationships with your brothers and sisters/other family	35	29	41
Your weight/body image	30	18	44

continued on p. 95

Table 2 (cont). How often do you feel stressed out?

	% Agree	% Agree *(Boys)*	% Agree *(Girls)*
Relationships with your boyfriend/girlfriend	29	24	33
The way you look	24	17	32
Your parents' relationship	23	20	26
Other people's health problems	14	10	19
Problems with your own health	14	9	19

Source: Mediamark Research Inc. (MRI) 2002 Teenmark Study

American Teens Say Quality of Life and Relationships Are Important

Reading Comprehension

Before you read the article, answer these questions:
1. What is a survey?
2. Read the title again. What is this article about?

Right There:
3. What do the majority of teenagers say is more important than being famous or going into the business world?
4. What is Teenmark?
5. What did 60% of the teenagers say about credit cards?
6. How many young people between 12 and 19 years old responded to the survey?

Think and Search:
7. Write 3 of the top goals among American teenagers.
8. How many teenagers said going into business was a future goal?
9. How many teenagers say they have significant stress in their lives?
10. Who gets more stressed about schoolwork: boys or girls?

On Your Own:
11. What does the word *stress* mean?
12. How important is money for these teenagers?
13. Find *your weight/body image* on the second chart. Weight means how much you weigh. What does *body image* mean?

Vocabulary — Contextual Guessing — Student A:

Word	What does it mean in the article?	Why do you think that?
	Things you want to get done, objectives	
	How you use your money	
Respond		
Ranked		
	Worry, stress, nervousness	
Significant		

Vocabulary — Contextual Guessing , Student B:

Word	What does it mean in the article?	Why do you think that?
	Answer	
Goals		
Finances		
	Say that something has a place or score, e.g., 1st place, 2nd place	
Tension		
	Big, large	

Appendix B: Materials for Lesson 6 in the Development Cube

Modification: Student-generated material from scaffolded questions and materials

Strategies: Advance organization, elaboration, relating new information to prior knowledge, relating different parts of new information to each other, or making meaningful personal associations with the new information.

Language: Vocabulary, present simple tense vs. past, expressing belief, opinion, expressing agreement and disagreement

Concepts: Individual, choices, change, additional subject area objectives

Artifacts of the Quality of Your Life
Past tense recycle, language of opinion

1. List the items in your artifact box and explain why you chose each one.
2. Now think about when you where a young child. What items would you have put in your artifact box when you were little? List and explain.
3. What items changed? Why?
4. What items remained the same? Why?
5. Go to http://puzzlemaker.school.discovery.com and create a word search from the words you used in your answers. Show me your work before you exchange with a partner.

Appendix C: Materials for Lessons 7 and 8 in the Development Cube

Modification: Student-generated material from scaffolded questions and materials

Strategies: Advance organization, using information in the text to guess meanings of new items, predict outcomes, or complete missing parts, elaboration, relating new information to prior knowledge, relating different parts of new information to each other, or making meaningful personal associations with the new information.

Language: Vocabulary, present simple tense vs. past, parts of speech, expressing belief, opinion, expressing agreement and disagreement

Concepts: Choices, change

Vocabulary for Argumentative Writing
When we write an argumentative essay, our opinions carry more weight if we look at both sides of the issue. In other words, we acknowledge our opponents' views but try to convince the reader that our own argument is stronger.

Our essay would be extremely dull if we used the words ***supporters*** and ***opponents*** all the way through. Similarly, it would be unimpressive if we only used the verb ***say*** to refer to people's opinions. The tables below contain lists of useful alternatives. Study them and then do the gap-fill task that follows.

+	−
Supporters	Opponents
Proponents	Opponents
Those in favour of …	Those opposed to …
Defenders of …	Critics of …
Advocates of …	Objectors
Pro-… (e.g. *Pro-abortionists*)	Anti-… (e.g. *Anti-abortionists*)
say that …	
Argue	
Claim	
Maintain	
Assert	
Contend	
Allege	
Insist	
Contend	
Suggest	
Point out	

Tasks

1. Complete the text below using words/phrases from the tables above. (Solid lines relate to the first table; dotted lines relate to the second.)

_____ of TV ………………….. that it exposes us to too much violence and, as a result, we become less sensitive to real-life violence. They also ……………………… that schoolchildren neglect homework and have problems concentrating in class as a result of spending too much time glued to the box. Finally, _____ ……………………… that television has turned many of us into over-weight, unfit "couch potatoes".

_____, on the other hand, …………….……… that it is a blessing for lonely, elderly or house-bound people. Furthermore, they …………………….., it does not simply entertain; it can be very educational as well. Another argument

_____ _____ of TV is that it sometimes plays an important role in fundraising for disaster relief and various charities. For example, the "Live Aid" rock concert in 1984 raised millions of pounds for victims of the Ethiopian famine.

2. Choose <u>another</u> controversial issue (e.g. hunting, car use, school uniforms, meat-eating, the use of animals in medical research, single sex schools, euthanasia). Write some sentences that express the views of people on both sides of the argument. Aim for variety in your choice of language.

Now you're ready to write.

Review "Guided writing process"

Go to writefix.com. Use the information on "How to Write Argument essays" to help you construct your essay.

Appendix D: Resources for Humanities Unit

Alberta Education. (1989). *Social studies K–9.*

Alberta Education. (2000b). *English language arts K–9.*

AOL. (2005). *All this technical wizardry.*

Gordimer, N. (1999). *Once upon a time.*

Mediamark Research Inc. (2003). *American teens say quality of life and relationships are important.*

Roessingh, H. (2005). *Learning by design.*

Seeq. (2005). *Embrace.*

Writefix. (2003). Writing argument and opinion essays.

A Mosaic of Change: An ESL Program's Journey to Meet the Challenges of Educating NNES Students

6

BARBARA FAGAN AND DEANNA BENAVIDES

If you've ever had the chance to admire the rich, colorful mosaics that line the walls and floors of European churches, you probably have marveled at how tiny, colorful stones could be designed to vividly depict detailed images of people and objects. Imagine bumping into a mosaic and releasing these intricately placed stones! What images could now be displayed with the mosaic pieces? Today, the mosaic analogy can be applied to how the Harrisonburg City Public School system, located in the state of Virginia's Shenandoah Valley in the United States, is rethinking, recreating, and redirecting its current English as a second language (ESL) program to meet the evolving and ever-changing needs of educating its nonnative-English-speaking (NNES) students.

This chapter focuses on two important changes that Harrisonburg High School implemented for its NNES students, starting in 2002 and continuing today—a change in content instruction and delivery and a change in its ESL instruction within the Intensive English Program. These changes involved ESL administrative and instructional staff, high school administrative and instructional staff, and the support services of an ESL educational consultant to help all stakeholders understand the academic needs of beginning level NNES students. The ESL and content teachers also learned how to incorporate effective reading and writing strategies into their instruction to help these students improve their English proficiency and attain success in mainstream content classes.

Curricular Context and Motivation for Change

Harrisonburg City Public Schools have seen rapid growth in the number of NNES students over the past 10 years, from 4% in 1995 to 38% in 2006. Harrisonburg was once known for its small pockets of Russian immigrants sponsored through various church groups and migrant Mexican farm workers, but its schools are now home to more than 1,658 NNES students from 64 countries. These students speak 44 languages (Harrisonburg City Public Schools, 2007).

Prior to 2003, the ESL program at Harrisonburg High School provided intensive English instruction for one or two periods daily to all levels of immigrant students. Newly arrived NNES students spent this time attending ESL classes that focused on oral language proficiency and grammar. Current research (Collier, 1995a, 1995b; Collier & Thomas, 1989; Cummins, 1979; Freeman & Freeman, 2000, 2002; Peregoy & Boyle, 2005) designates the need for today's NNES students to have academic knowledge of English as well as the interpersonal communicative skills necessary for school success. NNES students were placed in grade-level science, math, and social studies classes along with their ESL classes to make sure that they had these educational opportunities. However, these students were not able to keep up with their grade-level peers, and their low reading and writing skills caused failing grades. In addition, many were not able to pass the required End of Course (EOC) exams based on the Virginia Standards of Learning (SOL) for content subject areas.

Students were not the only ones experiencing difficulty. With the sudden influx of NNES students, classroom teachers, who were once comfortable delivering an instructional program that met the needs of their mostly English-speaking dominant learners, found themselves at a loss to communicate with students who had novice language skills and often lacked the expected academic preparation and content concepts that come with attending schools for many years in the same locality. In addition, Harrisonburg City Public Schools felt the pressure of having all students meet the goals of the No Child Left Behind Act and could find itself censured for failing to meet the expected educational targets in reading and math, especially the targets projected for subgroups such as Limited English Proficient (LEP) and Hispanic students. The educational mosaic of the 1990s for educating NNES students no longer met the academic needs of the current students and school system. The mosaic pieces did not fit and needed to be rearranged.

The Process of Reshaping a Program

Creating a culture of change is not easy. Program change requires the commitment of the entire educational community: central office staff, school principals, teachers, and school board members, as well as the use of community resources to begin to recreate the mosaic. In 2000, ESL researchers Dr. Virginia Collier and Dr. Wayne Thomas were invited to present their research on effective ESL programs to school administrators. They presented various options to meet the academic needs of NNES students and challenged the school division to move to the next level of effective instruction. Although the researchers reported that the greatest academic gains they found typically were for students in dual language immersion programs, they noted that there were also significant increases in student achievement in ESL programs that incorporated academic content into their English instruction. Although the majority of the NNES students in Harrisonburg City Public Schools are Spanish speakers, at this time, the school system is not able to implement bilingual or dual language immersion programs because of the lack of qualified bilingual teachers and the additional funds that would be needed to train or recruit teachers with a strong literacy foundation in both languages.

Therefore, for Harrisonburg City Public Schools, moving on to the next level of effectiveness has meant adding academic content to ESL instruction and a focus on literacy and language development to academic content. Administrators accepted the challenge and in the next few years looked for ways to move from a typical pull-out model of teaching English to a model that included teaching English through content. Collier and Thomas (1989) also emphasized that some of the instructional practices from the highly successful dual language programs can be applied to English content programs.

The Harrisonburg City Public Schools system has experienced gains from English content programs for its NNES students by providing specific training for ESL and grade-level content teachers. This training emphasizes the use of effective instructional practices that help NNES students access the content with greater understanding and provide opportunities for students to use their native language to help learn academic content. For example, when students do not understand new content vocabulary in their content classes, a student who speaks the same language can clarify information in their native language so students can refocus their attention on the lesson conducted in English. Content teachers generally have bilingual dictionaries in students' native languages available for use when additional clarification of unknown vocabulary is needed. Additionally, some content textbooks have bilingual components that have been ordered for those students who are able to read textbooks in their native languages.

While the increasing emphasis for the ESL department was on academic content, other high school departments were asked to increase their focus on literacy. During the 2000–2001 school year, Harrisonburg High School principal Irene Reynolds began work to create a school-wide expectation for literacy development across all curriculum areas by asking teachers to create literacy goals for all classes. During participation in a staff development session that compared students' instructional reading levels with the reading levels of current textbooks, Harrisonburg staff recognized the disconnect between what they expected their students to read and their native-English-speaking (NES) and NNES students' current reading abilities. Shockingly, almost 75% of the high school students were reading far below the instructional level of the content textbooks. Based on that realization, along with data from state assessments that showed that many students were struggling in reading and writing, most teachers realized that they had to make changes in their instructional delivery. The glue on the original teaching mosaic was now sufficiently loosened to make way for rearranging, recreating, and redirecting the stones.

ESL Content Models

Harrisonburg High School currently uses three models of sheltered content classes for its NNES students (see Figure 1). The first model is ESL integrated content classes. In the fall semester of 2002, Harrisonburg High School added integrated science and social studies classes to their course offerings in the ESL department. In this model, beginning level ESL students (typically reading below a third-grade level) study science and social studies with an ESL teacher in addition to their intensive English classes.

The ESL teacher works with newly arrived students on basic social studies and science concepts while focusing on English language development and vocabulary. For example, the ESL teacher might work on a unit about the U.S. government where students learn the vocabulary needed to write simple sentences about the three branches of government and the overall responsibilities of each branch. The ESL science class might work on a weather unit that introduces students to vocabulary and science concepts regarding hurricanes, volcanoes, and tornadoes. Students read and present short oral reports on these different weather phenomena. These classes begin to give students the basic vocabulary needed for science and social studies classes. However, it is unrealistic to think that this type of content class would be sufficient to prepare NNES students to meet the expectations for mainstream high school content classes.

The second model is based on content concepts classes. In the 2003–

Figure 1. ESL Content Models

Model 1: ESL Integrated Content Classes	Model 2: Content Concepts Classes	Model 3: Full-Year Content (SOL) Class
An ESL teacher delivers content to newly arrived and beginning level ESL students for one or two semesters. Students earn elective credit in ESL Content Classes.	A state-endorsed high school content teacher delivers content instruction to intermediate level ESL students for one semester as preparation for taking a SOL content course with another teacher the following semester. Students earn elective credit in Content Concepts classes.	A state-endorsed high school content teacher delivers an SOL content class to intermediate/advanced NNES students and NES for two semesters, with all students taking the state EOC test at the end of the second semester. Students earn both elective and state verified content credit in these classes.

2004 school year, content concepts classes such as Earth Science Concepts or World Geography Concepts were added to the science and social studies department offerings. These classes precede NNES students' entry into grade-level SOL content courses. Concepts classes are taught by Virginia certified content teachers and bridge the learning gap by introducing intermediate NNES students to important science and social studies topics and vocabulary of the content discipline that will be the foundation for future success in SOL content classes. Teachers use content materials at appropriate reading levels to help students learn not only the content objectives but also the learning strategies that are instrumental to become a successful student.

As an example of this approach, students in the mainstream World History class briefly cover all of the 30–32 civilizations required to pass the World History EOC exam, while students in the World History Concepts class cover only a few selected civilizations in greater depth. This allows time to work with students on reading, writing, and study skills as well as the history content. Content concepts teachers do not necessarily use a high-school-specific textbook but find other texts that support the necessary content, written at an appropriate reading instructional level. At the end of the course, the teacher may determine that some of the students are ready to take the EOC content exam for that course. If the students pass the state content exam, they then receive the necessary credit applied toward graduation and do not need to take the SOL course.

The third model, the full-year SOL class (e.g., U.S. History), is an adaptation of the content concepts class. Instead of a separate content concepts class followed by a grade-level SOL content class with each class taught by a different teacher, the third model designates one teacher with the same group of students studying grade-level content for two semesters. This model provides additional time for NNES students to learn the expected content and also provides explicit instruction in learning strategies, such as how to prepare an oral report, take notes from a textbook, and summarize important information about a topic. In the 2005–2006 school year, around 50 students were served in the integrated content ESL classes, 100 students in the content concepts classes, and 20 in the full-year U.S. History (SOL) class.

A key to the success of these classes is providing teachers with appropriate training in how to appropriately support the NNES students in learning academic content. All content teachers participated in a three-hour graduate course required of all Harrisonburg City Public Schools faculty, which provided strategies to integrate literacy skills into content area instruction and introduced the sheltered instructional observation protocol (SIOP) method (Echevarria & Short, 2004; Short & Echevarria, 1999, 2005). This class was offered on-site weekly over a 2- to 3-month period, and the high school content teachers learned how to plan language and content goals for each lesson and instructional strategies that provided scaffolding activities for teaching content.

To provide ongoing assistance to staff members who are teaching these various sheltered content models, the principal formed the Adolescent Literacy Department for teachers in science, social studies, math, ESL, and special education who work with students who are below grade level in reading. The school's literacy coordinator meets with these teachers several times a year, providing opportunities for teachers to learn from their peers and to focus on effective reading and writing instructional strategies. Additionally, the school media center provides multilevel books and generous resources on a wide range of topics for teacher and student use. Principal Irene Reynolds often reminds her staff that one textbook does not meet the needs of all students and that they should find books that make the content more accessible for all students.

In March 2005, Harrisonburg City Public Schools also benefited from another visit from Collier and Thomas, who reviewed their current research findings on effective instructional programs for NNES students (Thomas & Collier, 2003). These findings reaffirmed the method that the high school has chosen to integrate academic content into the ESL program and the continued commitment to curriculum and staff development.

ESL LANGUAGE ARTS

Once the sheltered content models were in place, it was time to continue rearranging and redesigning the mosaic stones to include the ESL classes in the Intensive English Program. Harrisonburg's secondary ESL program had benchmarks in reading and writing that were expected for different proficiency levels, but too few students were achieving these recommended scores. Fountas and Pinnell (1996) addressed the need to provide guided reading and writing within a balanced literacy program that includes elements such as reading aloud to students, guided reading, independent reading, guided writing, and independent writing. Based on teacher observations, it was clear that that the high school ESL teachers spent too much time on teaching isolated grammar items and not enough time incorporating grammar within the writing and reading curriculum.

The rearrangement of any instructional program can be frustrating for both the teachers and the administration. ESL teachers, who were once secure teaching basic English communication skills that often focused on grammar and vocabulary drills, now found themselves asked to teach English through content subjects like science, math, and social studies. Even more frustrating for many teachers was the emphasis on the reading process, which required a deep understanding of the stages of reading, especially at the emergent and beginning levels. Many of the high school ESL teachers had limited professional course work in teaching reading and writing and did not understand how to incorporate these different elements within their ESL classes.

Just as beginning NNES students need support and guidance to acquire English, teachers likewise need support and guidance with the changes expected in their instructional delivery. One-shot workshops on a new strategy can be uplifting and revitalizing for the workshop participants, but research points out that these new strategies, without direct support, often fade and diminish over time when other pressing needs arise (Gabriel, 2005; Routman, 2002). To effect change in the ESL program, the teachers needed to be involved in a long-term change process and be given an opportunity to voice their concerns about the changes they were facing.

From the time that the ESL program in Harrisonburg was established, secondary ESL teachers had met once a month after school for 2 hours, focusing primarily on program management issues. In 2004, ESL supervisor Wanda Hamilton and ESL specialist (and chapter co-author) Deanna Benavides decided to change the focus of these meetings. Barbara Fagan, a former ESL teacher and program coordinator (and chapter co-author) was invited to join the Harrisonburg City Public Schools ESL administrative team. Fagan was asked to use the monthly sessions as a vehicle to help the high school ESL teachers learn more about best practices in reading and writing strategies for NNES students and to help them learn how to make their language arts classes more balanced by incorporating oral language, teacher read alouds, and shared and guided reading and writing activities. The high school literacy coordinator was also invited to attend in an effort to strengthen the literacy–ESL connection. From 2004–2007, this core group, including the authors, has met regularly to organize and deliver teacher training for high school ESL teachers in the areas of literacy development and instructional models that meet the educational needs of NNES students, both of which are critical to reshape the ESL mosaic.

First, the secondary ESL program needs were reviewed, and a yearly framework with topics to be incorporated within the staff development plan was developed. For each session, literacy strategies that have been targeted in research on NNES students were modeled, such as the need for structured routines, activating students' prior knowledge, using a curriculum organized around themes or *big pictures*, helping students make connections with text, using authentic multicultural materials, and teaching reading and writing as a long-term developmental process (Collier, 1995b; Freeman & Freeman, 2000; Harvey & Goudvis, 2000).

Because the workshop meetings were monthly, the ESL teachers had an opportunity to practice new strategies and report back on their effectiveness or how they adapted the strategy for their students' needs. Immediately after each staff development session, teachers' feedback from the session was reviewed, and the next session was planned based on the needs of the ESL teachers or a topic that the teachers might not be familiar with but which was pertinent to their work with NNES students. Figure 2 shows the topics the high school ESL teachers covered in their monthly meetings during the first year together.

One major hurdle that was encountered in this process was the lack of available and appropriate instructional materials for ESL teachers who were expected to use fiction and nonfiction materials to improve the reading and writing skills of the students. In 2005, Harrisonburg City Public Schools allocated funds for the review and adoption of English and Language Arts textbooks that would be used in the schools for at least the next 5 years. The ESL supervisor decided this would be an appropriate time to adopt textbooks specifically for the ESL classes in the Intensive English Program. Some of the monthly meetings were used to guide teachers in the textbook and supplementary materials review process while they also learned the importance of explicitly helping students to use before, during, and after reading strategies in their lessons. The focus was on helping ESL staff review materials from a more comprehensive literacy approach that included selecting materials at the students' instructional reading levels as well as showing

Figure 2. Topics Covered in ESL Curriculum Meetings

Harrisonburg City Public Schools
ESL Curriculum Meetings 2004–05

Essential Outcomes

Participants will
- learn and implement the key components of a balanced language arts program for Level 1 English language learners (ELLs).
- learn, practice, and adapt effective instructional strategies that incorporate language, reading, and writing activities within the Level 1 language arts classroom.
- develop an instructional grid for curriculum delivery for beginning ESL students (1A, 1B, and 1C students) that includes classroom routines and potential thematic units.
- set goals for the 5-day curriculum project in June 2005.

Monthly Topics:

September 8	**Components of Balanced LA classroom for Level 1 students** • Oral Language • Reading • Writing for beginners
October 13	**Daily Routines** • Establishing a purpose for daily activities • Adapting instruction to meet group needs **Prioritizing Instruction**
November 10	**Application of State LEP & SOL Standards** **to Classroom Instruction**
January 12	**Planning Appropriate Reading Instruction** • Introduction to Harrisonburg Curriculum Grid • Examine State Curriculum Framework—Defining standards • Materials—Selection of appropriate resources for LA adoption
February 9	• Explicit strategy instruction • Practice before, during, and after strategies with sample text
March 9	**Textbook Adoption Process** • Review approved reading and language materials • Introduce the Instructional Delivery Model for Lesson Planning
April 13	**Overview of Year/ Planning for June Curriculum Writing** • Identify goals & end product • Using a template for unit development
June 7–10	**Curriculum Writing**

how the reading materials could introduce or reinforce important content concepts and vocabulary. Figure 3 details some of the reading and language texts that the ESL staff adopted in 2005 for the different levels of students who are designated as beginning proficiency; for example, recent arrivals, low beginning, and high beginning.

Harrisonburg High School follows a schedule with a 90-minute block for each class. As ESL teachers became more familiar with reading and writing strategies, they needed a framework to guide the process of incorporating these different language components within their daily lessons. Figure 4 shows the Balanced Literacy Instructional Framework that was developed and presented to the staff for review. ESL teachers' input regarding revisions to this model was important because teachers were expected to develop lessons based on the components of this model the following year.

As the textbook order was finalized, teachers expressed the need for pacing guides to assist them in integrating the components of the Balanced Literacy Instructional Framework and the chapters of the newly adopted texts. The pacing guides that were developed are structured overviews of the reading comprehension strategies, the writing and grammar focus, and the phonics and spelling patterns that are included in each unit or chapter of the newly adopted textbooks. In addition, the pacing guides give recommended

Figure 3. Reading and Language Texts for Different Levels of Beginning Proficiency

Intensive English A	Intensive English B	Intensive English C
Core Text		
High Point – Basic Level Hampton Brown Publishers	*Keys to Learning* Pearson Longman Publishers	*Shining Star* – **Introductory Level** Pearson Longman Publishers
Supplementary Materials		
Very Easy Stories from the Heart (Linmore Press) *Teen Stories* (Linmore Press) *Very Easy True Stories* (Longman) *Starting to Read* (Linmore Press)	*Easy Stories from the Heart* (Linmore Press) *Teen Scene* (Linmore Press) *Easy True Stories* (Addison-Wesley)	*Easy English News* (monthly subscription) *Long Way to A New Land* (Harper Trophy) *Dust for Dinner* (Tandem Library) *Pompeii—Buried Alive* (Random House Books)

Figure 4. The Balanced Literacy Instructional Framework

WARM–UP ROUTINE (10 minutes)

- *Purpose*
  — Engage students immediately
  — Present daily expectations
  — Integrate literacy skills into a meaningful routine
- *Format*
  — Daily Message or Daily Agenda
- *Guidelines*
  — Written or copied into notebook and discussed as class

ORAL LANGUAGE DEVELOPMENT (10–15 minutes)

- *Purpose*
  — Model reading & listening strategies
  — Introduce new vocabulary
- *Format*
  — Teacher Read-Aloud, Video clips, CD listening activities
  — Poems, Rhymes & Stories, Good & New, Jazz Chants, Mini-Dialogues, Scripts, Songs, Choral Reading
  — DLTA (Directed Listening Thinking Activity)
- *Guidelines*
  — Choose books that are personalized & related to students
  — Integrate oral activity content with reading & writing focus

JOURNAL WRITING or INDEPENDENT READING (15 minutes)

- *Purpose*
  — Develop fluency in reading & writing
  — Allow time for individual conferencing & informal assessment
- *Format*
  — Journal Activities
  — Independent Reading / Response Journal

GUIDED READING & WRITING (30–40 minutes)

- *Purpose*
  — Develop vocabulary
  — Introduce language structure
  — Modeling & introducing "before" & "during" reading strategies
  — Modeling & introducing writing process
- *Format*
  — Unit activities from textbooks or developed units
  — Integrated reading, writing, speaking, listening activities
  — Grammar mini-lesson applied to topic
  — Word study & spelling pattern lessons as needed
  — Extension activities & activities that apply to students' lives

continued on p. 112

Figure 4 (cont.). The Balanced Literacy Instructional Framework

- *Guidelines*
  — Integrate use of graphic organizers
  — Use a balance of grouping configurations (whole group, small group, paired work, individual work)

WRAP-UP ROUTINE (10–15 minutes)

- *Purpose*
  — Review key concepts & vocabulary
  — Reinforce understanding of homework assignment
- *Format*
  — Daily Review
  — Daily Summary
- *Guidelines*
  — Review of class may be oral or written
  — Homework assignment should be both written out & discussed

STUDENT MATERIALS:

Spiral Notebook & Composition Book in class
Planner & Binder for homework assignments

time frames that the teachers should spend on teaching specific units, either from the textbook or those supplementary units that were developed based on trade books. The pacing guides were developed during the summer of 2005, along with a trade book unit using some of the adopted supplementary books. The pacing guides are discussed in more detail in a later section.

Classroom and Curriculum Samples

INTEGRATING CONTENT AND LANGUAGE: A PEEK INTO A WORLD HISTORY CONCEPTS CLASSROOM

Jere Borg is a teacher who came to Harrisonburg from the state of California, where she received training in both second language acquisition and social studies. She started teaching in 2002 as an elementary ESL teacher and then moved to the high school the year after the concepts courses were put into place. She decided to take on the combination of ESL and social studies courses because, as she said to the authors in April 2006,

I noticed both my history students and the elementary ESL students I had taught in the past had one thing in common—they were not very literate in English, whether it was their first language or not. I love social studies, and I like teaching reading/ writing/literacy skills, so . . . it seemed like a good focus for both my interests. This way, my students and I get to read cool stories about history while becoming literate. How many social studies classes get to read a book about apartheid in South Africa (Journey to Jo'burg; Naido, 1986) through the eyes of a 13-year-old African teenager? (personal communication)

When visitors enter Borg's ESL World History Concepts classroom at Harrisonburg High School, they immediately realize that this is not a typical social studies classroom with a few maps hanging on the walls and students sitting in rows listening to lectures. Instead, they see NNES students who are immersed for 90 minutes daily in language activities that pertain to the social studies content. Upon entering the classroom, students immediately scan the Daily Agenda and SOL Objective Boards to see the World History SOLs as well as the reading and writing skills that they will practice that day. For example, students might have to find and highlight the topic sentences of textbook passages or write responses in complete sentences to questions that are posted about current topics. A word wall highlights pertinent vocabulary as well as the World Concepts and Big Ideas and Big Questions that students need to know about the current topic they are studying. The first activity of the day is for students to retrieve their classroom binders so they can spend 15 minutes reading a magazine, historical book, or novel that focuses on social studies topics. Once a week, they complete a Reading Response using four guided questions written in paragraph form. When asked about how she formulated her guided questions, Borg stated,

My guided questions are designed to elicit historical responses, not just literary responses. The questions correlate to the types of library books the students are reading each week. I give them a week to finish a small book—longer if it is a history resource book or long novel. I do not require a book summary or review because I want them to begin to enjoy their reading and use open-ended history questions. It gives the students a sense of accomplishment because they can write responses and actually get it right. They are always surprised that they have earned good grades for their writing, some for the first time in school!

Borg reviews these journal entries each week and responds to the students' entries. The following are examples of her guided questions:

- What was the most interesting history fact you learned? Why?
- What was the most surprising fact, or new information, you learned? Why?
- Would you want to visit or live in the time and place you read about? Why or why not?
- Would you recommend this book or magazine to another student? Why or why not?

Some of Borg's NNES students needed additional support to respond to the guided questions, so she developed a Skeleton Outline (see Figure 5) that provided a framework for what they were expected to do.

During an interview, Borg continually emphasized the need for her ESL students to have access to reading materials at both their independent and instructional reading levels. Grade-level texts and reading materials are generally too difficult for these beginning level NNES students. Students who read at an independent level have approximately 98% word recognition accuracy with about 90% comprehension, whereas at the instructional level, students have about 95% word recognition accuracy with about 70% comprehension. Students who are below 90% word recognition accuracy and have less than 70% comprehension are considered to be at the frustration level (Peregoy & Boyle, 2005).

Borg often plans *reading strategy* lessons to help her NNES students talk about the main idea of a social studies reading or compare and contrast opposing ideas. She plans her lessons using multiple reading sources and finds that the focus of the *History Alive* series (Teachers' Curriculum Institute, Rancho Cordova, CA) on prereading skills, vocabulary, and writing activities generally meets her students' reading and writing needs. In addition to reading groups, each ESL student has a buddy with whom they read

---

Figure 5. Skeleton Outline

The most interesting fact I learned was_____. It interested me because_____.

The most surprising fact I learned was _____because_____.

(Choose a fact)_____was new information for me. I would/would not want to visit/live in/during_____because _____.

I would recommend/not recommend this book because _____.

the text, review responses, and check each other's comprehension. Having a student partner immediately reduces the students' stress levels that come from having to individually understand new material.

Borg summarized the value of the concept class model by saying,

The real benefit of integrating language and content is that the students are able to see some order out of all the academic chaos of language. Reading and writing are taught as a process, not a product. Having to read, discuss, and write reading notes using graphic organizers involves the students in the reading process, and that's what makes the text accessible. When students encounter the words we've studied in their text or on a test, they have a variety of visual references to jog their memory and help them remember and apply the meaning. My target goal is to get students into reading for both pleasure and information. At the very least, they know how to read and write better, even if they do not become passionate readers. They can survive in regular classrooms and hopefully graduate. If they can read and write, my students will be able to choose jobs and careers.

Figure 6 captures the independent classroom library in Borg's room and Figure 7 shows an example of a social studies Big Question.

Planning and Pacing Effective Instruction

In June 2005, Harrisonburg's secondary ESL teachers spent 5 consecutive days developing units of study based on supplementary reading materials that correlated with topics in the recently adopted textbooks. The eight teachers who participated in the summer 2005 curriculum project to discuss and reflect were compensated for their daily time based on a district pay scale for curriculum writing activities. Figure 8 is an excerpt from one of the units developed by an ESL middle school and an ESL high school teacher who had ESL students at similar reading levels. These two ESL staff members decided to collaborate on the biography unit for overall goals, objectives, and activities but would designate different core biography books for their middle and high school students. This unit includes many of the reading and writing strategies that the ESL teachers learned during their staff development sessions.

Figure 9 is an excerpt from a semester pacing guide written by ESL teachers. The guide designates chapters of the adopted text and shows where the supplementary biographies unit should be incorporated into the yearly ESL language arts schedule.

Teachers used the summer 2005 curriculum project to discuss and reflect on how the program delivery changes required changes in their

Figure 6. The Independent Classroom Library

Figure 7. Example of a Social Studies Big Question

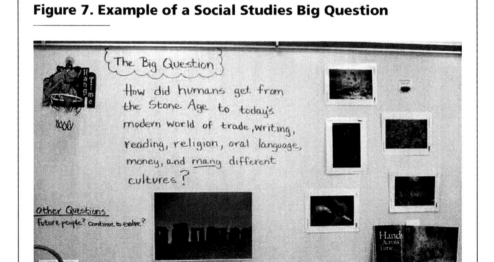

Figure 8. Unit Excerpt

SAMPLE SUPPLEMENTARY UNIT—"Biographies"			
BASIC INFORMATION			
Unit Title	Biographies		
ESL Level / Course	**Level 1 / Intensive English C**	*Approximate Length*	**3 Weeks**
Unit Theme	**Making A Difference** A study of people who have made significant contributions		
Subject Areas Addressed	**Language Arts** Reading, Writing, Oral Language		
Standards Addressed *(This unit is designed for ESL students and incorporates the Virginia English Language Proficiency (LEP) Standards. However, ESL teachers must also keep in mind the grade level English Standards of Learning (SOLs) expected of all secondary students.)*	**LEP 1.5, 2.4 & 2.6** Student will read, comprehend and analyze fiction/non-fiction. Answer simple factual questions about what is read; create artwork or a written response that shows comprehension; use knowledge of the story and topic to read words; name characters and tell about the setting of the story.; recognize the beginning, middle and end of narratives. **English 9.4** The student will read and analyze a variety of informational and non-fiction materials including biographies and autobiographies. Extend general and specialized vocabulary through speaking, reading and writing; read and follow instructions to complete an assigned project or task. **LEP 1.6 & 2.10** Student will write to communicate ideas. Write multiple sentences about a topic; use descriptive vocabulary; use pre-writing and planning strategies to organize information before writing; edit and revise writing; use available technology. **LEP 1.8 & 2.11** Student will use English punctuation and spelling conventions. **English 9.6** Student will develop narrative, expository and informational writings to inform, explain, analyze, or entertain. Generate, gather and organize ideas for writing; P\plan and organize writing; write clear, varied sentences; use specific vocabulary and information; revise writing for clarity.		
Materials Needed	*Helen Keller* (Class set for middle school students) *Rosa Parks* (Class set for high school students) Small sets of books on students' instructional level		
Unit Designers	Rachel Hershberger—Harrisonburg High School Pat Harmon—Thomas Harrison Middle School		

continued on p. 118

Figure 8 (cont.). Unit Excerpt

Unit Summary (General & Specific Goals)	Making a difference is a biography unit that includes a core book for modeling reading strategies, a read aloud biography for guided practice and additional biographies students will read in small groups/pairs. Each biography focuses on character traits that assisted the individual in overcoming their problems and/or accomplish their goals. Students will be able to: • compare and contrast character qualities of the individuals. • write a biography or an autobiography identifying and supporting selected character traits.

SAMPLE SUPPLEMENTARY UNIT—"Biographies"

GOALS

Essential Understandings (What students will understand by completing this unit— general concepts)	Reading the biographies in this unit will help students to: • think about how character is a quality that makes up or distinguishes an individual and to learn more about how a persons character defines what they can accomplish. • learn about people who developed unique character traits to fulfill lifelong desires. • learn about people who have tried to make life better for others. • think about how they can develop their own character traits/qualities.
Content Objectives (What students will be able to do & know in the content area by completing this unit—specific, procedural, product oriented)	The student will: • read and apply reading strategies such as: predicting, inferring, summarizing, and utilizing context clues. • learn about significant individuals in history. • associate the individual in the biography to a time period in history. • understand the significance role character traits play in helping people achieve their goals. • become familiar with characteristics of non-fiction text such as: bold face print, table of contents, glossary, and index.

continued on p. 119

Figure 8 (cont.). Unit Excerpt

Language Objectives (What students will be able to do with language or know about language by completing this unit—specific, procedural, product oriented)	The student will: • identify character traits exhibited by individuals in the biographies and compare and contrast these qualities. • summarize key information as they read. • retell the story and participate in discussions about the books. • become familiar with vocabulary used to identify character traits, in addition to vocabulary specifically related to each biography. • use present, past, and future tenses to respond orally as well as in writing. • use a poetry frame to write a Bio-Poem. • use the writing process to compose a biography or a personal autobiography.
Culminating Tasks (Ways students can demonstrate what they have learned)	The student will complete one of the following culminating projects: 1. Write a biography or create a PowerPoint presentation highlighting three character traits of a significant individual who made a difference in their life/country. 2. Write a personal autobiography or create a power point presentation that demonstrates three personal character traits. 3. Design a biographical or autobiographical poster depicting three character traits.

continued on p. 120

teaching strategies. The following section provides some of the ESL teachers' comments regarding their summer 2005 curriculum project experience.

WHAT WERE THE PARTS OF THIS CURRICULUM PROJECT THAT WERE MOST HELPFUL TO YOU?

• "It was motivational for me to have other people writing curriculum at the same time— much better than being alone in the school doing this. I really enjoyed having a template to work into rather than just starting from nothing."

• "Getting it on paper feels great! Having a skeleton [sample unit based on a novel] to work from was very helpful and will make the units more uniform and consist of more language acquisition activities."

Figure 8 (cont.). Unit Excerpt

SAMPLE SUPPLEMENTARY UNIT—"Biographies"	
UNIT PLAN—CORE BOOK	

Building Background Activities	• Introduce students to the genre of biography by presenting groups with a variety of pictures of famous people. Students will record information about what they **think** they know about the individuals and provide support for their ideas.
	• Use a timeline to associate the individuals pictured with a period of time in history.
	• Students respond in journals to essential questions focusing on personal character such as:
	    1. What character traits do you want to have?
	    2. What are your dreams?
	    3. What will you have to do to achieve your dreams?
	    4. How can we change things?
	• Students will free-write about a person they admire or who has inspired them. Include one or two characteristics of the individual they have selected. Teacher writes along with students and models the thoughts contained in the free-write assignment. Share responses as the teacher records on chart paper some of the characteristics that the students describe. Note which characteristics are mentioned the most.
	Why are these characteristics important in daily life?
	Why do these characteristics make these people successful in life?

Pre-Reading Activities	***Simulation Activity—Helen Keller—Courage in the Dark*** Have students experience Helen's world by blindfolding them. With a partner, have the blindfolded student walk around the room and try to identify objects by touch. Extend this idea by having the students make a sandwich blindfolded. Students should work in pairs so that the "sighted" partner can help verbally, as needed. When they are finished, have students write about their feelings while blindfolded. • Segment the story indicating where graphic organizers will be used to practice reading strategies. • Preview book cover and read title. Students discuss what they see and offer ideas regarding what the book might be about. • Preview the table of contents. Explain the table of contents helps to understand what the book is about. Use the table of contents to share what they already know about the individual.

continued on p. 121

Figure 8 (cont.). Unit Excerpt

SAMPLE SUPPLEMENTARY UNIT—"Biographies"	
UNIT PLAN—CORE BOOK	
During Reading Activities	• Model how to use features of non-fiction text such as: bold face print, table of contents, glossary and index. • Discuss and model reading strategies such as: predicting, inferring, summarizing, and utilizing context clues. • Complete graphic organizers focusing on questioning, connecting, summarizing and comparing and contrasting at designated sections of the book. • Identify the main idea of each section read by determining a "title" for the segments/chapters. • Maintain an ongoing word wall using vocabulary specific to each biography. • Maintain an ongoing character traits chart by recording behaviors the individual exemplifies (what the character says and feels, how the character acts, etc.) and identifying the character trait associated with the identified behaviors. • Students will respond to writing prompts that focus on character qualities throughout the unit.
After Reading Activities	• Sequence sentence strips containing important events in the life of the individual. • Retell (orally/written) important events in the life of the individual. • Complete a word study booklet of key vocabulary identified throughout the book. • Compare and contrast the individual to yourself.

• "The template and the hands-on help were invaluable. Also, having colleagues to bounce ideas off was good."

HOW WILL YOUR INSTRUCTION CHANGE NEXT YEAR AS A RESULT OF THIS PROJECT?

• "I feel I will be more focused on the purpose—that will drive my instruction."
• "My instruction will be more planned and deliberate."
• "It will be more focused on reading and writing activities. I will have more of a routine with different language activities."
• "It will be better organized. Instructional goals will be better focused."

Figure 9. Intensive English C—Pacing Guide for the Fifth and Sixth Marking Periods

Shining Star Unit 6: Exploring the Senses [2 weeks]

Vocabulary	Reading Strategies	Grammar	Writing	Phonics/ Spelling
• Ordinal numbers • Homographs	• Make inferences • Find main ideas	• Prepositional phrases • Combining simple sentences using *but* • Adjectives	• Writing a descriptive paragraph	• R-controlled vowels • Adding –ing –ed and –s to base words • Spelling patterns with *ir, ire, er, ere, ar, are, ur, ure, or, ore*

Supplementary Unit: Biographies [2 weeks]

Shining Star Unit: Wings [2 weeks]

Vocabulary	Reading Strategies	Grammar	Writing	Phonics/ Spelling
• Nouns and verbs • Same words in six languages	• Summarize • Understand the author's purpose	• Imperatives • Writing dates • Dialogue • Subject-verb agreement	• Writing instructions • Writing a review • Writing a short story	• Multi-syllabic words • Words with the schwa • Double letter words • oo in look and oo in food

The Ever Evolving Mosaic

As the ESL administrative team members step back to contemplate the new mosaic pattern, they are pleased with the progress that has been made, but they also realize that the work is not yet complete. The division between ESL and mainstream classes is no longer a bold line but has become a gradual shift from a completely sheltered, highly supportive environment that includes academic content to an integrated mainstream setting. Students continue to be assessed with the state-mandated English language proficiency assessment as well as with on-site literacy assessments, and the LEP status is removed according to Virginia state guidelines. However, the

ESL service they currently receive is based on their individual academic needs rather than a one-size-fits-all ESL class.

ESL staff development in the 2005–2006 school year focused on implementation of the adopted curriculum and provision of a forum for teachers to interact with each other. ESL teachers used their monthly meetings to share how they have reshaped their classrooms and instructional approach as they strengthened the reading and writing abilities of their NNES students. Teachers often used the Balanced Literacy Instructional Framework to show how they incorporated different components from this framework in their instruction throughout the week. In November 2005, ESL teachers used a district staff development day to meet and continue work on their curriculum units or pacing guides. The teachers revised the pacing guides based on the actual time it has taken for students to learn new topics. The curriculum units were implemented during the second semester, and the teachers used this staff development day to ensure that they had the necessary student texts and to put finishing touches on their units. Along with an ESL teacher, we presented some of these curriculum changes and units at a Virginia ESL state conference in February 2006.

During the 2006–2007 school year, student progress on local and state assessments was reviewed and analyzed to determine students' growth in all aspects of language acquisition, especially in reading and writing. One positive indicator that has already been seen is that after the first semester of instruction in 2005–2006, 42% of the students enrolled in intensive English courses had met the reading benchmarks to advance to the next level of instruction, compared with only 28% of the intensive English students at the end of the first semester in the 2004–2005 school year. Additionally, ESL students who participated in the three sheltered content models will be monitored to track their progress in SOL content classes and in passing the EOC tests. Preliminary data show that of the 232 students who have completed the SOL content class and taken the EOC test, 71% achieved a passing score.

For the past 2 years, the Harrisonburg ESL administrative team has met on a regular basis with Fagan to analyze and evaluate the changes in the ESL instructional program and to discuss teachers' reactions and comments regarding these changes. Communicating with the ESL teachers through e-mails, class visits, individual conferences, and monthly staff meetings has been the conduit for teachers to talk about their successes and difficulties with implementing new materials, new teaching strategies, and a new instructional framework. The Harrisonburg High School administrators and literacy coordinator have also been involved in the instructional change process and support the ESL teachers with supplementary instructional materials, hiring additional staff when classes become too large, and resolving scheduling conflicts.

In reflecting on this process, it is evident that many of the same effective teaching strategies that the ESL teachers were learning to use with their students were important in the sessions with the teachers as well:

- providing *background understanding* about why program changes were needed for the NNES students
- providing *data* that supported the need for change
- providing an opportunity to *learn and practice* new instructional strategies
- providing *collaborative support* from the ESL administrative team and the high school administration
- providing *time* for teachers to practice and talk about the new instructional strategies they were incorporating in their lessons
- *pacing* the staff development sessions so they would not overwhelm the teachers with too many strategies and not enough time for practice and reflection

In the future, the ESL administrative team will continue to work with teachers as they implement their pacing guides and make additional revisions to their units. They also will work with newly hired staff who need an understanding of the goals of the ESL program and the expectations of incorporating the Balanced Literacy Instructional Framework within their classes. As the central office and school-level administration work together with expert consultants and the ESL teachers to meet the needs of the students, the loose pieces of the former ESL program mosaic are slowly shifting into new positions, which will ultimately redesign the mosaic so that it represents a more effective and efficient ESL program.

Acknowledgments

Wanda Hamilton, Harrisonburg supervisor of language arts and ESL; and Irene Reynolds, principal of Harrisonburg High School, contributed to this chapter.

From a Spectrum of Language Learners to a Rainbow of Harmony: The International Baccalaureate Primary Years Programme

7

DIANE S. PRESSMAN AND EILEEN N. WHELAN ARIZA

How does a school with a diverse international student population celebrate that diversity while preparing students to succeed in learning the English language? Our school, Wilton Manors Elementary, Broward County, Florida, in the United States, sought to achieve these goals by incorporating the Primary Years Programme (PYP) of the International Baccalaureate Organization (IBO) into its curriculum. The IBO, established in 1968 and headquartered in Geneva, Switzerland, works with 1,597 schools to develop and offer three challenging programs in 122 countries to approximately 200,000 students (Graves, 2002). Our school deals solely with the North American office, International Baccalaureate North America (IBNA), which is located in New York City. The PYP is a relatively new addition to IBO's high school and the middle-school programs, which have been established internationally. Designed for children aged 3–12 years, the PYP recognizes many different forms of inquiry based on children's genuine curiosity and their desire and need to know more about the world. The program strives to develop the international person who is prepared to become a valuable, contributing member of today's global society. From the PYP perspective, an international person is someone with the attributes and dispositions described in the student profile identified in the PYP course design. These student profiles, which the PYP hopes will characterize its graduates, represent qualities of internationalism and are considered a key contribution of PYP schools to today's complex, challenging world (Mahoney, 2003). The PYP ideology does not impose time limits for teaching, nor does it limit the curriculum to certain subject areas. The program is a shift in thinking and teaching strategies, and this conceptual paradigm is integrated throughout the day. The PYP philosophy is a way to make overarching connections for the children—connections that range from reading to math to science—and shows them how to use what they learn and to implement this knowledge into their life, family, and community.

Wilton Manors Elementary (see Figure 1) is a public school that is 1.6 miles from the city of Fort Lauderdale. By virtue of its student population, it is a *de facto* international school with students from more than 36 countries who speak many languages. Broward County School District had IBO high school and middle-school programs in place but was searching for an elementary school to add. The district chose Wilton Manors to be a magnet school for the IBO PYP for several reasons. First, Wilton Manors recognizes and celebrates the heritage and languages of its students and encourages students to maintain their home language and culture while learning English. It also chose Wilton Manors based on its international student body and a declining student population. The faculty and staff discussed the possibility of becoming a PYP school and visited an established PYP school in Palm Beach County before the final decision to become a PYP school was made, a decision that was solely the district's.

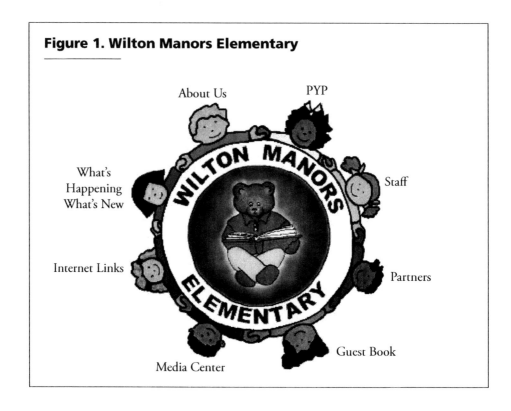

Figure 1. Wilton Manors Elementary

The Curricular Context

Wilton Manors Elementary School serves approximately 600 students. Students feed into the school from the surrounding neighborhood and from Kids in Distress, a program that provides safe housing for abused children and children who have been removed from their families for other reasons. It is a neighborhood school with a declining student population caused by changes in the neighborhood, such as aging demographics. The ethnic demographics show a student body that is 53% Black, 21% White, 20% Hispanic, 4% Asian, and 2% multiethnic. A large percentage of the Black students are Haitian. The school district does not identify the different nationalities or languages of students classified as Black; therefore, it is difficult to determine ethnic or language delineation. The student population of Wilton Manors is comprised of 21.3% nonnative-English-speaking (NNES) students, with an overall 77% minority population. Because of this diversity, a variety of programs are in place to ensure academic and behavioral success. One is the district's English for speakers of other languages (ESOL) program. Children are identified as NNES students when they register at the school. The Home Language Survey form determines the native language by asking three questions:

- Is a language other than English used in the home?
- Does the student have a first language other than English?
- Does the student most frequently speak a language other than English?

If any question is answered *yes*, students are further assessed to determine their language classification. If the student is classified as a nonnative-English speaker (A1), a limited-English speaker (A2), an intermediate-English speaker (B1 or B2), or an advanced-English speaker (C1), he or she is identified as needing ESOL services.

Broward County follows an inclusion model for NNES students, which means these students are taught in English the entire day in a mainstream classroom. Inclusive education calls for shared responsibility by all educational professionals. Each course is taught by qualified teachers, and appropriate materials are provided. The State of Florida requires teachers who work with NNES students to acquire an ESOL endorsement on their teaching certificate, which is attained through an in-service provided by the district or through college courses. The certification process ensures that all teachers who work with NNES students have an understanding of the methods, materials, and assessments that are appropriate for use in teaching these students. It also ensures that teachers have background knowledge about the language and cultural differences students from other countries bring to the classroom.

After a child is identified as a NNES student, he or she is assessed each year. Each assessment places the student at varying degrees of English speaking proficiency. When the student is considered a full-English speaker (C2) as identified through the district assessment scale, he/she is dismissed from the program. In keeping with the PYP's promotion of intercultural understanding and respect, we embrace the differences among our learners, including their languages and cultures, and incorporate these differences into the daily curriculum. This practice helps NNES students feel they are an important part of the class and makes it easier for them to share their histories.

In acknowledgment of the linguistic diversity of the students, the curriculum celebrates and teaches world languages. In recognition of the importance of teaching language, four full-time language teachers work with students for 1 hour each day, for 5 days, every other week. Upon matriculation, students are given the choice of studying Spanish or French in addition to English, and they study that language the entire time they are at the school. As a result, students become linguistically competent in at least two languages. Although students are permitted to choose between Spanish or French beginning in first grade, NNES students are encouraged to select their home language to continue native language literacy and fluency. We realize the benefits of having students continue to develop their first languages while adding English.

Developing the Primary Years Program at Wilton Manors Elementary

Developing a PYP school is a 3-year process that involves all stakeholders. The first step includes submitting an application for candidate status to IBO in New York. For the first 2 years after the program is accepted, the staff participates in training, including visits to established PYP schools, and develops the units of inquiry that will drive the curriculum. At the end of the second year, the school is assigned a consultant from IBO, who assists staff in recognizing the program's strengths and weaknesses. Before the school applies for authorization, the consultant makes recommendations to help ensure the program's success. At the end of the third year, the school submits the application for authorization. The process is complete at the beginning of the fourth year, when the authorization team visits the school and recommends revisions in the program or grants authorization. In the fall of 2007, Wilton Manors completed final visitation and is now a fully authorized PYP school.

The curriculum is organized around units of inquiry. During the first

3 years, each grade level creates two units of inquiry for a total of six, with each unit lasting 6 weeks. At the time this chapter was written, the school was in the third year of planning; however, at publication, the school had completed the three years and all six units. This chapter describes the process but does not show the completed school matrix of units. Appendixes A and B show examples of the school matrix and the second-grade matrix, respectively.

The PYP units of inquiry, which we refer to as PYP Planner Units, and the student profiles provide the framework for addressing the knowledge of learning strategies, understanding how to apply the framework, and helping to mitigate problematic social skills. In planning each unit of inquiry, one must consider several important components of the PYP international program. Six organizing themes are the foundational structure of transdisciplinary inquiry. These organizing themes are considered global concepts. The IBO's curriculum chooses global concepts about which students from all over the world can learn. These themes do not focus on area-specific topics, such as Lake Okeechobee in Florida, but rather on broader topics, such as Lake Habitats. These overlying themes help align the existing curriculum with the PYP format. The six themes are (a) Who We Are, (b) Where We Are in Place and Time, (c) How We Express Ourselves, (d) How the World Works, (e) How We Organize Ourselves, and (f) Sharing the Planet. Each theme lends itself to an in-depth study of certain curriculum areas. For example, Sounds All Around might be an inquiry-based unit categorized under How the World Works and be taught through a series of science or technology lessons. Storytelling from Different Countries, expressed by a series of language or reading lessons, might be an inquiry-based unit that demonstrates the theme How We Express Ourselves.

In addition to the six organizing themes, the PYP has a set of student profiles central to the work of the PYP that the administration hopes students will portray. The prescribed student profiles represent the primary objectives of the program and drive the curriculum framework central to the process of summative assessment.

The PYP profiles state that students are inquirers, thinkers, communicators, risk-takers, knowledgeable, principled, caring, open-minded, well-balanced, and reflective. A successful PYP depends on many factors, including the student's understanding of the different organizing themes as well as his or her success in displaying profiled behaviors. Because of its international makeup, the school strives to create curricula with a program that is truly international and reflective of the diversity prominent in the student body. An explicit expectation is that the PYP will lead to action as a result of the learning process. Our hope is that the children will learn, reflect, and act. An overview of the International Learner Profile was created through the IBNA office (see Appendix C). The profile is designed to show all aspects of the PYP and how the profile relates to the student expectations.

Our existing program accommodates our PYP ideals by expanding grade-level subjects to reflect PYP expectations. For example, in second grade, a thematic science unit, Sounds All Around, interconnects the PYP by including a variety of hands-on experiences, writing opportunities, math lessons, and reading tasks. The primary focus is on students and teachers in tandem, as opposed to having the teacher in front of the room or students working independently. Students share what they know and what they want to know and become engaged as learners who are actively involved in the process of learning. During this process, the teacher acts as a planner to create and facilitate opportunities for students to learn. The teacher continues to instruct using teachable moments while allowing inquiry to drive the curriculum, when possible. Finally, the teacher is responsible for assessing the students and the curriculum for ongoing revision and improvement.

Incorporating the PYP curriculum development plan in preparation for units of inquiry requires consideration of more than student academic learning. The curriculum must also consider the growth of students as lifelong learners and citizens of the world and provide the tools students need to be academically successful. Although Wilton Manors Elementary School follows the pedagogical approach set by IBO PYP, the school's program is closely aligned with district, state, and federal goals and encompasses our belief in the importance of the PYP's objective of promoting international-mindedness.

Planning a Unit of Inquiry

The process of planning a unit of inquiry for the PYP begins with a meeting of grade-level teachers to discuss the six organizing themes and grade-level areas of learning. Teachers discuss how the areas of learning could fit into the organizing themes, reflect on the grade-level expectations, and align with state standards. State standards drive the curriculum and assure students are being taught the necessary concepts to pass state requirements and be promoted to the next grade level. State achievement tests are also based on state standards. It is necessary that all units of inquiry align with those state expectations. In addition to the state, district, and school guidelines, the chosen theme must accommodate the school matrix (see Appendix A), which includes all grade-level themes without overlapping or repeating another grade theme. Each unit of inquiry is created using a PYP Planner template to maintain consistency and to ensure all units include the PYP-required components. The planner is described in the next section.

Teachers in Florida are required to be certified in the use of ESOL strategies. These strategies are used in every lesson to promote learning for students of other cultures and at all levels of English learning. Experiments, hands-on activities, small-group work, diagram labeling, pictures, and front-loading are all examples of ESOL strategies that are woven into the planners for the units of inquiry.

Part of the process of deciding which topic to use relates to what materials are available to teach the topic. Often, the group has a copy of each teacher's manual to browse through and to stimulate ideas. Discussion and material review continue until the group agrees on a topic. Group agreement is important because it ensures participation in the planning process by all teachers; as a result, each class will receive the same lessons and information. Once the group agrees on a topic, the PYP Planner template is used in the planning meetings.

The second grade at Wilton Manors Elementary consists of five classroom teachers. Teachers are provided a 1-hour planning block each day. Although 2 days a week are earmarked for PYP team planning meetings, the teams usually meet only 1 day a week. Although not mandatory, the meetings are necessary for the successful completion of the PYP Planners. Each grade-level group meets separately with the PYP school coordinator. The school coordinator leads the meetings and helps each group decide on which materials to use and assists in finding them; the coordinator often arrives at meetings with materials to share. She also monitors the schedule to ensure everyone completes their 6-week PYP Planners on time and that all Planners are completed within the school year.

During the planning meeting, the team reviews the PYP Planners that have been developed and discusses possible revisions. The PYP Planners are constantly in revision. Because the program is still in the third year of development, new plans are created until the third year of planning. Upon completion of plans and final authorization, plans continue to be refined and revised based on the success of the unit, the changes in available materials, and state standard changes. To decide what the next project will be, the team reviews the state standards, grade-level expectations, and programs of inquiry and then considers the materials that are available. With that information, the team agrees on the subject. Each week, the teams meet 1–2 days during the 1-hour planning time to work through the PYP Planner. The administration, teachers, support staff, and parents play a role in this process. All must support and participate in every stage of curriculum development for the program to be successful. Teachers are involved in the development, implementation, and evaluation of the units of inquiry for their respective grade levels. A summative evaluation will determine the success of the unit and student understanding, which will guide revision of the plan for the following year. Teachers must also determine the optimum time to teach each unit during the year.

The PYP Planner

The PYP Planner is a graphic organizer for teachers to use while planning the 6-week unit of inquiry (see Figure 2). It begins with the organizing theme, focus of the lesson, level of the lesson, names of teachers who will be delivering the lesson, and proposed duration of the lesson. This section is straightforward and includes a unit title. Although the PYP Planner is a flexible tool, teachers develop it in a specific order. As soon as the central idea and inquiry have been developed (Stage 1), teachers think about how they will assess students' understanding (Stage 5). Often, a teacher will ask questions (Stage 3) to help make the central idea clearer to the teachers. The activities (Stage 4) should not be developed before Stages 3 and 5 have been outlined; only after the teachers know what they want students to understand (Stages 1, 3, & 5) should they think about which activities will help guide the inquiry and what resources (Stage 2) they will need.

STAGE 1

Stage 1 of the planner articulates the purpose of the unit. The plan will include a concise description of the central idea to be addressed as well as the scope of the inquiry. The teachers' purpose in planning this stage is to give a general statement about the subject that will be learned.

STAGE 2

Stage 2 of the planner lists the resources that will be used to teach the unit. Resources can be people, places, audiovisual materials, related literature, music, art, computer software, textbooks, and other things specific to the unit. Teachers will find related chapters in textbooks and search the media center to find supplementary materials. They will also work with music teachers, art teachers, specials teachers (i.e., teachers on special topics), and foreign language teachers to develop related lessons and brainstorm ideas to bring the unit to life in the classroom. Some topics have more hands-on activities and resources than other topics. Teachers must often be creative and resourceful when looking for resources. For example, the Internet, as well as inviting community people to the classroom, are great resources.

STAGE 3

Stage 3 of the PYP Planner lists what teachers want the children to learn, but this section is phrased in inquiry form. A chart on the PYP Planner lists eight key concept questions. When planning this section, teachers look for

Figure 2. PYP Planner

Theme: PYP PLANNER

Unit Title:

Focus: π
Discipline(s) to receive the major emphasis.

Level:

Teacher(s): Proposed
School: duration:

Stage 1: What is our purpose?
A concise description of the central idea to be addressed and the scope of the inquiry

a) **Central idea:** Please begin typing here

b) **An inquiry into:** Please begin typing here

Stage 2: What resources will we use?
People, places, audio-visual materials, related literature, music, art, computer software, etc.

Please begin typing here

Stage 3: What do we want to learn?
The key questions which will drive the inquiry.

Form *What is it like?*			
Function *How does it work?*			
Causation *Why is it the way it is?*			
Change *How does it change?*			
Connection *How is it connected to other things?*			
Perspective *What are the points of view?*			
Responsibility *What is our responsibility?*			
Reflection *How do we know?*			

Teacher Questions:
Please begin typing here

Student Questions:
Please begin typing here

PYP Planner, ©IBO, September 2000

continued on p. 134

Figure 2 (cont.). PYP Planner

Stage 4: How best will we learn?
Teacher and/or student designed activities which will address the key questions.

Please begin typing here

Stage 5: How will we know what we have learned?
The strategies which will be used to assess learning.

Please begin typing here

Student self-assessment:
Please begin typing here

Stage 6: To what extent did we achieve our purpose?
To what extent: were the purposes fulfilled; was the unit relevant, engaging, challenging, and significant; were the resources adequate; were the concepts, skills, and attitudes addressed

Please begin typing here

How will we take action?
How the students will demonstrate their ability to choose, act, and reflect.

Please begin typing here

PYP Planner, ©IBO, September 2000

questions that will fit the format and result in the answers they are seeking. Teachers provide the students with question stems and examples so that students can also form inquiries that will help direct and drive the lessons. Creating questions to drive the unit of inquiry can be difficult. The first four of the eight question types are the easiest to design and the easiest for students to create. Figure 3 shows examples of these question types for a unit of inquiry on electricity.

Higher-order questions require students to use critical thinking skills and to stimulate their desire to learn. On the PYP Planner, "T" signifies teacher questions and "S" signifies student questions. Form questions are not listed because they are the easiest type to create and are part of the daily classroom discussions.

STAGE 4

Stage 4 includes teacher discussion about ways the students will best learn. Teachers plan activities that will address the key questions from Stage 3. Included in this section are frontloading activities designed to give the students basic information about the topic before the actual lessons begin.

Figure 3. Questions for Unit of Inquiry on Electricity

Order	Question Type	Key Question	Example
Lower	Form	What is it like?	What is electricity?
Lower	Function	How does it work?	How can we make electricity?
Lower	Causation	Why is it like it is?	Why is electricity important?
Lower	Change	How is it changing?	What happened between the discovery of electricity and now?
Higher	Connection	How is it connected to other things?	How does electricity make things work?
Higher	Perspective	What are the points of view?	Who discovered electricity?
Higher	Responsibility	What is our responsibility?	How can we use electricity in a responsible way?
Higher	Reflection	How do we know?	How did we learn about electricity?

Figure 4. The KWL Chart

K	W	L
What do you know?	*What do you want to know?*	*What have you learned?*

Frontloading activities provide visual and audio input that give students enough knowledge to begin forming questions and to drive the direction of their learning. After a week of frontloading, students are encouraged to write questions on topics; these topics are usually introduced with the KWL chart (which stands for What I **K**now, What I **W**ant to Know, and What I **L**earned). See Figure 4.

Using this KWL graphic organizer helps teachers decide what to add to the research and study topics. Following this KWL strategy, teachers move to the hands-on experiments and textbook lessons. Included in the next 4–5 weeks of study are group reports, writing assignments, science experiments, and class discussions. Math lessons also develop through this process. The PYP Planners provide an outline or framework from which to develop daily lesson plans.

Once teachers have completed the PYP Planner, they are ready to teach and provide the planned learning experiences. Information can be shared through videos related to the topic, library books placed in the room for students to read, pictures posted around the room to stimulate student questions, and discussion. Students are also given a chance to take action after they complete the unit. The unit may lend itself to a culminating activity that will allow students to demonstrate their ability to choose, act, and reflect. Examples of a PYP Planner using the theme Sharing the Planet and the unit titled Let's Talk Trash might lead to an investigation of natural resources and recycling. A result or student activity might be to develop and implement a recycling program in the school and then introduce it to the other students and classes.

STAGE 5

In Stage 5, teachers determine how students and teachers will know when they have gained the required knowledge. Stage 5 has a list of strategies that can be used to assess formative and summative learning during and after the unit is completed. Evaluations may include formal assessment, informal assessment, projects, group presentations, or any other form of assessment the group decides will accurately show student learning. Determining how to assess a student's learning may be done through projects, formal tests, oral presentations, multimedia presentations, or writing and performing a play.

STAGE 6

Stage 6, the final stage of the PYP Planner, questions to what extent teachers have achieved their purposes. This section gives teachers a chance to reflect on the lesson and determine whether the goals of the lesson were achieved; if the unit was relevant, engaging, challenging, and significant; if the resources were adequate; and if the concepts, skills, and attitudes were addressed. This reflection stage allows teachers to adjust or change things that did not work and note the things that worked well.

Sample Unit of Inquiry: Sounds All Around

Let's look at one unit of inquiry—Sounds All Around. The purpose of this unit of study is to teach children how sounds are formed, how sounds travel, how the properties of sound can be altered, and how we hear sounds. This planned duration of this unit of study is 6 weeks. The unit interconnects the existing science program with the PYP by including a variety of hands-on experiences, writing opportunities, math lessons, and reading tasks.

DEVELOPING THE PLANNER

When developing the Sounds All Around Unit Planner (see Figures 5 and 6), we began by examining the science textbook (Deman et al., 2000), which provided a concrete set of materials upon which the unit is based. The grade-level teachers met weekly for several weeks to complete the PYP Planner template and to share the ideas and materials they had gathered. This process continued until enough materials and activities were gathered to provide a quality unit that would last approximately 6 weeks. Problems that arose during this period included a paucity of materials, perhaps from a loss of materials from the library, and outdated materials that were ineffective. Some materials were consumable and had to be replaced, which required funding that was not readily available. Many materials in the media center were outdated, although media center staff continued to update and increase the number of titles available for each planned unit of study. Time frequently was a challenge because the amount of time needed to complete a project or unit was often underestimated.

RESOURCES

The unit incorporated the science benchmarks and state standards. The textbook was used for the introduction of the lesson, and a laser disc provided additional information. Many books related to the topic were found in the media center and provided independent reading as well as material for whole-class read-alouds. An audiologist provided an additional piece of information. During the music period, students were exposed to many different types of sounds through instruments. During art class, students were given different types of music and were asked to provide their reactions through drawings. Students were provided materials and designed an instrument of their own. In groups, students explored different aspects of sound and then presented their study to the class.

STAGE 1

Stage 1 of the planner addresses the purpose of the unit. An example of the central idea for the Sounds All Around Unit would be *Sounds work in various ways*. Stage 1 also shows that the unit is an inquiry. For the Sounds All Around Unit, the inquiry seeks to answer the following:

- How do we hear vibrations?
- How do sounds travel?
- What are the properties of sound (pitch and loudness, higher and softer)?
- How can sounds be altered?

STAGE 2

Stage 2 of the PYP Planner lists the resources that will be implemented to teach the unit. In the Sounds All Around Unit, the resources are the science text, an audiologist demonstration, a laser disc, and a list of books. The PYP Planner for Sounds All Around shows a completed copy of the PYP Planner created for this unit.

STAGE 3

Stage 3 of the planner lists what we want the children to learn, but this section is phrased in inquiry form. The chart provided on the PYP Planner gives eight key concept questions. Questions for the Sounds All Around Unit of Inquiry gives examples of these question types for this unit.

STAGE 4

Stage 4 includes teacher discussion about ways the students will best learn. Teachers plan activities that will address the key questions from Stage 3. Books, pictures, and videos related to sound will be displayed in the room. Students will be permitted to view and read materials before the unit is introduced with the KWL chart.

Figure 5. PYP Planner for Sounds All Around

continued on p. 140

PYP PLANNER

Theme: How the World Works

Unit Title: "Sounds All Around"

Proposed duration:

Focus: Science
Discipline(s) to receive the major emphasis.
Level: Second grade
Teacher(s) Allwein, Pressnan, Compton, Hildreth, Nazien
School: Wilton Manors Elementary

Stage 1: What is our purpose?
A concise description of the central idea to be addressed and the scope of the inquiry

a) **Central Idea:** Sounds have various properties

b) **An inquiry into:**

How vibrations may be heard.
How sounds travel
The properties of sound (pitch and loudness) and how they can be altered.

Stage 2: What resources will we use?
People, places, audio-visual materials, related literature, music, art, computer software etc.

Harcourt Science Book Unit F chapter 2
Audiologist demonstration
Discover the Wonder Laser Disc-Sound #3
Big Book - Polar Bear, Polar Bear What Do You Hear?
Student violin demonstration
See attached lists of books

Stage 6: To what extent did we achieve our purpose?
To what extent were the purposes fulfilled; was the unit relevant, engaging, challenging and significant; were the resources adequate; were the concepts, skills and attitudes address

This unit was a high interest unit for our students. They were engaged during the hands on activities and they were able to communicate real world application of what they learned. Students applied their newly learned vocabulary when discussing the unit with others. Our science book was a great resource that provided several activities that the students were able to do independently. The audiologist demonstration was extremely valuable and students were very interested in how the ear works to hear sound.

The students showed curiosity when participating in activities such as the pitch experiment. They filled glasses to different levels with water and listened as they tapped the glasses to hear the different pitches. They showed cooperation while working in groups. They were creative in designing their musical instruments and demonstrating ways sounds can be altered.

What's Needed

It would be valuable to also have a county audiologist demonstration as they have more high tech equipment and more materials to share with students.
It would be beneficial to form research groups. Divide children into groups and have each group research a different topic (pitch, loudness, how sounds are heard.) and present it to the class. This will enhance communication skills and serve as an assessment.
More integration of music class would be helpful in understanding how different instruments produce and alter sound.

Music and language sounds differ for different cultures. Share the sounds of different cultures.

PYP Planner, ©IBO, September 2000

STAGE 5

In Stage 5, teachers determine how the students and teachers will know when they have learned what is required. For example, during the Sounds All Around Unit, students were formally evaluated and gave an oral group presentation to the other students in the class. As an alternate assessment, students designed and created a musical instrument using household items.

Figure 5 (cont.). PYP Planner for Sounds All Around

Stage 3: What do we want to learn?
The key questions which will drive the inquiry.

			S3
Form *What is it like?*			S4
Function *How does it work?*	T1	S1	
Causation *Why is it the way it is?*	T2	T4	
Change *How does it change?*	T3	S2	
Connection *How is it connected to other things?*			
Perspective *What are the points of view?*			
Responsibility *What is our responsibility?*			
Reflection *How do we know?*			

Teacher Questions:
1. What makes a vibrating object vibrate?
2. How does a sound get from a vibrating object to your ears?
3. How do sounds change when they travel through matter?
4. How can you change the pitch or loudness of a musical instrument?

Student Questions:
1. How do animals make sounds?
2. How does the same instrument make high and low sounds?
3. How does sound travel for cell phones and cordless phones?
4. How do vocal cords work?

Stage 4: How best will we learn?
Teacher and/or student designed activities which will address the key questions.

Frontloading:
Display of resources to support the unit. Students are provided with books and videos about sound.

Activities
* Science book page F22 Investigation "What is Sound?"
* Listening walk–students walk around campus and record the sounds they hear. Teacher led discussion of results.
* Students observe sound level machine in the cafeteria and record the sound level. Compare/contrast days, times, and grade levels.
* Audiologist Demonstration – pitch, loudness
* Laser Disc sound demonstration
* "Chicken in a Cup" Students make a hole in the bottom of a paper cup and pull a string through. The friction causes a chicken-like sound
* Telephone with cups- students observe how the phone works with the string loose compared to the string being tight.
* Students observe pitch by filling water glasses to different levels. They tap the glass and observe the difference in pitch and how it relates to the amount of water and air in the glass.

How will we take action?
How the students will demonstrate their ability to choose, act and reflect.

Stage 5: How will we know what we have learned?
The strategies which will be used to assess learning.
Informal Assessment & Classroom observation

Chapter 2 Science Test

Demonstration of ways sounds can be altered-water in a cup; string loose or tight; thick/thin rubber band

Student self-assessment:

PYP Planner, ©IBO, September 2000

STAGE 6

Stage 6, the final stage for the PYP Planner, questions to what extent we have achieved our purposes. The Sounds All Around Unit was a high-interest study for the students. They were engaged and able to communicate using appropriate vocabulary they had learned during the lessons. Some

Figure 6. Questions for the Sounds All Around Unit of Inquiry

Order	Question Type	Key Question	Example
Lower	Form	What is it like?	What is sound?
Lower	Function	How does it work?	What makes a vibrating object vibrate?
Lower	Causation	Why is it like it is?	How does a sound get from vibrating object to your ear?
Lower	Change	How is it changing?	How do sounds change when they travel through matter?
Higher	Connection	How is it connected to other things?	How does sound affect other things?
Higher	Perspective	What are the points of view?	Who discovered sound?
Higher	Responsibility	What is our responsibility?	How can we use sound in a responsible way?
Higher	Reflection	How do we know?	How did we learn about sound?

suggestions that would improve the unit of inquiry include inviting a district audiologist as a guest speaker, forming student research groups to provide additional learning opportunities, and integrating music classes into the lessons.

The Sounds All Around Unit of inquiry fits into the organizing theme of How the World Works. In addition to the planner activities, students were assigned group reports. Students were given worksheets, textbooks, and media center time to find additional materials, word boxes, and pictures to assist them in their report. After they completed their work together, students were given a paper with notes and empty blanks (see Figure 7, Sounds Report) that the teacher created for the unit. As they listened to the group presentations, students were asked to listen for the words that were missing. These words appeared in a word box on the paper and were repeated three times by the group reporters. Each topic that was discussed was included on the end of the unit assessment. Hands-on experiments were provided to give students an opportunity to see how different aspects of sound work. An example is the Chicken in a Cup activity (see Figure 8). After children are given the opportunity to explore the world of sound through lessons, videos,

Figure 7. Sounds Report

NAME_____

SOUNDS REPORT

WORD BOX					
higher	lower	vibrate	pitch	loud	soft

SOUNDS VARY IN MANY WAYS.

1. A man's voice sounds _____ than a child's voice.
2. A lion's roar sounds _____ than a cat's meow.
3. A whistle sounds _____ than a truck engine.
4. A mouse's squeak sounds _____ than a dog's bark.
5. A car engine is _____.
6. A dog's bark is _____.
7. A _____ sound is soft.

SOUNDS TRAVEL THROUGH THREE KINDS OF MATTER.

1. A bird singing is an example of sound traveling through
   _____.
2. A dolphin using _____ is an example of sound traveling through water.
3. Scratching a piece of tape on your desk is an example of sound traveling through a _____.

HOW CAN WE MAKE DIFFERENT SOUNDS?

1. Thin strings _____ faster and make higher sounds.
2. Making a string longer makes it _____ slower.
3. If you hit a drum hard it makes a _____ sound.

SOUND DEFINITIONS

1. _____ is what is made when things vibrate.
2. _____ is using sound to locate things under water.
3. _____ is how high or low a sound is.
4. _____ is how loud or soft something is.

HOW YOUR EAR WORKS

WORD BANK
outer ear   eardrum

1. First sound enters the _____.
2. Next it reaches the _____ where it vibrates.
3. After that it goes to the _____, which carries it to the _____.

books, experiments, research, and creative projects, they are given a short assessment to determine their comprehension of the way the ear works (see Figure 9).

To assess this unit of study, we used a triangular approach. The science

---

Figure 8. Chicken in a Cup

CHICKEN IN A CUP

Experiment
Sound is produced when an object vibrates. To practice this idea and also tie it into a fun art project, we are going to make a chicken in a cup.

Concepts to Remember
1. Sound is produced when an object vibrates.
2. Sound waves can be transmitted through solids, liquids, and gases but never through a vacuum. The denser the medium, the faster the sound waves travel.
3. Sound waves can be collected and amplified.

What you will need:
1 5 oz. wax cup (plastic is ok, but the teacher must make the hole)
1 12-inch length of string (must be cotton)
1 paper clip (large)
1 piece of masking tape
   Water

Procedure
1. Open the paper clip up and punch a small hole in the center of the bottom of the wax cup. Put the end of the string over the hole and push it through to the other side using the paper clip. Try to keep the hole as small as possible so that more of the vibration is transferred to the cup and is amplified.
2. Tie the paper clip to the outside end of the string. Reach into the cup and pull the string tightly so that the paper clip is right on the bottom of the cup. Tape the paper clip to the bottom of the cup.
3. Grab the string with your thumb and forefinger near the bottom of the cup. Pull downward with short pulls and listen. Little to no sound should be produced.
4. Now wet the string with the water and pull down again. With a little bit of practice you will be winning the chicken calling contest at the state fair.

Why Does This Happen?
The water on your fingers creates friction between your skin and the cotton string. The friction produces vibrations, which travel up the string. When they hit the bottom of the cup, it starts to vibrate too and this is amplified (made louder) by the shape of the cup. Good luck at the county fair!

Figure 9. Short Assessment: How Our Ear Works

How Our Ear Works

When you hit a drum, you hear a sound. At that moment, many things happen.

- When the drum is hit, the top vibrates, or moves back and forth.
- The *vibrations* make sound waves that travel through the air.
- When the *sound waves* enter your ear, they hit your *eardrum* (which is like a drum) and makes it vibrate.
- *Nerves* then carry the message to your brain and your *brain* tells you about the sound.

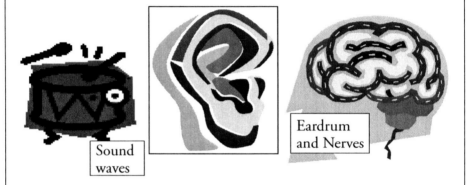

Sound waves

Eardrum and Nerves

Short Assessment: How Our Ear Works

Paste ✂

1	Your eardrum begins to vibrate.
2	Nerves carry the message to the brain.
3	The drum is hit and the top vibrates.
4	Your brain tells you about the sound.
5	Sound waves move through the air and enter your ear.

book provided a chapter test with pictures. The Create an Instrument assignment was evaluated by the student's ability to describe and explain the instrument using the appropriate terminology. Finally, the group reports provided the teacher with additional information related to the students' ability to explain and demonstrate their understanding of the topic. Further program assessment is gained through portfolios, a student action that culminates in the fifth grade. Students are required to complete a program-specific project that demonstrates a consolidation of what they have learned.

Evaluating the Effectiveness of the PYP

Since August 2003, when Wilton Manors Elementary began the process of becoming a PYP school, we have watched our state standardized test scores continue to rise. In 2003, 66% of students scored at or above grade level in reading and 63% in math. In 2004, the percentage of students scoring at or above grade level rose to 73% in reading and 66% in math. We saw further improvement in 2005, when students scored 75% in reading and 72% in math. In 2006, we proudly watched as scores increased to 80% in reading and 76% in math.

Of particular note is the improvement in social behavior. Because of the program's Attitudes and the Passport to Peace ideology, which highlights attitudes through weekly activities, there was a decrease in aggressive behavior, as evidenced in the decrease in referrals. In addition, more students began requesting Chill Out time, which is encouraging. Chill Out is when a child requests time away from a potentially volatile situation that is beginning to escalate rather than allowing the behavior to build up to aggression. Although an increase in academic scores is impressive, this demonstration of self-control is also noteworthy.

Conclusion

As our school continues to take shape as an international community, it is becoming a microcosm of the greater world. The role educators play in providing opportunities for their students to grow into thriving world citizens is critical. Educators are charged with developing and providing a global education that will teach students to function successfully in a variety of ways, modalities, circumstances, and cultures. Promoting high expectations for student achievement, including opportunities for students to learn the essential elements of the curriculum, and helping students understand how the elements fit into the world scheme, is our primary goal. Because of this universal approach to educating the international citizen, students can readily comprehend the interrelatedness of knowledge, concepts, skills, attitudes, and action. This program also recognizes the importance of the attributes and dispositions of an international person and tries to prepare students who will be sensitive to the experiences of others. Success of the PYP is substantiated by the enthusiasm, understanding, and excitement children convey when they complete a unit of inquiry and continue to share their knowledge using appropriate terminology. Finally, the most demonstrable evaluative tool is action. Students reveal their command of the PYP objectives by engaging in culminating projects designed by their own hands and implemented in their own school and communities. The pride they feel in their accomplishments reinforces the objectives and perpetuates the sphere of dynamic teaching and learning. Student interest and excitement are obvious when youngsters connect what they have learned and apply it to actions outside school. Hands-on activities, cooperative learning opportunities, building on previous knowledge, language development, visual aids, and family involvement all play an important part in making the PYP work for all students.

As teachers working with students from many cultures and many languages, we have found the PYP has helped us focus on the ESOL strategies we are taught in the process of receiving our ESOL endorsement. We find that when we use these strategies, all students learn better, act better, and show academic achievement.

The journey to PYP has not been easy, but it has been beneficial and rewarding. Along the way, teachers have been expected to spend far more time planning with their teams, find more ways to provide inquiry based activities and lessons, change their way of teaching from mainly lecture to more student centered, and take part in weekly in-services to continue the journey to IBO authorization. During this journey, obvious positive changes have taken place. Students are getting along better and showing academic improvement while enjoying the process. This program gives our school a sense of community and helps students become active, compassionate, lifelong learners who understand that others, no matter how different, can also be right.

Appendix A: School Matrix

PYP Inquiries by Grade Level

	Who We Are	Where We Are in Place and Time	How We Express Ourselves	How the World Works	How We Organize Ourselves	Sharing the Planet
K	Central idea: Personal relationship is a lifelong process. An Inquiry Into: • Who I am • How we can make and keep friends • Why people need family and friends			Central idea: Weather affects the earth and it's inhabitants. An Inquiry Into: • How weather changes from day to day • The seasons of the year • Using measurement to keep track of weather	Central idea: Our senses help us discover the world. An Inquiry Into: • The five senses and how we use them daily • Ways our senses tell us about our surroundings • Ways to extend the senses	Central idea: Water is important to people around the world. An Inquiry Into: • Different types of water • Ways people use water • Ways to use water wisely • How to keep our waters clean
1	Central idea: The symbols a country chooses tell about its people and history. An Inquiry Into: • The meaning of symbols • Selected American symbols and their history • Ways important buildings, statues, and monuments tell about national history			Central idea: The world is made up of solids, liquids, and gases. An Inquiry Into: • Ways to group matter by its physical characteristics • The properties of solids, liquids and gases • The effects of heating and cooling on solids, liquids and gases	Central idea: Transportation is important to our world and has changed the way we live. An Inquiry Into: • Modes of transportation • Transportation through history • How transportation has affected the way we live	Central idea: Living things grow, change, and have basic needs. An Inquiry Into: • Living and non-living things • How living things grow and change • The basic needs of plants and animals
2		Central idea: People use maps to locate and identify places. An Inquiry Into: • Why maps are used • Different types of maps • Map legends and symbols • Ways maps have changed over time	Central idea: People share stories in different ways to explain the world around them. An Inquiry Into: • The ways stories are shared • The reasons people share stories • The different types of stories	Central idea: Sounds have various properties. An Inquiry Into: • How vibrations may be heard • How sound travels • The properties of sound (pitch, loudness) and how they can be altered		Central idea: People can help our planet by taking care of it's natural resources. An Inquiry Into: • Ways people use natural resources • Ways human activity affects the environment • Ways to care for the earth at home and at school

3	**Central Idea:** A community is characterized by the customs and cultures of its people. An Inquiry Into: • Similarities and differences attached to customs and cultures • Beliefs and values • Ways regions are constructed according to physical and human criteria	**Central Idea:** Inventions and inventions continually change our world through communication and technology An Inquiry Into: • An inventor's process • Significant inventions in the area of communication and technology • The impact specific inventions have had on our world		**Central Idea:** People around the world use machines to make work easier. An Inquiry Into: • The six types of simple machines • Ways machines make work easier • Uses of machines around the world	**Central Idea:** Living things have behavioral and structural adaptations that enable them to survive. An Inquiry Into: • Organisms within an ecosystem • How organisms with similar needs compete • How environmental changes may cause some organisms to thrive, become ill or perish
4	**Central Idea:** Throughout history significant individuals have contributed to the development of places where people live An Inquiry Into: • The early exploration of Florida • Key events in Florida's history • Contributions of significant men and women in Florida's history	**Central Idea:** Our life on earth is effected by the sun and the planets that travel around it. An Inquiry Into: • The force of gravity • The characteristics of the inner and outer planets • How the tilt of the earth causes the seasons and length of day		**Central Idea:** The surface of the earth is constantly changing. An Inquiry Into: • The rock cycle • The water cycle • Weathering and erosion	**Central Idea:** People create positive and negative impacts on their environment. An Inquiry Into: • Ecosystems • The relationships between humans and ecosystems • Protection of the ecosystems • Case study: The Everglades
5	**Central Idea:** Different systems work together to keep the human body working properly. An Inquiry Into: • How plant and animal cells differ • Cells as the building blocks of the body • Main Human body systems	**Central Idea:** A country's natural and economic resources affects the supply and demand of consumer goods causing interdependence among countries An Inquiry Into: • US regions and their geographical features • Economic and natural resources of US regions • Regional specialization and interdependence		**Central Idea:** Energy is a finite resource and its use impacts the way we live our lives everyday. An Inquiry Into: • Why energy is a finite resource • Different forms of energy • Alternative forms of energy • Uses of energy	**Central Idea:** The way governments are structured affects the rights of their people. An Inquiry Into: • Structure, function and purpose of government • Types of government • Importance of government

Appendix B: Second-Grade Matrix

Wilton Manors Elementary
Program of Inquiry and Correlation of Curriculum Guidelines

Second	Who We Are	Where We Are in Place and Time	How We Express Ourselves	How the World Works	How we Organize Ourselves	Sharing the Planet
Title:		Where in the world...?	Sharing Stories	Sounds All Around		Let's Talk Trash
Subject Focus:		Social Studies	Language Arts, Reading	Science		Science
Central Idea:		People use maps to locate and identify places	People share stories in different ways	Sounds work in various ways		People influence the quality of life of those around them
An Inquiry Into:		• Why maps are used • Different types of maps • Map legends and symbols • Ways maps have changed over time	• The ways stories are shared • The reasons people share stories • How people share stories through music and art	• How vibrations may be heard • How sounds travel • The properties of sound (pitch, loudness) and how they can be altered		• Ways people use natural resources • Ways human activity affects the environment • Ways to care for the earth at home and at school
Critical Content Addressed:		SS.B Geography	LA.C Listening, asking questions LA.E Story characteristics LA.A Retelling, rereading discussing	SC.C Force and motion		SC. D Processes That Shape the Earth

Appendix C: Learner Profile

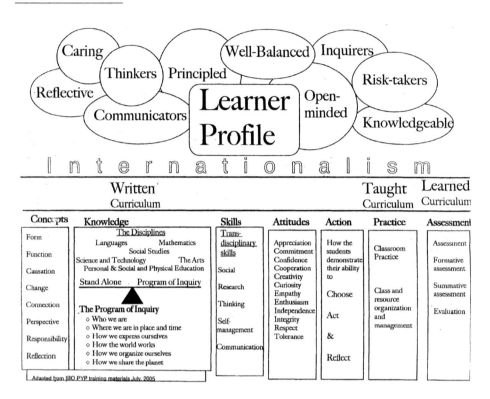

Adapted from IBO PYP training materials July, 2005

Learning From Families for Curricular Change

8

MARGARET HAWKINS, CAROLINE JOHNSON,
KELLY JONES, AND LYNN LEGLER

Although there is general agreement in the fields of English as a second language (ESL) and education in the United States that many English learners are not adequately served in schools—as amply evidenced by research, assessments, and drop-out rates—there is no consensus on how to best structure programs and deliver instruction to remedy this situation. In this chapter, we explore the efforts of one K–2 school (serving primarily 5 to 8-year-old children) in a Midwestern city located in the state of Wisconsin, in the United States to re-design instructional approaches to better support the language and literacy development of their English learner population.

Lakeview Elementary School's[1] demographic profile is roughly one third White middle-class students, one third African American students (most of whom live in poverty), and one third English learners (primarily Hmong and Spanish speakers, most of whom also live in poverty). In 1997, when the current principal arrived, English learners received only pull-out services, as did other students for remedial work. The principal arranged a retreat for her staff and asked them for a vision of how they would like their school to be. The staff agreed that they wanted more cohesiveness in programmatic and instructional approaches and a more integrated community. The principal applied for and received a Comprehensive School

---

[1] All names of people and places in this chapter are pseudonyms, with the exception of the identified school staff members and university faculty members.

Reform Grant[2] and began to redesign, starting with restructuring service delivery. All pull-out support was ended, and professional development was required for teachers in the area of ESL, as all classroom teachers would have the primary responsibility of supporting the English language development of their students. There were a number of facets to this new initiative, some of which were mandated by the principal, others of which were organic and emerged from teachers' interests. Examples of principal-mandated initiatives were a new hiring policy (all new teachers must have both an early childhood or elementary teaching license and an ESL teaching license or be hired under emergency licensure and obtain the ESL license) and offering an in-house course on teaching ESL for current teachers (this course was offered by Maggie, the university faculty member co-authoring this chapter). Examples of teacher initiatives were involvement with the Latino, Hmong, and African-American communities in various ways, and, ultimately, the creation of *study groups* to read and discuss relevant issues. This chapter is co-authored by three teachers in the school (Carol, Kelly, and Lynn), and the university faculty member who has worked with the school throughout the transition period (Maggie).

Although there have been many changes within individual classrooms as to how teachers design curriculum and scaffold learning, they are not the specific focus of this chapter. One bottom-line tenet for the school staff is that in order for children to succeed, teachers and parents need to work together as partners. There has been much research documenting the importance of parental involvement in schools (Foster & Loven, 1992; Hoover-Dempsey & Sandler, 1997). The discrepancy between the involvement of mainstream White parents and that of minority parents also has been documented, as have the complexities of making connections between teachers and schools and parents from diverse linguistic and cultural backgrounds (Compton-Lilly, 2003; Gonzalez, Moll, & Amanti, 2005; Valdes, 1996). Much of the literature centers on the differing cultural perspectives on schooling, including different conceptions of parental and teacher roles in the education process (Delgado-Gaitan, 1990; Flor Ada & Zubizarreta, 2001; Valdes, 1996). However, improving home–school connections is not just a matter of getting parents into the classroom, teaching them new and better practices to implement at home (e.g., read stories aloud to their children or help with homework), or representing the families' foods, traditions, and customs in the classroom. It is finding ways for two-way communication to occur, with the ultimate goal of connecting classroom curriculum and families together. We conceptualize this as involving shifts

---

[2] Competitive state funding for school restructuring.

in understanding for both teachers and families. Thus, it is initiatives that speak to connecting families and curriculum that we address; these are fully integrated with our curricular and instructional approaches.

There are many such initiatives in place school-wide as the community of teachers attempts to build bridges with families. These range from more traditional institutionalized events such as conferences; parents serving as classroom volunteers; children's performances; and family nights, which are now sometimes centered around themes such as math night, the book fair, and authors' circles; to more teacher-initiated events such as staff committees and home visits (some, though not all, teachers conduct these). In addition, the school sponsors *parent empowerment groups* with separate monthly meetings for Latino, Hmong, and African American parents. Teachers attend, and the topics and activities are a blend of teachers' agendas and those of the parents. The school has also instituted a *backpack program* in which backpacks go home with the children with a book in the families' native language, a tape-recorded reading of that book, and a tape player, to enable parents—even those who are not literate—to participate in literacy events with their children.

To further exemplify how committed teachers are to forging strong con- nections with families, two university faculty members (chapter co-author Maggie & Beth Graue) facilitated a monthly discussion group focused on home–school relations at the school during after-school hours for 2 years. Roughly 15 staff members—mostly teachers, but including the schools' two bilingual support staff—attended on a regular basis. These participants received no compensation or any kind of educational credit for their partici- pation. Some of the teachers involved chose to conduct research projects on their practices, and others simply attended the meetings. Meeting agendas were set by the group. Staff used this time to air concerns, share ideas and specific strategies, and brainstorm together. Samples of issues addressed were (a) how to improve minority parents' participation in school events, (b) conference formats and content, (c) making report cards meaningful and accessible, (d) what sorts of information parents and teachers could and should share, (e) how to make homework relevant and equitable, (f) how to best represent and support families' home languages and home cultures in the classrooms, and (g) conducting home visits. Sometimes teachers came to the meeting with just a topic for open discussion, sometimes the facilitators organized activities to focus the conversation on topics the staff had previ- ously identified, and sometimes teachers who were conducting their own studies on parent–school relations shared their work. Thus, the monthly dis- cussion group evolved into a space for collaborative reflection and support.

There has been a focus in the professional teacher education literature, both within and outside of the field of ESL, on teacher study groups.

Virtually all of the groups identified in the literature are put together and mentored or directed by a university faculty member. The groups have varied foci and purposes, such as using books as catalysts for cultural conversations (Florio-Ruane, 2001), ESL teachers analyzing students' work to improve teaching (Clair, 1998), or rural teachers' discussions on teaching multicultural young adult literature (Lewis & Ketter, 2004). Although these groups have been widely touted as providing time, space, and structure for reflection (Freeman & Hawkins, 2004), rarely does the group determine the focus and content of discussion and activities. Less common, too, are groups where teachers engage in individual teacher–research projects and receive support and feedback from the group (though see Toohey & Waterstone, 2004, for a wonderful example of a group that does this).

This chapter focuses specifically on initiatives from Carrie, Kelly, and Lynn, who designed individual year-long projects to improve instruction for ESL children and to connect ESL families to the academic practices of their classrooms. Each project is centered on the notion that, although parents can learn from teachers, partnerships must be reciprocal, and teachers must listen to and learn from parents as well to support English learners' linguistic and academic development in school. Each involves designing and implementing curricular initiatives but also has a research component. The teachers began with authentic questions about their practices and gathered information to hypothesize answers. They tried new approaches based on this information and collected and analyzed data to assess effectiveness. Thus, the following accounts are of teacher researchers researching their classroom practices to better support their English learners. Each section is written by the teacher and is presented in the teacher's voice. The teachers' projects span the content areas of mathematics, reading, and science education for young learners and portray the processes of change but also the struggles and successes of their endeavors.

Carrie: Involving Families in Mathematics Education

CURRICULAR CONTEXT

As a first-grade teacher, a major focus in my mathematics curriculum was helping children develop their number sense. As I became more comfortable in my approaches, I also became increasingly concerned about my Latino students. They presented themselves in unique ways but with amazingly similar results. Although no two families were alike, their stories had commonalities. My students were all first generation, born either in the United States or abroad, all with foreign-born parents. Their parents had varying levels of English. All spoke Spanish at home, although English began to creep in as children entered school. Few parents had much formal education in their home countries; all of the children had attended school only in the United States. All parents had attended school outside of the United States, but most of them had not graduated from high school. Almost all were living in poverty, with parents working two or more jobs to support their family. Yet every family wanted the best for their child, and to them this included a good education. They were willing to do whatever was necessary to help their children in school but often didn't know exactly what to do.

Gabriela was a second-grade Mexican American child in my class during the 2003–2004 school year. Her parents had requested a conference to discuss concerns about her progress in math. As I prepared for the conference, I found myself at a loss. I knew her parents had a strong desire to work with Gabriela at home. I also knew that any materials I gave them needed to be in Spanish. I struggled to pull together activities or games that were in Spanish. Of the few I found, not many promoted the kind of mathematical thinking and reasoning I was trying to develop. I also knew that I would need to be very explicit in how I wanted them to work with Gabriela at home. Gabriela's parents' reference point for mathematics was drastically different than my own, having developed in a very different system and style of education. I knew there had to be a better way to provide parents with opportunities to understand how our school teaches mathematics and interacts with their children around mathematics. Yet there never were any satisfactory answers or ideas to offer my Latino parents because I myself didn't understand what caused barriers in these students' achievement.

Drawing from a project I had created at our school 3 years earlier to support native language literacy with books and tapes in Spanish and English, I thought this model could be effectively adapted to bring mathematics activities home to families as well. I felt that most families would be enthusiastic participants if given easily accessible activities in Spanish. Although I began the project with a focus on the Spanish-speaking students in my classroom, other teachers requested to be included. Thus, the project was expanded to include first- and second-grade Spanish-speaking families.

The divide between home and school practices and lack of communication between home and school has been well documented through research. De La Cruz (1999) found that school programs face a difficulty in communication between teachers and the parents of English learners and often fail to include families in a teaching partnership. Unfortunately, much blame has been misplaced, faulting parents for a lack of involvement. My experience has consistently been that parents are eager for information and willing to be involved, although the literal and figurative barriers put up between schools and parents often prevent this. I hoped to overcome these barriers while discovering their deep-seated roots.

As the school year began, I identified first- and second-grade Latino families that spoke Spanish at home. Nine first-grade families and 8 second-grade families met the qualifications. Of the 17 students, 4 were in my classroom, while the other 13 were spread among 3 other classrooms, each of which had a Spanish-speaking teacher. The vast majority of the students were Mexican, with one Peruvian child and one child of Mexican and Brazilian descent.

Of the Latino student population participating in the study, 88% were living in poverty (defined as qualifying for free lunch at school). Of the families who completed the study, nine of the parents had not completed high school, three were high school graduates, and four had attended at least some college.

PROCESS OF DESIGNING, ADOPTING, AND EVALUATING

I contacted all eligible families in person or through written communication to inform them about the study. As I speak Spanish, all communication between families and myself was done in Spanish, without an interpreter. All 17 families agreed to participate in the study, an excellent participation rate and an indication of parents' interest in participating in their child's education.

Before implementing the math activities, I wanted to collected baseline data from the families on their understandings of our math pedagogy, feelings of connection between home and school, and ideas of what math is. Because of my concerns about the distance between parents and teachers (Peressini, 1998), I hypothesized that conducting home visits would make families more comfortable. Although home visits are infrequently used, they can result in an increased trust between parents and teachers and provide teachers with insights into families within their home environment (Gestwicki, 2004; Gonzalez, Moll, & Amanti, 2005).

In early October, I scheduled a home visit with each first-grade family. I asked each family a specific list of questions, although much valuable information came from discussions after the interviews, as parents continued to talk to me and ask questions. The interview questions addressed demographic information, their perceptions of how they (the parents) use mathematics, how their children use mathematics, their goals for their children, and the role mathematics played in these goals. In addition, the questions sought the level of information parents had about the mathematics curriculum, expectations at Lakeview, and their children's math skills.

At the end of October, after the interviews, I held a meeting for all families participating in the project. As I met with the parents, the children made the materials they would need for the semester. Similar to the literacy program, students would receive a folder with a new math game in it each

Friday. Parents were asked to play the game at home with their child, using materials the child had created at school. In addition to a game, a brief optional evaluation was included in the folder that parents and students were asked to complete weekly. The students also were provided a box in which to keep their materials and a folder in which to keep the previous weeks' games.

As students received new games each week, parents were encouraged to continue playing previous games to build fluency. Each of the games had been specifically chosen because they met the grade-level standards set by the school district, were easily implemented at home, and required the participation of more than one person. I specifically designed, chose, and adapted games that required mathematical reasoning and communication (for sample games, see Appendixes A and B). None of the activities could be done with memorized formulas; they all required independent thinking.

During the meeting, parents were informed about the purpose of the project and brainstormed with other parents about how families can include mathematics in their daily lives at home and in the community. They also watched a videotape of a bilingual teacher playing a game with students to model how teachers interact with children around mathematics in the instructional system our district uses. The meeting ended with a brief overview of how we teach mathematics at Lakeview and how this may be reproduced in a home setting.

Each week during the fall semester, families received a new game. When school resumed after winter break, I again scheduled home visit interviews. This time, the questions were designed to build upon information collected in the fall. I wanted to know with whom and how families used the games, if they encountered specific problems, how many games they played and how often, if families continued to use the games, and if parents saw a change in their child's math thinking. I also wanted to find out if responses to earlier questions regarding understanding of the Lakeview curriculum and of their child's math understanding had changed since implementing the program. Results from the winter interviews, although they did not specifically affect the games chosen for second semester, showed a need for more specific explanation to the parents about how math was being taught and the pedagogical reasoning behind it.

Once the interviews were completed, an additional parent meeting was scheduled. This meeting was a bit less structured and was held to respond to questions and concerns raised in the parent interviews. The meeting began with feedback on the games and program overall and was followed by some discussion of various mathematical terms used in the games that parents had not understood, as well as explanations of mathematical concepts parents would need to understand for second semester games. The students again created the materials necessary for the second semester during the parent meeting.

The second semester proceeded much as the first, with families receiving a new game each week that the math folder was returned to school. Participation rates remained constant throughout the second semester.

Finally, end-of-the-year interviews were conducted and another round of home visits was made. At the conclusion of the project, all participating families were invited to come to school for an end-of-the-year celebration.

After analyzing information from many interviews, three meetings, and weekly evaluation sheets from families, I found both expected and surprising results. Each interview and meeting I held gave further support to the many assertions about parental involvement in the literature. Dauber and Epstein (1993), De La Cruz (1999), Ehnebuske (1998), Fillmore (1990), and Peressini (1998), all assert that parents want to be involved in their children's educations but that they are distanced by teachers and are left uninformed of specific practices that schools desire. Each of these researchers believes that given information and guidance, parents are eager to help their children at home. Would this be true at Lakeview? Would our parents indeed want to be involved?

A number of qualitative factors support the claim that Lakeview parents do indeed desire to be involved, given the opportunities. I was pleasantly surprised when every family I approached agreed to participate in the project. No family was pressured to participate. Not only did each family voluntarily agree, but the vast majority of the families continued participation throughout the year at very high levels. All families who remained at the school continued participation until the end. Given the time required to play the games, complete the evaluations, and participate in interviews, this involvement spoke volumes about parental desire to be involved.

The high levels of at-home participation and meeting attendance signaled support for my theory that given appropriate, easy-to-use materials in Spanish, families would actively participate in their child's education in a way that would support their child's work at school. Dauber and Epstein (1993) found that giving parents specific guidance increases the type of help and time spent by parents with their children, a need especially asserted by parents with less formal education. Lakeview parents substantiated this finding. As a result of the study, I have been more intentional in providing parents with information about what is happening in the classroom and in making specific suggestions about ways to work with their children at home.

One of the most surprising outcomes for me was the extent to which parents were aware of their children's understanding of mathematics. Perhaps because I had rarely asked a parent what they understood about their child's knowledge, I had not expected this. It was something I had rarely contemplated prior to this project yet something that struck me strongly during the course of the year. Although parents were often unaware of what their child specifically needed to know at each grade level, they had clear understandings of what concepts their child had mastered. I had never asked one of my Latino parents about the mathematics understandings they saw their child demonstrate at home. Often, it had been me telling the parent what I saw at school and what the child needed to learn. Yet these parents offered valuable information to me. I gained a glimpse into the perspectives on education that the parents held and gained a different perspective on the children's mathematical understandings and progress. This was, in large part, because parents were able to see their child in another environment, in a one-on-one situation, and utilizing their native language.

Given a safe space and the opportunities, parents had important questions and opinions that I needed to hear. During interviews and meetings, parents asked why we taught concepts in specific ways. They had opinions about the concepts that were taught at specific grade levels, the materials used, and the pedagogical style in the classroom. They were able to give specific examples of what their children knew and ways they were adapting materials to meet their child's needs. Clearly these parents had great stores of valuable information for me. Since completing this project, I have made a practice of beginning parent–teacher conferences by requesting parents to share observations of their child, rather than using this time solely to deliver information.

Although I generally experienced many successes and received positive feedback from parents, I found one challenge that is a very real barrier for many families. De La Cruz (1999) found that parents want to be involved but believe they do not know enough about mathematics. Even though the students in the program were learning first- and second-grade mathematical concepts, they were gradually being exposed to algebra and higher level problem solving, which their parents may have never encountered.

This was brought home to me in a unique situation during a home visit. The family began an interesting conversation by telling me that they did not always understand the directions given for the math games. After some discussion, the father elaborated by saying the Spanish was *más alta*, a *high* form of Spanish that *"solo usan los presidentes"* ("only presidents use"), not people like his family. I heard his frustration with the language and his difficulties understanding the one-page directions.

As the conversation progressed, the father gave me a specific example. He said he did not use the word *ecuaciones*, a word I used frequently for "equations." It was clear to me that if he did not understand this word, he would have difficulty understanding many of the games. When I asked what word he would use, he said *restas* and *sumas,* literally translated into *subtraction* and *addition*. I was confused about this limited vocabulary, as it would only work for an equation restricted to addition or subtraction operations. I wrote an equation like $4 + 3 - 2 = $ ___, a fairly simple equation, and asked him what he would call this equation. He responded by telling me he never saw equations like that in Mexico.

At that moment, I underwent a profound change in my understanding of this process. How would I be able to teach parents to work with their children on concepts they themselves had not been exposed to? How could I reach parents if I was using academic vocabulary they did not understand? This seemed to be a step backward in my process of encouraging parental involvement. I had entered the journey believing that simply providing opportunities in families' native languages would provide immediate results and meet everyone's needs. I realized it was not as simple as I had thought: The parents were entering this process at a dramatically different place than I, in my White middle-class and formally educated way of thinking, had assumed. This conversation led to many more conversations with families about everything from algebraic concepts to measurement.

Short of providing mathematics courses to parents, I would be unable to provide them with a more comprehensive understanding of mathematics. This will be a much more complex problem for these families as their children grow. During my project, I was able to meet this need by showing some basic principles and examples that would assist parents in understanding the activities. In addition, I defined important concepts that parents may not know as part of the game directions. By using these simple techniques, parents were informed in a respectful manner. Despite attempts to inform parents about the definitions of terms, I continued to encounter instances when parents simply did not have the mathematical knowledge they needed.

Other teachers may have success in providing information to parents by translating mathematical terms, though with a need to provide more than a definition—they may also need to give an explanation with examples. Schools with large Latino populations may also find success in conducting parent math nights to introduce parents to their children's mathematics curriculum. This becomes increasingly important with older students as mathematics concepts become more difficult. Regardless, an environment must be created where parents feel safe asking questions and are respected for the knowledge they bring.

Most of the documented changes revolved around parental attitudes and information. Because only a fraction of the students involved in the study were in my class, I was not able to directly observe all of the students' classroom work throughout the year. Data in student achievement were not collected because of the various confounding variables—even if students showed improvement in mathematics, it wasn't necessarily attributable to this program. I was able to collect anecdotal data from the home visits I conducted. Often students were present during interviews and wanted to share their own thoughts. Many expressed to me how much they enjoyed playing the games with their families, their delight in teaching and involving younger siblings, and some also demonstrated to me their new mathematical knowledge. To me, simply seeing students at such a young age display a positive attitude toward math and share those experiences with their families was just as important as possible increases in achievement scores.

CONCLUSION

Reflecting back on the data from October 2003 in the 2003–2004 school year, a clear gap was present between Latino and White student math achievement in my classroom, as well as a lack of understanding and communication with Latino families about math. It appears that Lakeview is further along the road than the inner-city schools that Dauber and Epstein (1993) studied. Teachers at Lakeview, for the most part, have moved beyond blaming parents and seek active involvement with parents. We also have parents who are eager for information and ways to participate. The teachers and parents each make attempts, yet neither side quite meets halfway. Had the environment been different and this groundwork was not in place, this project may not have been successful.

The project ended upon the completion of the school year only because I left Lakeview to embark upon a new adventure teaching first grade in Mexico, inspired largely by the families I met and a desire to be able to return with a deeper understanding of how to better work with Latino immigrants in the United States.

Certainly, other questions worthy of exploration are left at the termination of this project. Issues of language and culture are complicated by the bicultural world in which the children live. While they were learning at school in English, learning at home was done in Spanish. Although this provided them with first language support in learning at home, we are not usually able to offer such support at school. In addition, the activities were not necessarily culturally relevant for the families but rather, activities used within a school setting translated into Spanish. Thus, families were asked to adjust to school practices, but school staff did not need to adjust their teaching to accommodate cultural differences.

At the end of the year, my perspectives had changed about the families involved in the study. The parents shared their lives, their hopes for their children, and their fears and concerns with me. For many of the women with whom I spoke, it was as if I had removed the cork from a tightly closed bottle. When I was in their homes, only a portion of the time was spent with interview questions. They had many other things to tell me about their families. The insights I was able to gain were so valuable. Perhaps this is what Peressini (1998) was hoping for as he defined a growing distance between parents and teachers. The simple act of going to their homes, showing that I cared about their children, and creating a relationship altered the fabric of parent involvement. Although the project ended, the lessons I learned from them certainly have transferred to my classroom. Connecting with these families showed me the importance of connecting with other families I will meet, remembering the impact that their out-of-school lives have on what happens in my classroom.

Undertaking a project like this required an immense amount of work. Given a core group of teachers who are committed to finding and translating math games and activities, the project could easily be replicated in other schools, even without the home visits and interviews. Those components, however, enabled me to learn about the families and forge more meaningful relationships with them. In schools where one teacher might have to work on his or her own or where there are many language groups represented without a concentration of one language, teachers can certainly find ways to incorporate aspects of the project. Knowing that families are indeed very interested in their children's education and are willing to help, given the tools and materials needed, should be an assumption in parent–teacher communication. Small intentional steps are a good place to start. Perhaps teachers can make extra copies of an activity or game students do in class to send home; give parents an opportunity to share information, observations, and concerns at conferences; and provide families with key academic words and concepts that students are learning at school (e.g., *Ask your child about the tens and ones in two-digit numbers* or *Have your child tell you about our evaporation demonstration*). In addition, teachers can connect with families outside of school on their turf by going to their homes, their children's sporting events, or the neighborhood after-school center for informal conversation. By doing these things, teachers will become more visible within their families' communities. As scary as it may initially sound and feel, parents are usually more nervous than the teachers. The relationships that are built speak volumes to students about how much teachers care about their lives and families and open the doors of communication for parents.

What I saw more than anything through this project was the parents' desire for opportunities and for a good education for their children. Each family was finding ways to fit into their new culture and to negotiate the culture of a school. Although small steps such as this project will not be enough to reverse the trends of the achievement gap, it supports the ideals involved. We need to be explicit in our expectations and intentional in our relationships, and we need to value different experiences. The families in this study showed me the power of their perseverance, love, and commitment to their children. By capitalizing on our strengths as teachers and parents, we can work to create the best educational environment for our students.

Kelly: Learning From Families to Redesign Literacy Instruction

Early in my teaching career as a first-grade teacher, I became interested in how my students learning English learned to read. I began to notice that although they could make initial progress in reading, many of the students stalled when it became necessary to comprehend the text. It seemed that I was able to successfully teach my English learners how to decode words but when it came to comprehension, my techniques were not as effective.

I generally followed a balanced literacy approach that included a range of literacy activities that I carefully selected to move each learner to a higher level of skills and understanding. This approach included activities to enhance phonemic awareness, comprehension, fluency, high-frequency word knowledge, reading strategies, and literacy appreciation. I regularly assessed children and organized them into different groups based on reading levels. Throughout the year, students moved in and out of groups based on their performance and needs. After a quarter of the school year had passed, it shocked me to realize who was in each of the four groups. Based on scores generated from our district's language arts assessment, my two highest group of readers consisted entirely of White students, and my two lower groups consisted entirely of English learners. At this point, I knew it was necessary to look critically at my literacy practices to discover why my English learners were behind in reading and what factors contributed to the achievement gap clearly present in my classroom.

My research began in a classroom of 15 first graders. These students came from diverse cultural and economic backgrounds. All of my minority students came from working- class families and qualified for free or reduced lunch. All of my White students came from middle- or upper-class families. There were three Hmong students who had lived in Wisconsin for the majority of their lives. One student moved from Korea and had lived in the United States for less than 2 years. Another student's family had moved to Wisconsin from Laos, and another student's family came as refugees from Vietnam. There was one African-American child who moved to our district in the middle of the year and eight White students.

I began by talking with experienced teachers at my school about what I noticed with my English learners and their reading comprehension. I was curious as to whether they had discovered teaching strategies that supported their English learners' reading comprehension. I was disappointed to hear that teachers who were considered the best reading instructors in our school also experienced lower achievement with their English learners. I was even more disappointed when the response to my questioning continued to be "That is typical for students learning English." It frustrated me to think that because lower achievement was considered typical, it was not critically examined. The message I received was that the students were unable to comprehend because of their limited English vocabulary and that they would continue to be behind in reading until their vocabulary improved to the level of their native-English-speaking peers. I wondered if vocabulary was the only factor contributing to students' difficulties with reading comprehension. I believed that connections between home and school, how reading instruction was presented in school, and family-reading practices also may have been contributing factors.

It appeared that to enhance reading instruction for my English learners and ensure they would leave my classroom as proficient readers, I would not only have to discover new ways to teach reading, I also would have to find out what was happening at home.

My research focused on the students and their families. I wanted first-hand information about how they find meaning in written English. The focus of my study was to discover what teachers could do to help enhance reading comprehension for English learners. To research this question, I gathered data through home visits, parent and student interviews, and classroom observations. My goal was to learn more about students' literacy practices both at home and in school. I wanted to explore the parents' perceptions and attitudes about reading and see what literacy experiences might be available in the homes.

After many classroom observations, student interviews, and home visits, I still felt that a critical piece of information was missing. I wanted to observe parents reading with their children so that I could see what strategies they were using when reading together. I wanted to hear the conversations that were happening around the text and witness the interactions between parent and child while reading. To do this, I designed a family reading night. At the family reading night, students would share both self-written stories and classroom books with their families. I would be able to observe parents and children reading together. My assumption was that regardless of the language, the reading strategies would be consistent and transfer across languages.

What I observed at my family reading night was priceless and gave me new insight that would change the way I taught reading forever. It didn't take long to notice that there was much less interaction while reading among the families of students learning English than among my White families. The conversations of the former group had rarely deviated from decoding the current word being read. The parents would tell their child a difficult word or help them sound it out, but that was the extent of the discussions. Virtually all of my White families, on the other hand, were constantly commenting on illustrations, making predictions about what would happen next, or making connections from the book to their own lives.

These observations did not give me answers to my initial questions; rather, I was left with more questions. I instantly began to ask myself: Why are families of English learners not having conversations about books? Is it because that is not how books are experienced in their cultures and that is how their parents read with them? Is it because they do not feel that is what U.S. teachers want them to be doing? Is it because books are solely for school purposes to help students become better decoders of words, or is it because parents do not know how to discuss the stories? I also questioned: What should teachers do about this lack of conversation that is happening around books? It was crucial that parents did not receive the message that the way they read with their child was wrong. Should teachers try to share reading comprehension strategies with parents of English learners and have conversations about engaging with literature at home, or should teachers just realize that they need to be aware of the different reading styles that students may experience at home and increase the instruction of reading comprehension strategies at school to make up for communication about books that may not happen at home?

All of these questions led me to what I believe are three basic principles that follow and that have become the foundation of my teaching of reading to English learners. These principles have allowed me to enhance my instructional practices at school, strengthen my relationships with the families of English learners, and connect home and school literacy practices.

1. COLLECT INFORMATION ON THE STUDENTS' LITERACY SKILLS IN THEIR FIRST LANGUAGE

Home visits and parent interviews allowed me to find out information that was not easily available to me in the classroom. I was able to learn that a Hmong student viewed herself as speaking limited English as well as limited Hmong. She did not feel she had a language with which she could be successful. She had not been exposed to Hmong literature at home and had very little print displayed in her home. I also learned that one of my students attended a Korean kindergarten, had Korean books at home that were often read to him before bed, and had a mother teaching him to read and write in Korean.

These two students experienced different exposure to books and print at home. Although both of them struggled with reading comprehension in the classroom, their needs varied greatly. The first student needed instruction about how print worked and needed to gain an understanding of how letters combine to make sounds. The second student, while also needing to learn English letters and sounds, had many literacy experiences at home and would be able to make connections from experiences he had with Korean books to the English texts he encountered in school.

2. READ TO STUDENTS DAILY, AND EXPLICITLY TEACH STUDENTS HOW TO INTERACT WITH TEXT

Daily read-alouds were already happening in my classroom. However, I noticed that many of my English learners seemed to be uninterested in the stories I was reading. After examining my read-aloud practices, I realized I would often rapidly read a story from beginning to end, leave little time for conversations after the book, and encourage students to hold all of their questions and comments for the end. An article by Copenhaver called "Running Out of Time: Rushed Read-Alouds in a Primary Classroom" (2001) caused me to drastically change my approach to stories. I no longer used stories to fill short periods of time. Instead I made story time a priority in the classroom. I incorporated stories from many different genres, included stories read in various languages, invited parents to read stories that were native to their cultures, and, most importantly, encouraged conversation before, during, and after a story. I began to realize that the connections students were making during a story were more important than finishing the whole story.

Many of my White middle- and upper-class children grow up with story times and parents who constantly encourage them to interact with text. Parents point to pictures and ask, "What is that called?" and "Who is this?" thousands of times before children even reach the age of 3. Heath (1982) gives the following example of a mother interacting with her child. A mother and child sit down for a bedtime story. They alternate turns in a dialogue: The mother directs the child's attention to the book and asks, "What is this?" The child responds with a verbal or nonverbal answer, and the mother provides feedback to the child. Although the mother may not realize what she is doing, she is preparing her child for what will be expected of him or her in school.

As discovered in my observations during family reading night, the same questioning strategies and ways of interacting with texts may not be embedded in the cultures of families who are learning English. This does not mean English learners are unable to learn these strategies. It simply means that teachers need to consciously teach the strategies. Teachers can most effectively do this by verbalizing their own thinking about reading. I began to read chapter books aloud to students and think out loud about the connections I was making. While reading, I would stop and say, "Wow! That is interesting. It makes me think of a time when I. . . ." Or, "This character really reminds me of the character we read about last week in. . . ." Before long, I heard students making the connections themselves when reading with friends.

I also created mini-lessons to accompany stories that would require students to listen and make connections. One such activity had students draw pictures at different times during the story to help them remember what happened at that point in the story. The students then used those pictures to retell the story to a friend at a later time. Another activity had students make three connections with the book they were listening to or reading. They had to draw a picture to show connections to something that happened in their life, in someone else's life, and to another story. Many of these lessons were extremely difficult for my English learners. Slowly, as the first-grade year came to an end, students began to not only read and listen to books but also to understand them.

3. INVOLVE PARENTS

This suggestion may be the most important factor to increase reading achievement in school. Literacy starts at home, and much of the literacy development of a child throughout their schooling is affected by home experiences. Teachers and families need to collaborate so that literacy development can flourish. This collaboration does not happen automatically. Many teachers are unaware of home literacy practices and make assumptions about what is or is not happening in the homes of their students, especially their English learners. In addition, many parents may feel like their input is not valuable or wanted by their child's classroom teachers.

In *Reading Families: The Literate Life of Urban Children,* Compton Lilly (2003) observed that many educational professionals bring negative assumptions to the classroom that deny the many resources and sources of support that children's families offer. She found in her studies that it was a common mainstream teacher belief that urban parents did not read, cannot read, and did not care about reading or their child's learning. I believe this statement can be extended to many families of English learners. Because students are not succeeding in literacy practices, assumptions are made about the home. Excuses for minimal achievement need to be made so that blame can be diverted from the classroom. Through interviews, Compton Lilly found that every parent she talked with valued reading and wanted their child to learn to read. However, she found that parents often felt unrecognized, unappreciated, dismissed, and considered by the public school system as having little to offer.

One parent interview brought to light the confusion that some of my parents had about my commitment to involve parents in the classroom.

In January, while conducting an interview with the mother of my Korean student, I found that she never believed my repeated offers for volunteers in the classroom extended to her. She did not feel like she was the parent I was asking for when I sent home letters to recruit parents. She did not feel her English was good enough, and assumed that I wanted more educated parents who could help *teach*. When I explained different ways that she could help, she was more than willing to volunteer weekly in my classroom. She needed a specific volunteer invitation that she felt comfortable with and needed to know that my reasons for having parents volunteer was more about connecting homes and school than about helping me. On the other hand, I needed to understand her feelings and perspectives to know how to negotiate her involvement.

In time, I found that with many families of my English learners, when parents understood that my desire to learn from them was sincere, they became more willing to build a working relationship. Often this came from one-on-one conversations rather than notes that were sent home. When I began looking *outside the box* in terms of how I could involve parents, I received more participation in classroom related activities. Parents came in to share family immigration stories, play instruments, do cultural demonstrations, and listen to children read books. All of these interactions allowed parents to become more closely connected to their child's education and gave me a better understanding of what I needed to do to help each child succeed. By the end of the year, every child had a parent who had visibly contributed to our classroom repeatedly. It was a fantastic experience to realize that with every conversation came more comfort and more trust.

CONCLUSION

In my project, I focused on reading issues I noticed related to my Asian English learners who lived in poverty. I realize that the specific issues I identify here may not be standard for all English learners, including English learners not living in poverty or native-English-speaking students who are minorities. However, students come to schools from different literacy backgrounds. Regardless of the child's background, teachers need to be aware that not all students come to school with the same literacy and preliteracy backgrounds or familiarity with school literacy practices, and we must work to make literacy instruction accessible to each child.

The purpose of my research was to discover what literacy practices were happening in the homes of my English learners and how those practices could enhance instructional practices in school. Although not all of my English learners ended the year at a proficient reading level, they made great progress. Most importantly, this was the beginning of my learning that has continued to benefit students well beyond my year of research. I continue to learn from my families and believe that the partnership I have developed with my parents has led to more effective literacy instruction for all students in my classroom. In the end, my focus changed from what could I do to change home literacy practices to what could I do to change my classroom practices based on what I learned from families.

Lynn: Connecting Parents to the Curricular Practices of School

I am a kindergarten teacher who has been teaching young children, including English learners, for many years, and I have developed strong beliefs that I think are critical to their learning and growth. I feel that if I develop a positive, personal relationship with a child, they will be available for learning. I feel that if I provide an environment conducive to learning, a child will learn. I am knowledgeable about the developmental levels of children and what is appropriate. I have been comfortable in my role as a teacher and have felt successful in the classroom. However, I was prepared in a traditional program, and, in my early years of practice, I taught in classrooms where all students spoke English as their native language. As Lakeview saw an increasing population of English learners, we hired ESL teachers, and mainstream teachers felt that it was the ESL teachers' responsibility to teach English to the newcomers.

Several things precipitated a change in my attitude and beliefs. First, the school went through a restructuring process, and we no longer had a specific ESL staff member; all teachers had the responsibility of teaching all students in their classrooms. As part of this restructuring, professional development opportunities were offered to increase our expertise in teaching English learners. I took classes led by Maggie Hawkins (a co-author of this chapter), and that led to a research collaboration. I was interested in how I could better teach my English learners, and she wanted to better understand what was going on in terms of language and literacy development for young English learners when they entered school (Hawkins, 2004; Hawkins & Legler, 2004). She challenged many of my assumptions and was forever asking, "So what?" I slowly began to realize that my fundamental beliefs were sound but there was so much more to learn. I had never taken a critical look at my practices, questioned my curriculum, or evaluated my relationship with parents until I started working with Maggie.

Maggie and I have now worked together for 7 years. Here I discuss some general insights from our collaboration, but I focus particularly on the initiatives we undertook in the 2003–2004 academic year. In the preceding years, we had examined aspects of interaction and learning within the school environment, including a focus on developing curriculum. During that school year, we looked intensively at home-school relations and connecting parents to the curricular practices of school. First, I describe our thinking about the specific curriculum we were using, then I discuss our attempts to involve parents in our work.

At the kindergarten level, much of the curriculum has a hands-on approach. The children are exposed to materials and encouraged to explore, sometimes with questions stated by the teacher. After the experience, there is time for the children to tell about what they experienced. This procedure usually works well for children from White middle-class homes because the curriculum matches their way of engaging in explorations and learning experiences at home, although I now believe that all children need more than this type of learning experience to maximize their learning. For children from a different language or cultural background, this type of learning needs an infusion of modifications. The children in my classroom came from a wide variety of language and cultural backgrounds. The children's languages include Spanish, Korean, Chinese, Hmong, Russian, and Vietnamese. Some of the children are first-generation immigrants, some have been adopted by U.S. families, and some are newly arrived immigrants with little knowledge of U.S. culture or the English language. Providing optimal learning experiences for these children is a challenge. Working with the parents is a must because parents hold the information that is so necessary to their children's success in school.

Early on in our research partnership, Maggie and I realized that not all children were fully participating in classroom activities. In response, we designed activities around topics to which we felt children from all cultures could relate, such as family meals. Although the topics were familiar, as I became more aware of the comfort levels of the children, I began to realize that most of my English learners were avoiding speech and participating only at a nonverbal level. For example, we had children in small groups put together skits to perform for their classmates. They were supposed to enact a family meal, with each child choosing a role of someone at the table. My two English learners chose to be a dog, with only barking required; and a baby, who simply cried. They avoided using language. We then turned our attention to devising language-rich activities, paying particular attention to incorporating the need to speak for activities to be successfully used.

Our research became a variation of an action research model. We planned an activity, implemented the activity, gathered data on the implementation, and then evaluated what happened. Based on what we learned, we redesigned activities (Hawkins & Legler, 2004). It was an eye-opening experience. I realized that I needed to be much more involved in the hands-on learning that was supposed to take place in my classroom. Many of the children did not have the *language* of the classroom, the language that is required for success in school. There is language specific to academic disciplines but also to the routines and practices of school that these children didn't bring from home. This was the case not just with my English learners but with most of my students. I needed to think about how I could scaffold language development. The more I thought about it, the more complex the issue became. I was overwhelmed. I knew about preteaching vocabulary, connecting to students' previous experiences, and using realia in my teaching, but this seemed to demand more. Maggie and I decided to work with the science curriculum because it seemed to lend itself well to my goals: (a) it was concrete and hands-on, (b) it had specific school-based language and concepts children needed to know to be successful in school, and (c) it lent itself to children working together (collaboratively) and using language to solve problems.

I examined a variety of science curricula for young children. Together, Maggie and I developed a sample curriculum called Bugs. Our goals were to incorporate the processes of science (i.e., observing, describing, comparing, predicting, classifying, experimenting, measuring, recording, analyzing) and scientific vocabulary into the activities we created as well as involve the parents. We wanted parents to understand the sorts of activities and expectations their children encountered in school, be able to incorporate the experiences (in this case with the natural world) that children brought with them to school, and for children to bring the worlds of home and school together. We designed the unit to include classroom lessons and activities and a homework component. We wanted to infuse the classroom activities with language and ensure the necessity of using language for everyone. After each activity, we would examine what worked and what did not work, then modify the activity. The homework was intended to bridge the gap between the learning at school and the parents. It was a cooperative activity that the child and parent would do together to enhance the child's learning and increase the parent's understanding of what was happening at school. It was translated into the child's first language, and we encouraged the parents to use their first language when helping their child.

For example, as part of the unit, we sent home a sheet with four empty lines at the top and four large boxes below them. The children were to hypothesize where they might find bugs, and list four places on the lines. Then, with a parent, they would look in those places to see if their predictions were correct. Then, in each box they were to draw a picture of a bug they found in the place where they found it. The homework went home each Friday to be done over the weekend and returned to school on Monday. Each Monday morning, the children shared their homework with each other, thus providing practice in using the science-related language and in presenting and asking and answering questions. This sharing was videotaped, and Maggie and I analyzed the children's use of language and mastery of concepts.

One particular challenge we faced was that not all children brought the homework back with them on Monday mornings. This became visible because of the group sharing format. Because of our concern that no child be embarrassed or upset, we devised alternate ways of sharing. In most cases, it was an occasional lapse. But one child's family never did the homework activities. We made sure to take him out earlier in the morning to complete the activity with one of us, so that he, too, had something to share.

We surveyed all the parents in my classroom about the homework midway through the school year. They were very positive in their responses and felt that it helped them understand what their child was learning in school.

Because of our strong belief that we needed to connect the parents with the curriculum of school, we made homework only one of three initiatives involving parents that year. In addition to the weekend activities we sent home, we also conducted home visits, and we required parents to come into the classroom at least once during the school year. They could help with an activity, present something of their choosing, or just observe. We worked with them to decide what they would do. We tried very hard to get the parents to come into the classroom and attempted to make the experience as comfortable as possible. When they did come in, Maggie would interview them after the experience to gain some insight into their feelings about the experience. These interviews contained compelling data about parents' changing understandings of what their children do in school, who their children are at school, and what learning looks like in school.

We met with all the parents in individual conferences before school started to tell them about our research, explain our initiatives, and elicit their cooperation. In October, we did a home visit with all families of our English learners to discuss their family histories, their children, their feelings about school, and to address concerns and questions. In some cases, as necessary, a translator went with us. During the visits, we also modeled working with books and math patterning so the parents could observe the ways in which interactions occur around math and literacy in school. The children were thrilled to have us come and were eager to share their homes with us. We did two to three home visits with each family during the school year.

CONCLUSION

My experiences have led me to several understandings:

- Teachers need to be involved with parents to gain insight into the lives of the children in their classrooms. Knowing about a child's life at home, who (if anyone) reads to him, where they hear English other than at school, who the significant people are in the child's life, and what the parents expect from the school are all important pieces of information for the teacher to have.

- Providing a language-rich curriculum with ample opportunities to use language is an absolute necessity. Rethinking activities so that children use language in their learning is critical.
- I still strongly believe that developing a positive relationship with the child is important, but the relationship has to also involve the family.
- Creating an environment conducive to learning is important, but the role of the teacher is much more involved than setting things up and hoping the learning takes place. Even the unstructured parts of a kindergarten day need to be thought out. How can the objects in the doll corner be used to facilitate interaction? Where should the blocks be placed to encourage shared use and use of language? Does the learning environment reflect the images of the children using it? Is each child an equal member of the learning community?

I feel fortunate that I was part of a research team that looked at children's learning or lack of learning, then went through the painstaking process of examining *why*. I think that even the best of teachers work on so many ingrained assumptions about who our students are, what learning in schools looks like, and what should happen in classrooms, but we don't have the opportunities to really research and reflect on our practices. Through my work with Maggie, my teaching practice has evolved to look much different than it did before. I have eliminated many of the time-filling activities that didn't require students to use language in favor of a curriculum that puts the building blocks for academic skills and language in place—although it is still kindergarten, with lots of wiggle songs and creative play. I pay attention to the language I use and provide opportunities for children to practice new language and concepts. I try to find out as much as I can about children's lives out of school and incorporate their families, cultures, and experiences into the classroom and curriculum. I reach out to families in different ways. There are many other issues to contemplate, but being aware of each child as an individual with a unique family, a unique language and cultural background, and unique learning needs is a good place to start.

Conclusion

This chapter represents three teachers' efforts at curriculum revitalization within the context of school restructuring to meet the needs of a rapidly expanding population of students from diverse linguistic and cultural backgrounds. The stories we tell are not unique, but they are compelling.

They illustrate that simply being sensitive to cultural differences is not enough; it takes a rigorous ongoing examination of assumptions, practices, and environments to effect real change. We advocate for teacher research, whether as a single defined initiative or as an action research cycle, knowing that no matter what we find, and what new practices we implement, there will always be more to discover, understand, and change.

Our focus here has been on families. Generally, education acknowledges the importance of partnerships between schools and parents, especially for young children. As a whole, from experience, Lakeview teachers have identified this as a key component of success in restructuring to better meet the educational needs of English learners. This topic has a rapidly expanding knowledge base in the field of educational research and is even the target of legislation in the United States. However, all too common are well-intentioned approaches that position educators to *help* or *fix* families—these approaches are intended to guide them to change beliefs, behaviors, and practices. Not only does this suggest that families with diverse beliefs and practices are somehow inferior or inadequate, but it places the blame on them for their children's lack of success in school. This chapter illustrates how programs and curricula across disciplinary areas can be more effectively redesigned and implemented through collaborations between teachers and families. The three teachers represented all undertook initiatives in which gaining information from parents, listening seriously and respectfully to their voices, and including them in instructional design and implementation were central and led to changes in the teachers' perspectives and practices. Changes in schools and schooling that reflect and respond to the heterogeneity of student populations are clearly necessary. We believe that, at core, it is the teachers' willingness to engage in reciprocal learning with families, to modify and change curriculum and instructional approaches, and to work as authentic partners with families in establishing educational support for children, that will shift the tide of school achievement for linguistically and culturally diverse learners.

Resources

Adgar, C. T., Clair, N., & Smith, D. (Producers). (2001). *Why reading is hard* [Video]. Washington, DC: Center for Applied Linguistics.

Alexander, R. B. (1998). *Number jugglers: Math card games.* New York: Workman Publishing.

Cary, S. (2000). *Working with second language learners.* Portsmouth, NH: Heinemann Publishing.

Chamot, A. J., & O'Malley, M. (1994). Instructional approaches and teaching procedures. In K. Spangenberg-Urbschat & R. Prichard (Eds.), *Kids come in all languages: Reading instruction for ESL students* (pp. 82–107). Newark, DE: International Reading Association.

Claire, N. (2001). *Why reading is hard* [Viewers guide]. Washington, DC: Center for Applied Linguistics.

Gibbons, P. (1991). *Learning to learn in a second language*. Portsmouth, NH: Heinemann Publishing.

Harden, W. (2000). *The teaching of science in primary schools*. London: David Fulton Publishing.

Kaye, P. (1987). *Games for math*. New York: Pantheon Books.

Rosebery, A. S., & Warren, B. (Eds.). (1998). *Boats, balloons, and classroom video*. Portsmouth, NH: Heinemann Publishing.

Saul, W., & Reardon, J. (Eds.). (1996). *Beyond the science kit*. Portsmouth, NH: Heinemann Publishing.

Shockley, B., Michalove, B., & Allen J. (1995). *Engaging families: Connecting home and school literacy communities*. Portsmouth, NH: Heinemann Publishing.

Stanmark, J. K., Thompson, V., & Cossey, R. (1997). *Family math*. Huntington Beach, CA: Creative Teaching Press.

Appendix A: Can You Find the Difference? (English/Spanish)

Game: Can You Find the Difference?

Materials: Deck of cards, beans

Number of Players: 2

Directions:

1. Divide the pile of cards into two groups.
   How can you divide the cards so both people get the same number?

2. Each person gets one pile of cards. Put the beans in the middle.

3. Each person chooses a card. Look at it and show it to your partner.

4. The person with the biggest card subtracts the difference and takes that many beans.

   Example: Player 1: 9 Player 2: 5 9 − 5 = 4
   Player 1 gets 4 beans.
   If your card has a face, it is worth 10.

5. When all the cards have been drawn, add up all your beans.

Challenge:
Can you think of a faster way to add your beans than counting by 1s?

ENCUENTRE LA DIFERENCIA

Juego: Encuentre la diferencia

Materiales: Una baraja de cartas, frijoles

Número de jugadores: 2

Instrucciones:

1. Divida las cartas en dos grupos.
   ¿Cómo pueden dividir las tarjetas para recibir el mismo número?

2. Cada persona recibe un montón de cartas. Ponen todos los frijoles en el centro.

3. Cada persona voltea la primera carta de su montón. Mira su carta y la enseñe a la otra persona.

4. La persona con la carta con el número más grande suma la diferencia y toma el mismo número de frijoles.
   Por ejemplo: Jugador 1: 9 Jugador 2: 5 9 − 5 = 4
   Jugador 1 toma 4 frijoles.
   Si su tarjeta tiene una cara, la carta vale 10.

5. Cuando todas las cartas se han vuelto, cuente cada uno desus frijoles.

Reto:
¿Puede contar sus frijoles en una manera más rápida que de 1 en 1? Inténtalo de 2 en 2 o 5 en 5.

Appendix B: Addition Top-It (English/Spanish)

Game: Addition Top-It

Materials: a deck of playing cards

Number of Players: 2

Directions:

1. Divide the cards into two equal groups.

2. Each person gets one group of cards.

3. Both players turn over their top two cards. Add your two cards together.

4. Say the sum of your two cards. The person with the larger sum takes all four cards.

5. If the sum is the same, each player turns over two more cards. The player with the larger sum takes all eight cards.

6. Continue until all of the cards have been turned over. The person with the most cards wins.

Subtraction Top-It

Play the game the same way, this time subtracting your two cards. The person with the larger difference takes the cards.

SUME CON CARTAS

Juego: Sume con cartas

Materiales: una baraja de cartas

Número de jugadores: 2

Instrucciones:

1. Divida las cartas en dos grupos.

2. Cada persona recibe un montón de cartas.

3. Cada persona voltea las dos primeras cartas en su montón. Sume las dos tarjetas.

4. Diga la suma. La persona con la suma mayor, toma todas las cartas.

5. Si las sumas son la misma, voltean dos cartas más. La persona con la suma mayor toma las ocho cartas.

6. Continúen hasta que todas las cartas se han volteado. La persona con más cartas gana.

Resta con cartas

Puede jugar el mismo juego pero restando. Cuando voltea las dos cartas, reste. La persona con la resta mayor toma las cartas.

Living Things Are Interdependent: An Ecological Perspective on Curriculum Revitalization

9

JUDY SHARKEY AND LYNN CADE

Living things are interdependent. This was the overarching concept for a 4-week interdisciplinary unit on biomes in chapter co-author Lynn Cade's fifth-grade self-contained English as a second language (ESOL) classroom in February 2004. As we reflected on the learning that occurred during our collaborative classroom research project that school year, we realized that the concept *living things are interdependent* was analogous to our understanding of and approach to curriculum. We view curriculum as a living and lived phenomenon that encompasses a rich variety of interacting components: teachers, learners, school community, and resources. In this chapter, we highlight *ecosystem* as both curriculum content and a metaphor for the process of revitalizing a fifth-grade ESOL curriculum to include a more intentional focus on academic language and content. We write from the perspective of an elementary school teacher with 20 years experience (10 of those years with English learners) and a university-based teacher educator who supervises ESOL and elementary education interns and conducts collaborative research with classroom teachers.

Motivation for the Adaptation

ACKNOWLEDGING A CLIMATE CHANGE

Leading up to the 2003–2004 school year, several local and national factors began to converge that warranted curricular attention and reflected our shared professional interests. Student demographics in our district had been changing over the past 2–3 years. There was an increase in English learners who had had little or no formal schooling and who were not print literate in their first language (L1). As a result, more English learners were staying in self-contained, or what the school district called *magnet* ESOL classrooms, for 2, 3, or 4 years. Previous groups of English learners, students with stronger academic backgrounds in their L1, had typically exited the magnet program after 1 year. The assumption was that the magnet was the place where students learned social language and school culture. It did not explicitly teach mainstream content and concepts; rather, it helped students prepare to enter those classrooms. One problem many ESOL teachers in the district recognized was that the longer the students stayed in the magnet, the more grade-level content and opportunities to interact with English-speaking peers they were denied. Thus, conversations and calls to respond to these changing needs of the population were heard throughout the district.

Second, in January 2002, the No Child Left Behind Act (NCLB), Pub. L. No. 107-110, was signed into law, bringing numerous changes to policy and practices in public schools in the United States. One of those changes was the increased level of accountability for particular populations or *subgroups*: low-income students, minority students, students with special needs, and English learners. Under the mandates of NCLB, English learners were to be assessed annually in two areas: English language proficiency and academic content (as defined by each state's curriculum standards). No less than 95% (on average over a 3-year period) of English learners would be required to participate in these assessments. If one subgroup did not attain adequate yearly progress (AYP), the entire school would be labeled as having failed to make AYP.

In 2003, our state, New Hampshire, had K–12 curriculum frameworks for language arts, math, social studies, science, and the arts—but not for ESOL. Although teachers were advised to use the TESOL pre-K–12 standards (Kornblum & Kupetz, 1997) with the state frameworks when designing curriculum for their students, there were no coordinated or sustained efforts to help teachers with this process. In our school district, efforts to develop an ESOL curriculum aligned with the district curriculum had stalled because of uncertainty about the kinds of changes NCLB would actually bring. Teachers were hesitant to spend time and energy developing a curriculum if it might be trumped by a state or federal initiative.

Given the changing demographics and pressures from NCLB, chapter co-author Lynn Cade, like many of her colleagues throughout the district, realized that the current curriculum for the ESOL population had to adapt to this change in climate. It had to recognize the increased numbers and variety of learners and their needs while acknowledging external pressures to improve test scores. The revitalized curriculum had to help students develop language and grade-level content simultaneously. The magnet classroom could not be a place where students just learned social language and school culture while their mainstream English-speaking peers were busy learning content. If this were the case, English learners would never catch up to their peers.

In terms of personal professional interests, we were both interested in understanding how English language learners develop academic language and literacy in English. We were familiar with Cummins' (1981, 2000) distinction between basic interpersonal communicative skills and cognitive academic language proficiency and his instructional recommendations for facilitating academic language proficiency. We were also familiar with sheltered instruction (SI), an instructional approach to teaching academic content to language learners (Freeman & Freeman, 1988), and had been exploring and experimenting with the SI observation protocol (SIOP), an instructional framework that grew out of Echevarria, Vogt, and Short's (2000) efforts to operationalize SI. Lynn, who had always used theme-based approaches to curriculum, was interested in incorporating more aspects of SI into her teaching because it would increase the academic rigor of her curriculum and reflect the national shift to standards-based instruction. Chapter co-author Judy Sharkey was interested in two broad topics: (a) understanding teachers' knowledge and processes in revising their curriculum and (b) documenting the teaching and learning of academic language and literacy within an SI classroom. We were familiar with the research stating that it takes second language learners 4–7 years to develop academic proficiency (Cummins, 1981; Thomas & Collier, 1997, 2002) but wanted to know what the first and second years of this process might look and sound like.

During the 2003–2004 school year, we were both participating in a school–university literacy collaborative guided by the overarching question: How do we bridge the gap between mainstream literacy reforms and the literacy needs and challenges of English learners? A principal objective for the collaborative was to develop curriculum that used mainstream materials as much as possible and was based on research and best practices in second language learning. Within the structure of the collaborative, we developed a classroom-based inquiry project investigating how SI would affect teaching and learning in an ESOL magnet classroom. As part of our project, we carefully documented the classroom events of the school year and met weekly to discuss impressions of students' learning, analyze work they had produced; reflect on the week's learning and teaching; and discuss future lessons, units, and school events (e.g., upcoming field trips and testing). Judy spent 1 day a week in Lynn's classroom during the school year. She videotaped approximately 15 hours of classroom activities over a 6-month span, and formally interviewed students four times between January and June.

The Curricular Context

HAVE TO HAVE A HABITAT TO CARRY ON: THE ECOSYSTEM OF BEECH STREET COMMUNITY SCHOOL

An ecological perspective on classroom activity emphasizes the highly contextualized, complex, and interactive nature of teaching and learning. It highlights the nested contexts of classroom, school, and community and views learning as an interactive, co-constructed activity (Shulman, 1986; Van Lier, 2000). "Have to have a habitat to carry on" (Oliver, 1995) is the key line from one of several songs Lynn uses when teaching about ecosystems. The message is that we need to appreciate the special features of a habitat that aid our survival (e.g., the importance of healthy forests in producing oxygen). A classroom is a habitat nestled within the larger ecosystem of a particular school and city. Understanding the various layers of our habitat and ecosystem helps us identify key resources and realities, an awareness that allows us to "carry on." In the following paragraphs, we provide a brief overview of our curricular ecosystem.

Beech Street Community School is located in a historic mill city in the Northeastern United States. Manchester, with a population of approximately 109,000, is the largest city in the state of New Hampshire and since the 1980s has been a refugee resettlement city. In the past half dozen years, the largest groups have been from Bosnia and several African countries, including Sudan, the Congo, and Somalia Bantus. In addition to the refugee population, the city's immigrant population boasts a growing and diverse Hispanic community with families from Mexico, Puerto Rico, the Dominican Republic, and countries in Central America and South America. New Hampshire is a low-incidence ESOL state; only 1.3% of the state's K–12 students receive ESOL services. However, Manchester is home to more than 45% of the state's ESOL population, and 7.3% of the district's 17,500 students receive ESOL services. More than 70 languages are spoken in the district. Although education for English learners is a low priority for the state, it is one of the most pressing issues for a collection of Manchester schools that have significant populations of English learners, one of which is Beech Street Community School.

Beech Street is the most culturally and linguistically diverse elementary school in a predominantly White (95%) state. It also has the state's highest concentration of poor students. During the 2003–2004 school year,

85% of the 685 students enrolled in grades K–5 were eligible for free or reduced-price lunches. Approximately one third of Beech students received ESOL services, and these students represented over 20 languages. There were ESOL magnet classrooms in grades 2–5. Two pullout ESOL teachers worked with individual and small groups of students.

Because of its high population of students from low-income families, Beech Street is a Title I school, a federal designation that brings additional resources into the school. The Title I resource room at the school has an extensive collection of literacy support materials that teachers can check out and use in their classrooms. One of the most valuable resources is the guided reading collection, which consists of more than 500 titles, often with multiple copies for teachers to use with small groups of students. These small books, usually between 12 and 20 pages, are organized according to 26 (*a* to *z*) reading levels that fall under four broad levels (aligned with approximate grade level): early emergent (kindergarten), emergent (grade 1), early fluent (grade 2), and fluent (grades 3–5). Beech Street also has a site license to use the Reading A to Z Web site (www.readinga-z.com). This allows teachers to print out additional titles. Many of the titles on the Web site are available in Spanish as well as English.

The cultural and linguistic diversity that the English learners bring to the school is acknowledged and welcomed. The ESOL teachers and their students are an integral part of the school's identity, and this is visible everywhere in the school, from the multilingual and multicultural murals, the welcome signs that decorate the halls, and the welcome message on the school's Web site. The ESOL team is quick to acknowledge the support they receive from their principal, as it is this support that has helped the team be proactive in program design and classroom instruction in a state where ESOL education is a low priority.

The goal of the magnet program is to transition the English learners to mainstream classrooms as soon as they can be successful in those classrooms. The ESOL magnet teachers are part of their grade-level teams and participate in weekly grade-level meetings. Thus, Lynn's magnet class is part of the fifth-grade community. All fifth graders, typically 10–11 years old, follow the same schedule: School begins at 8:30 a.m. and ends at 2:35 p.m. The students stay in their respective classrooms all day except for one 45-minute *special*, when they have a different subject each day (e.g., art, health, physical education, library, and computer lab). In addition to knowing the mainstream curriculum, the content objectives, and so forth, Lynn makes sure that she is asking her colleagues questions such as, "What do students in your classrooms need to do to be successful?" and "What are your expectations for students?"

During the time of our project, there were 16 students in the fifth-grade

ESOL classroom (9 girls; 7 boys) from 7 countries: Bosnia (4 students), China (1), the Dominican Republic (3), Mexico (5), Puerto Rico (1), Russia (1), and Ukraine (1). Viktor[1] knew no English when he arrived in August 2003, but he was a very good student in Ukraine and on grade level. Manuel knew no English when he arrived in June 2003 from the Dominican Republic, and he had weak Spanish literacy skills; his parents reported that he was "not a good student" in his previous school. Mahir, from Bosnia, had excellent social and oral English skills but struggled with reading and writing. At the start of the fifth grade, his second year at Beech Street, Mahir was performing on a second-grade literacy level. Alexandra, in her third year in the magnet program, had missed 2 years of schooling in Russia before her family immigrated to the United States. Thus, she had only rudimentary literacy skills in Russian. At the beginning of the school year, she could demonstrate her ability and skill at memorizing and reciting chunks of texts without really comprehending them.

The diversity of students; their personalities; and their cultural, linguistic, and academic backgrounds creates a rich biodiversity for a classroom habitat. However, this population can change quickly over the course of a year. Newcomers may arrive at any time, and others will be exited to mainstream classrooms when they are ready. The student population in Lynn's classroom during our project was fairly stable, with the largest changes coming between April and June 2004. Six of the 16 students were mainstreamed for the last 8 weeks of school. In addition, two new children, Faisel and Gaul, Somali Bantus with no English and no L1 print literacy, arrived in April and May, respectively. In December, Tania left for Mexico and returned in April. In January, Alana returned to Beech Street after having been in Mexico for 3 years.

Process of Revitalizing the Curriculum

ADAPTATION AND SURVIVAL

Understanding the curricular context is the first step in any curriculum development process. Specifically, the context is composed of the students' abilities, needs, and personalities; the institutional expectations; and the available resources. For our project, the next piece was making the shift from theme-based instruction to SI. This required identifying and articulating what we understood to be the differences between the two approaches as

---

[1] All student names are pseudonyms.

they applied to elementary ESOL education and then deciding which pieces would inform revising the curriculum.

Sheltered instruction and theme-based instruction are content-based and feature contextualized and multimodal (listening, speaking, reading, writing) language use. Vocabulary is recycled and reinforced. There are many visual supports and hands-on activities as well as numerous opportunities for interaction. In terms of differences, SI is built around academic concepts whereas theme-based instruction is built around a topic or subject. For example, *living things are interdependent* is an academic concept, whereas the environment and life in the rainforest are themes. Lynn's theme-based instruction has always been interdisciplinary, whereas many SI materials and examples seemed to focus on one subject area. The SIOP (Echevarria et al., 2000) organizes the components of SI into eight broad categories: preparation, building background, comprehensible input, strategies, interaction, practice and application, lesson delivery, and review and assessment. Each category of the SIOP has three or more subcategories or indicators. For example, *language* and *content objectives* are under the preparation category.

Lynn used the SIOP to guide her planning. Some SIOP categories served as places to list resources or ideas for activities; others served as gentle reminders of what to address in planning. (See the section Curriculum Products for an example.) For Lynn, using the SIOP meant articulating explicit content and language objectives and making those objectives accessible to the students, including more explicit teaching of grammar and learning strategies and placing an increased focus on assessment—specifically, on making assessment criteria accessible to students and involving them in the assessment process.

Writing content and language objectives and making those objectives accessible to the students affected Lynn's planning significantly. It forced her to change from what she called her shoot- from-the-hip style and do more long-term and organized planning. By *accessible*, we mean writing and posting objectives in language that students can understand. The planning started by working with the standards (i.e., state curriculum frameworks, grade-level concepts) and then thinking about ways to make them accessible to students. This was a subtle but significant shift from thinking about general topics and themes to asking, "What kinds of things can students do with these topics?" It meant bringing students up to the content rather than watering down the content for the students. As a result, the 2003–2004 academic standards for the ESOL fifth graders were more challenging than those for the previous year.

The greatest challenge in helping students access the concepts was finding appropriate materials. The Internet was invaluable in meeting the challenge. The Web sites listed in Appendix A have excellent visuals—including maps, charts, and texts—and some wonderful ideas for hands-on activities. Because the students had a wide range of language and literacy abilities, we needed to identify topic-related textbooks written at a variety of reading levels. One project the university–school literacy collaborative completed was a database that listed all the guided reading material in the Title I resource room according to topic and then reading level. This helped Lynn put together a collection of 20–30 books that related to biomes (e.g., *Tundra*, Cefrey, 2002; *Life in a Rainforest*, Gibbons, 2001) and make them available to students. She also used the Reading A–Z Web site to print out books in Spanish for the Spanish-speaking students who could benefit from accessing the concepts in their L1.

Building on her knowledge and experience with theme-based instruction, Lynn sought to make her SI units as interdisciplinary as possible so that key concepts and vocabulary could be recycled and practiced in meaningful ways. For example, in the Biomes Unit, one math lesson is related to changing fractions to percentages. For the content of this lesson, Lynn used informational profiles on specific animals and their typical daily diets (www.seaworld.org/just-for-teachers/guides/index.htm). Thus, words such as *consume*, *omnivore*, and *natural habitat* were used in meaningful ways in the math class as students compared the animals' daily intake to body weight. In language arts, the picture book *Sarah Saw a Blue Macaw* (Bogart, 1991) served as a great introduction to a mini-lesson on irregular forms of past-tense verbs. The topic and pictures were connected to the Biomes Unit, while the text was filled with numerous examples of the irregular past tense. For example,

> *Where did Sarah swing? Sarah swung where branches hung. Big branches hung where Sarah swung and trees were towering. What did Sarah see? Sarah saw a blue macaw. The blue macaw that Sarah saw was sleeping in a tree. (Bogart, 1991, pp. 4–5)*

Another prominent feature of the adaptation was an increased focus on assessment, specifically on increasing student involvement in assessment and creating more opportunities for formative assessment. The first step in this process was making sure students knew what the learning objectives were, why those objectives were important and then consistently encouraging students to identify and reflect on what they were learning and how they were learning it. The learning objectives, key vocabulary, and concepts were posted in a prominent position in the classroom, and students became accustomed to referring to them at different points of the day and throughout the week. For larger projects, Lynn told the students what the criteria for evaluation would be and involved students in the process. For example, when students gave oral presentations to the whole class, the audience completed the same rubric that Lynn had. During a 4-week unit on the 19th century U.S. explorers Lewis and Clark, the students kept learning logs. At the end of each day, they spent 5–10 minutes writing about what they had learned that day. When Judy visited the classroom each week, she would often ask individual students to fill her in on what they were learning. Starting in late fall, students used peer-editing for their writing assignments. All these activities and interactions worked together to create an environment in which students were accustomed to thinking about and articulating what they were learning.

Curriculum Products

THE FLORA AND FAUNA OF OUR HABITAT

The goal for the entire school year was to incorporate more pieces from SI into the curriculum. In this chapter, we explain the process by highlighting products and activities from a 4-week interdisciplinary unit on biomes that occurred in January and February. The unit did not occur in isolation. In the fall, students had studied plants and animals, including classification systems, characteristics of particular species and their habits, and processes such as photosynthesis. The Biomes Unit built on this knowledge and helped students apply and extend their learning to understanding more complex interactions of plants, animals, and habitats.

The culminating project of the Biomes Unit was an oral presentation explaining the life systems within a particular biome. Working in groups of two or three, students investigated an assigned biome (taiga, desert, grasslands, tundra, rainforest, or deciduous forest), and created a poster illustrating the interdependence of plants and animals within their biome. They gave an oral presentation to the whole class, which was followed by a question-and-answer session.

We have selected several curriculum products to illustrate some of the teaching and learning that occurred in Lynn's classroom during and shortly after the Biomes Unit. These products include a range of materials and texts that address planning, students' varying reading levels, classroom activities, and student-generated products (oral and written). After each heading, we describe the product and how it was used in the classroom.

Planning Using the State Standards and the SIOP Categories
In addition to knowing the content and expectations of the fifth-grade mainstream curriculum at Beech Street, Lynn worked with the state curriculum frameworks (Figure 1) in planning her instruction and

**Figure 1. State Standards
(New Hampshire Curriculum Frameworks)**

Social Studies: Geography

10: Students will use maps and graphic tools to acquire, process, report, and analyze geographical information.

11: Students will use geographical features to understand places and regions.

12: Students will analyze landform patterns on the Earth's surface.
- Students will describe characteristics of biomes and associated plants and animals.
- Students will study the carrying capacity of different ecosystems

14: Students will analyze the connections between the Earth's physical and human systems.

Science: Life Science

3a. Students will recognize patterns of evolution with a focus on specialization and adaptation.

3b. Students will understand how environmental factors affect all living systems (biomes). Students will identify basic requirements for sustaining life.

3c. Students will recognize how organisms are linked to each other and their physical setting by transfer of energy to maintain a dynamic equilibrium.

3d. Students will identify life processes in plants and animals and their functions.

6a. Students will analyze parts of a system and their interrelationships.

assessment. Our state's frameworks are organized by broad topics under the content areas (e.g., Geography under Social Studies and Life Sciences under Science). For each topic, there are several proficiency indicators.

Using the SIOP Categories as a Planning Framework

Lynn typed up the SIOP categories and used them to help her organize and plan her curriculum. Figure 2 shows the SIOP notes Lynn made for the Biomes Unit. The intent was not to implement the SIOP model but rather see how its framework could aid planning and instruction. It is for this reason that Lynn's notes do not include all 30 SIOP indicators. The content objectives reflect the state standards but are written in language that is more accessible to fifth-grade English learners.

Examples of Texts at Different Reading Levels

Here we include mockups of examples of texts that students had access to during the Biomes Unit. The four texts shown (Figures 3–6) represent four reading levels. The first three are from the guided reading collection at Beech Street. Each book is approximately 5 inches × 7 inches (12.5 cm × 17.5 cm) and is illustrated with beautiful, rich photographs or illustrations.

Figure 2. Lynn's Notes for the Biomes Unit

CATEGORY 1: PREPARATION

Content Objectives

Students will demonstrate an understanding that all biomes depend on the relationships of living things within that ecosystem.

Students will work in groups to create a diagram that illustrates the interdependence of plants and animals within a specific biome

Language Objectives

Students will give an oral presentation of their biome project, appropriately using target vocabulary.

Students will evaluate each other's group projects through listening and questioning.

Content Concepts

An ecosystem is a group of interdependent organisms together with the environment that they inhabit and depend on.

A biome is an ecosystem that covers a large area of land.

Plants and animals within a particular ecosystem have interdependent relationships.

A food chain is a series of steps showing the transfer of energy among living things.

New Vocabulary

Ecosystem, habitat, producer, consumer, decomposer, omnivore, herbivore, carnivore

Supplementary Materials

Posters of biomes and food chains

Wall charts of plant and animal classification

Nonfiction books about biomes (at a variety of reading levels)

Overhead transparencies of food webs (downloaded from various Web sites)

Poster board and markers for students

Printouts of information about different animals (from various Web sites)

Adaptation of Content

Charts

Books

Songs (e.g., "Habitat")

The ways in which students use the maps and charts from the textbook

Meaningful Activities

Computer searches for information on assigned biomes

Group work creating biomes posters

Read-alouds during snack time and other transition times

Class discussions

Vocabulary classification activities

Singing content songs at the end of each day

continued on p. 190

Figure 2 (cont.). Lynn's Notes for the Biomes Unit

CATEGORY 2: BUILDING BACKGROUND

Students completed several units in the fall on animals and geographical regions of the world. They have had practice reading and gleaning information from charts and maps. They will use this information as they learn about food chains and ecosystems.

CATEGORY 3: COMPREHENSIBLE INPUT

In a clear, step-by-step manner, the teacher will model both process and product for the completion of the project (poster and oral presentation). Students will be able to conference with teachers and group members as well as members of other groups.

CATEGORY 4: STRATEGIES

The teacher will model strategies for reading and locating important information from nonfiction picture books. Students will use a teacher-designed graphic organizer to demonstrate their understanding of the strategies.

CATEGORY 5: INTERACTION

Students will have numerous opportunities to interact with classmates and the teacher. Group brainstorming, pair work, small group work, oral presentations, and individual student-teacher conferences.

CATEGORY 6: PRACTICE AND APPLICATION

First, students will listen to teacher lecture and read-alouds highlighting key content concepts. Then, they will discuss and read adapted material about the content. They will learn and sing content songs. In small groups, they will create a poster representing the central features and characteristics of a particular biome and the food chain within that biome. They will then orally present their research to the large class. Depending on their language proficiency levels and comfort doing a formal presentation, some students may choose to script their lines for the presentation.

CATEGORY 7: LESSON DELIVERY

Students' comprehension and engagement level will dictate the pacing of the project. If students show interest in continuing their independent research for their biomes, they will be given more time to do so.

CATEGORY 8: REVIEW AND ASSESSMENT

The teacher will be giving the students constant feedback as they work on their projects. The criteria on which their projects will be assessed will be distributed before students begin their projects. They will have copies of the project rubric and will use this as they create their projects and give feedback on their classmates' presentations.

Lynn had assembled approximately 30 titles and of those, about one-third had multiple copies. During any 1- or 2-week period, each student may have read 10–12 of these short books. The last example (Figure 6) is a passage from the fifth-grade mainstream social studies textbook.

Figure 3. Example of an Upper Emergent Level Text

Title of text: *What Is a Mountain?*

Picture of Mountains	*Picture of Mt. Everest*
A mountain is a group of rocks that has pushed through the ground and that rises high into the air. [Note: 20 words on this page]	The tallest mountain in the world is Mount Everest. Mount Everest is over five-and-a-half miles high! [Note: 19 words on this page]

(Adapted from Braidich, 2001, pp. 2–3)

Classroom Pocket Chart With Objectives

Clearly articulated objectives that are accessible to the students is one of the key aspects of the SIOP. Lynn used a large (3 foot × 5 foot; 0.9 meter × 1.5 meter) pocket chart to post objectives. The chart is constructed of a cloth back with clear plastic pockets. Lynn wrote objectives and key vocabulary on strips of paper or index cards and posted them in the pocket chart. Objectives were color-coded according to subject area (e.g., black for Social Studies, red for Science). The top line held the key concept for the unit. The bottom three rows contained key vocabulary. Figure 7 shows what the

Figure 4. Example of an Early Fluency Level Text

Title of text: *Life in the Rain Forest*

What Is a Rain Forest?	
A rain forest is a forest in a place where it rains more than 100 inches a year. There are rain forests in many different parts of the world. The Amazon rain forest in South America is the world's largest rain forest. [Note: 42 words on this page]	*A picture of a South American rain forest*

(Adapted from Gibbons, 2001, pp. 6–7)

Figure 5. Example of Text From a Higher Level Chapter Book

(not in the guided reading collection)

Title of text: *The Battle for Survival*

Herbivores

Herbivores eat plant foods such as grass, moss, lichen, leaves, flowers, berries, fruits, nuts, and roots. Many, but not all, plant-eaters have sharp front teeth (called incisors) to bite off food, and large back teeth (called molars) to grind it. Some herbivores, such as rabbits, have incisors but not molars.

Kangaroos are herbivores

More text

Elephants are herbivores

(240 words on this page)

A picture of an elephant and her calf

(Adapted from Bird & Short, 1993, pp. 6–7)

chart looked like on an afternoon when Lynn was about to teach a lesson on strategies.

Graphic Organizer Used to Model Strategies

During one lesson on strategies, the objective was for students to learn how to use picture books to gather a variety of information. The specific strategies were to learn how to use the parts of a book (e.g., charts, index, and the table of contents) to obtain information. This would help students as they did their research on their biomes and on a later project on endangered animals. Lynn taught the lesson by pointing students' attention to the objectives and then starting a whole group discussion on what the students knew about the different features of a book. Next, she drew a graphic organizer on the board (Figure 8) and asked students to copy it in their notebooks. She distributed copies of the book, *The Whale's Year* (Butterworth, 2001) and led the students through some previewing questions, such as, "What's the first thing you do when you pick up a book?", "OK, so what do you

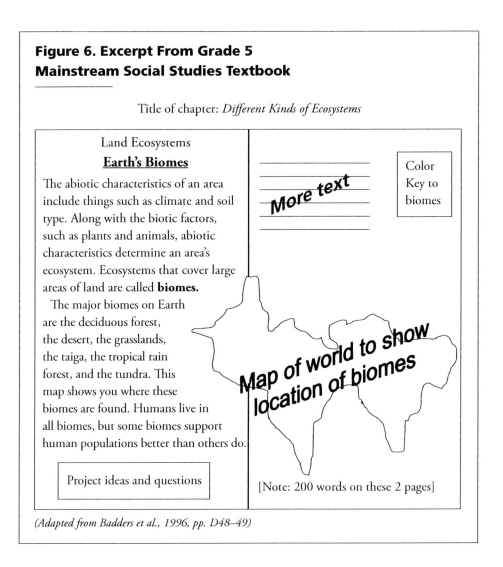

Figure 6. Excerpt From Grade 5 Mainstream Social Studies Textbook

Title of chapter: *Different Kinds of Ecosystems*

Land Ecosystems

Earth's Biomes

The abiotic characteristics of an area include things such as climate and soil type. Along with the biotic factors, such as plants and animals, abiotic characteristics determine an area's ecosystem. Ecosystems that cover large areas of land are called **biomes.**

The major biomes on Earth are the deciduous forest, the desert, the grasslands, the taiga, the tropical rain forest, and the tundra. This map shows you where these biomes are found. Humans live in all biomes, but some biomes support human populations better than others do.

More text

Color Key to biomes

Map of world to show location of biomes

Project ideas and questions

[Note: 200 words on these 2 pages]

(Adapted from Badders et al., 1996, pp. D48–49)

already know about whales?", "What information do you think will be in the book?", and "What additional information do you want to know?" The students' responses to these questions were written in the appropriate boxes on the graphic organizer. The point was to focus on the strategies, so the reading level of the text was accessible to all students and the content was fairly familiar. The class read the book *The Whale's Year*, page by page, together. Then, Lynn solicited information they learned from the different features of the book and recorded it on the graphic organizer. At the end of the lesson, students were allowed to select books that related to their projects. For homework, they completed a graphic organizer similar to the one they had just completed in class.

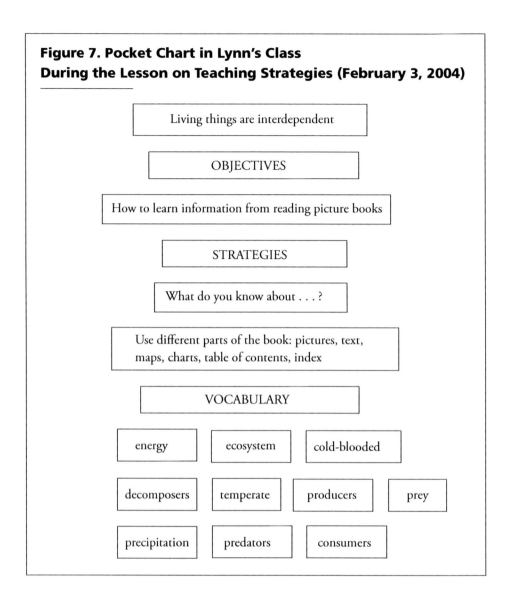

Figure 7. Pocket Chart in Lynn's Class During the Lesson on Teaching Strategies (February 3, 2004)

Living things are interdependent

OBJECTIVES

How to learn information from reading picture books

STRATEGIES

What do you know about . . . ?

Use different parts of the book: pictures, text, maps, charts, table of contents, index

VOCABULARY

energy ecosystem cold-blooded

decomposers temperate producers prey

precipitation predators consumers

Excerpt From the Exchange Between Lynn and the Students During a Read-Aloud

Every period of the school day can be used as an opportunity to reinforce the content and language in meaningful ways. At Beech Street, like many other elementary schools in the United States, teachers often find time to read aloud to students at various parts of the day. Usually, the purpose is to share good stories and foster enjoyment of reading. It can also serve to model fluency and reading with expression. Lynn read aloud to students at least twice a day, but always during the afternoon snack period because it helped students transition between two class periods. It served as a mental break for the students and helped them regain their focus for the subsequent lesson. The following passage, videotaped by Judy, represents a 1-minute

Figure 8. Graphic Organizer Completed by Lynn and Her Students

Animal: Whale Name of the book: *The Whale's Year: Butterworth, 2001*	
What I know • warm-blooded • mammal • breathes • live babies – calf • many types • ocean • carnivore • migrates • some can swim in cold water	What I predict? What do I want to know? • what do they eat? • do they lay eggs? • which oceans? • how do they use pressure to throw the water out of their hole?
What I learned	
Text • about blue whales • in winter, they are in cold water • babies are born in spring	Picture • size of the baby when it's born • krill [whales eat these]
Maps • show where whales migrate	Charts
Index • krill, page 8 • migrate, page 6	Table of Contents • title of chapters

excerpt from a 10-minute read-aloud. We include it here to emphasize the interdependent pieces of the school day.

Scene: It's 1:40 p.m. and the students have just finished Social Studies class. They have a 10-minute snack break. Lynn gathers the students at the back of the room. They sit on the floor in a circle around her chair. She holds up a book that she will read aloud, *Who Eats What? Food Chains and Food Webs* (Lauber, 1995). The atmosphere is very relaxed.

Monica: Can I read the title?

Lynn: Yes.

Monica (*reads title*): Who Eats What? Food Chains and Food Webs. (*Adds*) It's the one about the food chain.

Lynn (*to group*): What do you know about food chains?

Antigone: One animal eats something and is eaten by another and another and another.

Lynn (*reads*): A caterpillar is eating a leaf on an apple tree [p. 4]. (*asks the group*) What do we know about the caterpillar?

Mahir: It's an herbivore.

Lynn (*reads*): Later, the caterpillar is spotted by a wren. It becomes part of the wren's dinner. (*asks the group*) What do we know about a wren?

Several students: Insectivore!

Lynn: Or a carnivore. Good. (*reads*) All food chains start with green plants. (*asks*) What's one difference between animals and plants?

Marielena: Animals have to find their food, but plants produce their food.

Lynn: Everyone remember Marielena's word "produce." (*reads*) Green plants take their energy from the sun using water and air. All animals need green plants for food. (*asks*) Is that true? Raise your hand if you think that's true.

Tania: Carnivores!

Juan: What about people?

Lynn: What do you think? You tell me.

[*3 minutes later*]:

Lynn: What we're going to be doing in science today is learn that there are special food chains for every biome. First, we're going to try to remember some of the things we already know about food chains and biomes. [February 3, 2004]

Songs

Two or three new songs were introduced every Monday and sung at the end of the school day throughout the week. Here is an excerpt from "Habitat" (Oliver, 1995).

Title: "Habitat" ("Have to Have a Habitat")
(Sung to the tune "Lollipop, Lollipop")

Chorus
  Habitat, habitat, have to have a habitat
  Habitat, habitat, have to have a habitat
  You have to have a habitat to carry on.

Verse

> The ocean is a habitat, a very special habitat
> It's where the deepest water's at
> It's where the biggest mammal's at
> It's where our future food is at
> It keeps the atmosphere intact
> The ocean is a habitat we depend on!

(*Chorus*)

Excerpts From Students' Work

The students produced a wide range of oral and written texts during the unit. Below are excerpts of the work of two very different students, Mahir and Mei. The texts fairly capture these students' language proficiency levels but more important, the content knowledge they were attaining. The examples included in this chapter of texts at different reading levels reflect just one way the varying level of students' English proficiency levels affected Lynn's planning and teaching. During collaborative learning projects and activities, she made strategic decisions for grouping students so that their personalities, learning styles, academic abilities, and language levels would facilitate individual and group learning. In the example below, Mahir had strong oral skills but struggled with reading and writing. His partner, Murat, was a strong reader and writer but lacked confidence in presenting academic knowledge in class presentations.

The culminating project for the Biomes Unit was an oral presentation of the students' research on their particular biomes. Students worked in groups of two or three. Judy videotaped the presentations. The following is an excerpt, verbatim, of Mahir and Murat's presentation. They referred to a poster they had created illustrating the food chain in their biome but they did not use any note cards. Mahir spoke at native-speaker speed.

> Hello and welcome to our show. Our desert, our biome name is desert and everything starts first with, ah, precipitation. The precipitation gives us the energy to the plants so plants grow. When plants grow the harbivores [*sic*], the herbivores eat the plants that [*pointing to pictures on the poster*] the jackrabbit and kangaroo and iguana eats the plants. They are called, they're called predators, no herbivores. OK, you take it. [*signals Murat to continue*]

A few minutes later, Mahir continues his part:

> And, the, when the omnivore dies and he goes in the ground and the decomposers split the animal up to pieces and put it in dirt and new plants grow. [pointing to poster] This animal is called

prey because this, these two animals can't eat this animal because it's at the top of the food chain. These animals are called predator because uh, they are, this animal can eat them? [looking to Lynn for confirmation]

Lynn: Show me where desert is on the chart.

Mahir: OK. [*The boys move over a few steps so that they are in front of the a large classroom chart constructed during a science class.*] OK. In the desert the precipitation we get only 10 percentile of rain and, ah, we get 300 days of sun and food we get only 500, ah, kilograms. And, ah, in the biome of the dessert there is some [*has moved back over to their poster*] animal called reptiles, animals, and this animals [*pointing to poster*] is a vertebrae and the iguana is an invertebrate because it don't eat, it doesn't have the back bone [February 16, 2004].

Mahir has confused *predator* and *prey* and mistakenly calls an iguana an invertebrate, but his presentation demonstrates that he understands the defining characteristics of his selected biome and the interrelationships between the living organisms in the biome, and that he is building his academic vocabulary. Mahir, however, struggles with reading and writing. On the spring 2004 English language proficiency test, his scores labeled him as a limited-English writer and a nonreader.

Immediately after the Biomes Unit, students started learning about endangered habitats and endangered animals. This unit built on students' knowledge of the interrelationship of plant and animal species. Now, they were investigating the negative impact humans can have on the different habitats and their inhabitants. Each student selected an endangered animal to investigate, completed research on the animal, and wrote a one-page essay on the animal. Judy interviewed the students immediately after their 40-minute research session in the computer lab. Listed below are excerpts from an interview with Mei and her final essay, completed 1 week after the interview. Although the students were used to Judy being in the classroom once a week and she had already videotaped their presentations, they did not know that she would interview them on this particular day and they did not have any notes with them.

Interview Excerpt

Judy: In Mrs. Cade's class you've been doing a lot of reading.

Mei: Yeah, we read about, like we do with the bats [*reference to work done in October*]. And we read about Martin Luther King and we read the food chain. We read about endangered animals. We read about biomes.

Judy: Oh, you're reading about so many things. Now you're reading about endangered animals?

Mei: Yup.

Judy: What's your animal?

Mei: Giraffe.

Judy: Giraffes are endangered? Why?

Mei: 'Cause people hunt the, their, like their meat.

Judy: For their meat.

Mei: Yeah, for their coats.

Judy: For their coats.

Mei: And for their tails.

Judy: Their tails? Why do they want their tails?

Mei: 'Cause they want to make uh, I don't know what that is called. [*pause*] That . . . giraffe is the tallest mammal and he eats the acacia tree and . . . [*trails off*].

Judy: Where does the giraffe live?

Mei: In the grasslands of Africa.

Judy: Are there giraffes in China?

Mei: Some of them, like in a zoo. I go to a zoo and see a giraffe [Febuary 21, 2004].

Mei's strategic ability to steer the conversation to introduce new information when she could not remember why hunters wanted the giraffe's tail reflects her motivation to keep the conversation going and to assert her knowledge of the topic. Here is the essay she completed the following week:

I am giraffe. I am one of the vulnerable animals. I am the tallest mammal. I have a longneck and longlegs. I weigh between 2,400 and 3000 pounds. When I stand up I can be 19 feet tall from head to tail. My knobs are use to protect my head in fights. I live 25 years long. I can be found in central eastern and southern Africa. My habitat is the Savannas of Africa. I am a herbivore. I eat leaves, plants and I drink water everyday on the river. My long neck helps me to eat leaves from the tall acacia tree. I am a social animal. I travel in a group. I have a baby called calf. When my baby can stand up and walk after about an hour. People hunt my meat, coat and tail. People use my meat to eat. People use my coat for shield covering. People use my tail for good luck bracelets. There is no protection for me now but I may soon be endangered [February 28, 2004].

Process of Evaluating the Revitalization

HOW A CLIMATE CHANGE CAN ENDANGER A HABITAT

In addressing the question, "How do we know this is working?" we looked to the students and their learning and considered two types of assessments: internal and external. Internal assessment was the learning we could see and document in the classrooms at Beech Street, including observations of students, their interactions with one another, and analysis of their work (written and oral). The external assessment was the language proficiency test (also known as the IDEA Proficiency Test or IPT), the state-approved annual assessment instrument for English language learners (*IDEA proficiency tests*, 1993).

In our ongoing conversations throughout the year, we could see and document that the students were rising to meet the increased academic challenge of the curriculum. They were making connections across the curriculum, using more academic language in their written and oral work, constructing meaning from numerous texts, and using learning strategies. In addition, the students who were mainstreamed into the other fifth-grade classrooms late in the year were successful academically and socially. Lynn remarked, "I'm trying to challenge them a little more [this year], and they continually amaze me by how they meet the challenges . . . [E]ven the newcomers are showing me they can meet some of the challenges" (February 20, 2004).

Mahir's oral presentation, Mei's interview and essay, and the student–teacher exchange in the read-aloud on food chains exemplified the kind of academic language and content students were learning and acquiring just in the Biomes Unit. This level of language use was consistent with students' production throughout the year, and it was substantially different from the work the students the previous year had produced. For example, the culminating project for the Biomes Unit in February 2003 was an illustrated class book. Each student drew a picture of an animal and wrote a simple sentence to accompany it. Examples included the following:

- In the desrt [*sic*], the animals get water from the plans [*sic*] they eat. The kangaroo hops across the deserts of Australia.
- The snake slithers through the ground in the desert.
- The owl is looking for animals to eat in the desert.
- A lion walks in the grasslands.

It was exciting for us to see the students making connections and applying their language and content knowledge across the curriculum. For example, in a social studies lesson using the fifth-grade textbook, Danny pointed out several irregular past-tense forms he noticed (March 11, 2004). In a grammar review of the present progressive, Lynn had a sample sentence on the board: "The boys are eating lunch." She asked the students to generate some more examples. Alexandra offered, "The whales are migrating now" (February 21, 2004). In a language arts class featuring a folktale with a toad and a frog, Antigone asked about an illustration in the text, "Who is the frog?" Marielena, her partner, replied "Remember, frogs have longer legs than toads, so this must be the frog" (March 18, 2004).

Students were constructing meaning using multiple texts. In his essay on the endangered gray wolf, Luis had only written five sentences; however, he had read three different texts and information from all three were in his passage. He had not copied any sentence verbatim from a book. During a classroom observation in the fall, Judy noticed Mei using a *hunt and copy* strategy when she was answering comprehension questions. Mei seemed to be focused on getting the answer correct rather than on understanding the question and answer. In an April classroom videotape capturing the students' independent work time, Mei reads a page from a book, closes it, and then tries to write what she understood in her notebook. In a June interview, Mei read a three-page biography she had written on Harriet Tubman, and discussed her writing process: She read and viewed multiple texts, wrote several drafts, and used peer feedback sessions before handing in her final draft (June 4, 2004).

Stephanie, Murat, Antigone, Marielena, Ivana, and Monica were mainstreamed in late April, and their teachers reported that these students' work and work habits were positive additions to their classrooms. Because they had been using fifth-grade materials in their magnet classroom, the students were not intimidated by the mainstream content. They actively participated in small-group and large-group discussions in their new classrooms.

Unfortunately, the amazing amount of learning students achieved individually and collectively was not captured on the IPT, the state-sanctioned annual assessment tool for English language learners. The results were disappointing to all of us. For 6 months, the students had been actively engaged in learning content and language-rich, grade-level appropriate instruction; however, the IPT did not measure content knowledge. Rather, it gave students a proficiency score in three domains: reading, writing, and speaking. Mei was labeled as a non-English speaker and writer and a limited-English reader. Mahir was labeled as a non-English reader and writer. This conflict or mismatch between documented classroom achievement and sanctioned state level assessments leads us to our final reflections and conclusion on our project.

Conclusion

Writing this chapter afforded us the opportunity to carefully reflect on our project, read and reread our notes and student work, review the videotapes from the year, and better articulate what we understand the challenges and rewards of explicitly attending to academic content and concepts when teaching English learners. It is also reinforced our ecological perspective on curriculum and on teaching and learning. Classrooms are habitats nested in larger ecosystems, and events that occur on a more global (e.g., national) level reverberate down to and affect the smallest habitats and niches. In our case, we refer to the effects of the NCLB Act. Although the grand goal of demanding success for all students is worthy—and in our case it helped us raise the academic expectations of the fifth-grade ESOL curriculum—the sanctioned assessments for the policy have been woefully inadequate (see, e.g., Abedi, 2004; Wright, 2005 for a larger analysis of NCLB assessments and English language learners). The last line from Mei's essay on giraffes reminds us why it is so important to fight for the legitimate value of the teaching and learning that occurred in our classroom community: "There is no protection for me now. I may soon be endangered."

Rather than end on that negative note, we would like to stress two positive insights from our project: (a) students' engagement as a renewable source of energy and (b) professional collaboration as symbiosis. Implementing SI can be incredibly labor intensive for the teacher. Lynn spent countless hours searching and assembling appropriate materials, from multiple texts to Web sites. However, seeing the students' engagement and growth energized her and emphasized the creative aspect of planning. This, in turn, created a dynamic learning environment in which teacher and student learning fostered continued learning.

Professional collaboration between classroom teachers and university researchers is a symbiotic relationship. Our collaborative inquiry enriched our individual knowledge and in turn generated shared knowledge in ways that would not have been possible if we had been working alone. The daily demands of teaching often do not allow for systematic documentation and analysis of teaching and learning. University researchers often do not have opportunities to understand the rich details and complexities of the teaching and learning that occurs in one classroom over the course of a school year. We look forward to continuing our collaboration and thank the students for allowing us to learn so much from them.

Appendix: Internet Resources

www.blueplanetbiomes.org/world_biomes
www.enchantedlearning.com/biomes
www.mbgnet.net
www.mrhabitat.net/songbook.html#habitat
www.readinga-z.com
www.siopinstitute.net/lessonplans.shtml
www.seaworld.org/just-for-teachers/guides/index.htm
www.worldbiomes.com

Curriculum Revitalization in a Japanese High School: Teacher–Teacher and Teacher–University Collaboration

10

KAZUYOSHI SATO AND KEIKO TAKAHASHI

This chapter describes curriculum development toward communication-oriented English in a Japanese public high school over a 5-year period. It compares and contrasts two 2-year projects in the same school, the first beginning in April 2001 and the second in April 2004 (see Table 1), to determine what factors contributed to the successful revitalization of the curriculum. In the first project, teachers resisted the program; they struggled and learned through trial and error, yet they lacked the communication and collaboration necessary for sustained revitalization of the curriculum. In contrast, in the second project, four teachers volunteered and formed a team. As these teachers collaborated to develop the curriculum, they generated more learning opportunities for teachers in the context of their school. Furthermore, they found that their students' learning improved.

In this chapter, we first describe the school context and provide details on the roles we assumed. Then, we delineate each project, incorporating stories. We believe these stories offer valuable insights from a teacher's perspective of how teachers revitalized their curriculum in the school.

The School and Curricular Context

The public high school charged with incorporating the programs is coeducational and located in a central regional area of Japan. Each grade has six classes with, on average, 38–40 students per class. Some students begin working directly after graduation, and others enter university. To cater to the

Table 1. Overview of Projects

Year (Grade Level)	Class	Goals (Improving...)
2001 (1st grade)	Oral Communication I	Oral communication skills
2002 (2nd grade)	Writing	Speaking and writing skills
2003 (3rd grade)	Writing: Teachers work in different ways	
2004 (2nd grade)	Writing	Speaking and writing skills
2005 (3rd grade)	Writing	Discussion and debate skills, writing skills

Note. Project 1 took place during the school years of 2001 and 2002; project 2 took place during the school years of 2004 and 2005.

latter group, two of the six classes in each grade prepare students for university entrance examinations. When the first project started in 2001, there were 10 English teachers in the school, including one native-English-speaking teacher, who was an assistant language teacher. The average teaching experience was 15.6 years (range 0–31 years).

The main goal of the projects was to improve students' communication skills in English in accordance with the guidelines on communication-oriented English implemented by the Ministry of Education, Culture, Sports, Science and Technology (MEXT). These guidelines, which were renewed with a further emphasis on communication skills in 2003, were designed to address a perceived need to improve the *typical* high school student's ability to communicate in English, which was felt to be inadequate despite several years of instruction in English. The overall objectives of the guidelines were "to develop students' practical communication abilities such as understanding information and the speaker's or writer's intentions, and expressing their own ideas, deepening the understanding of language and culture, and fostering a positive attitude toward communication through foreign languages" (MEXT, 2003, p. 7). Although the guidelines required teaching Oral Communication twice a week to 1st-year students, most teachers had been replacing it with a grammar class as they thought grammar was essential to prepare students for university entrance examinations.

Oral Communication was taught only when the native-English-speaking assistant language teacher visited each classroom approximately once a week. Oral Communication was taught using student-centered activities, such as games. For other English classes, such as English I and II, most teachers relied on the textbook. They focused on grammar explanation and translation, with little or no instruction in communication-oriented English. This type of covert curriculum and traditional way of teaching, which is contrary to official guidelines, has been the norm in Japan for many years (Sato, 2002). Table 2 shows the structure of the English curriculum of the school.

In 2001, the project began with Oral Communication for 1st-year students and Writing for 2nd-year students. In 2004, the second project started with Writing for 2nd-year students followed by Writing for 3rd-year students. The goal was to continue to improve students' communication skills (vertical articulation—coordinated, coherent curriculum over several years) over 3 years. Although there were some attempts to integrate the two English classes (e.g., Oral Communication and English I) in the same grade (horizontal articulation—coordinated, coherent curriculum among different subjects), the teachers did not succeed in achieving this. Therefore, this chapter focuses solely on vertical articulation (Oral Communication and Writing; see Table 2).

With respect to the teaching culture at the school, initial interviews with teachers at the outset of the project revealed three distinctive characteristics:

- Teachers had low expectations of students' performance and often complained about their students.
- Managing students and keeping classroom order were particularly important to teachers.
- There was little communication among teachers regarding teaching issues and goals.

McLaughlin and Talbert (2001) categorize this as a weak school teaching culture in which most teachers are isolated and rely on routine practices (see also Kleinsasser, 1993; Sato & Kleinsasser, 2004).

Roles and Motivations

In spring 2001, chapter co-author Sato, a university teacher, was asked by fellow chapter co-author Takahashi, a member of the Communicative Language Teaching Study Group organized by Sato (see Sato, 2003), for advice. The prefectural Board of Education had just unexpectedly assigned

Table 2. The School's English Curriculum

Year (grade level)	Classes where projects were implemented (vertical articulation)	Other classes
1st year	Oral Communication I (2 hours)	English I (4 hours)
2nd year	Writing (2 hours)	English II (4 hours)
3rd year	Writing (2 hours)	Reading (4 hours) English II—elective (2 hours)

Takahashi's public senior high school to experiment with a 2-year project (the project name, translated from Japanese, is the Communication Power-Up Plan). Sato was interested in the project, and asked for permission to do research. It took 6 months for the principal of the school to accept Sato as a researcher and curriculum adviser, after which Sato was allowed to visit the school and collect data. Sato visited the high school once a week, observed classes, and gave advice to the teachers involved in the projects. Multiple data sources, including interviews (teachers and groups of students), classroom observations, documents (e.g., teachers' materials, videotapes of students' speaking tests, students' portfolios), and student surveys, were used to document how the teachers revitalized the curriculum and how students improved their communication skills. Sato interviewed teachers and groups of students twice a year (September and February–March). He collected and analyzed all data except for the students' speaking tests, portfolios, and surveys.

Takahashi, who became the coordinator of the projects, collaborated with Sato and met with him every week after his visit. She received additional advice from Sato through online communication. Based on this advice, Takahashi created lesson plans and developed materials, which she then shared with other teachers. She also created a student survey, and asked other teachers to administer it in their classes twice a year (October and February). Takahashi was responsible for summarizing the survey data. She also collected comments from students' portfolios in July, December, and February and translated them into English.

Project 1 (2001 and 2002 School Years): Revitalizing 1st-Year Oral Communication and 2nd-Year Writing

INTRODUCTION

The first project started in April 2001, although Sato did not become involved until September 2001. Most teachers were not sure how to teach Oral Communication and thought students might perceive it as a *fun* class. They thought it would not be useful to students taking university entrance examinations. The teachers had to change their curriculum, and to some degree their teaching approaches, because of the top-down reform initiatives. During the first 3 months of the project, teachers often complained about the students' lack of progress on their speaking tests. However, as the teachers began to discuss assessment criteria during meetings in October and collaborate to assess speaking tests, they witnessed a remarkable change in the students' performance. The second year started in April 2002. Even after engaging in a long discussion, three teachers did not agree to integrate writing and speaking to further improve their students' communication skills. Takahashi took the initiative and tried the new approach recommended by Sato; the other two teachers relied on the textbook. Over time, the other teachers began taking risks, and moved away from the textbook as they observed Takahashi's class and saw how well Sato's approach worked. The following sections describe how the Oral Communication curriculum was revitalized when the textbook was changed and speaking tests were implemented and how the revitalization continued in the second year as writing and speaking were integrated.

THE FIRST YEAR: ORAL COMMUNICATION FOR 1ST-YEAR STUDENTS

The Process of Revitalization: Changing the Textbook and Adding Speaking Tests

Oral Communication (twice a week) started with five Japanese English teachers and one assistant language teacher. One class (approximately 40 students) was divided into two, and the assistant language teacher team-taught one of the two classes a week with each Japanese English teacher. Teachers were uncertain how to teach Oral Communication, and the prefectural Board of Education had not provided guidelines. Sato immediately suggested the following:

- Use a different textbook, *Impact Intro* (Ellis & Sano, 1997), which has many pair and self-expression activities, including a teacher's manual with clear directions in English. (The manual is attached to the textbook.)
- Give a speaking test[1] after finishing each unit, and make sure speaking test results are incorporated into the total grades of the Oral Communication class.
- Have a weekly meeting for teachers who teach Oral Communication classes.

Following Sato's advice, teachers stopped using the required textbook approved by MEXT in June and made it a supplementary text.[2] They began

---

[1] Although the term *test* is used, the tests would be more appropriately thought of as a form of continuous assessment based on performance. However, as formal tests are highly valued in the context, the term *test* was retained for these assessments.

[2] Senior high school teachers in Japan can choose textbooks from a list of MEXT-approved books. The municipal or prefectural Board of Education decides which textbooks are used in junior and elementary schools. Teachers are required to teach using the approved textbook. Therefore, the school retained the MEXT-approved textbook as a supplementary resource, although teachers used *Impact Intro* as the main textbook.

using *Impact Intro* in July, after the midterm examination of the first semester. The teachers were motivated to use speaking tests as they thought the tests would encourage students to engage in oral activities in class. However, attending a weekly meeting was difficult for the teachers because of their tight schedules and reluctance to do so. Table 3 shows the structure for Oral Communication classes in the 2001 school year. Nine speaking tests (i.e., assessments) were administered: four individual speeches, four pair presentations, and one group presentation. Presentations 1–4 were scheduled for the first semester of the year (April to September) and presentations 5–9, for the second semester (October to March). Appendix A shows sample handouts for the presentations. *Hello There* was the required MEXT-approved textbook.

Five speaking tests were administered from April to July, before Sato began visiting the school. The tests involved individual, pair, and group presentations on predetermined topics. Students prepared for the presenta-

Table 3. Structure for Oral Communication Classes in the 2001 School Year

	Lesson/Unit	Topic	Speaking Test
1	Introduction (*Hello There!*)	Self-introduction	Individual presentation
2	Lesson 1 (*Hello There!*)	What are you interested in?	Individual presentation (What I am interested in)
3	Lesson 2 (*Hello There!*)	This is my class schedule.	Individual presentation (My favorite subject)
4	Lesson 3 (*Hello There!*)	What club do you belong to?	Pair presentation (Club activity)
5	Unit 1 (*Impact Intro*)	My family	Pair presentation (My…won't let me go!)
6	Unit 2 (*Impact Intro*)	My friends	Pair presentation (Nice to meet you!)
7	Unit 3 (*Impact Intro*)	My pastimes	Pair presentation (Are you doing anything on…?)
8	Unit 6 (*Impact Intro*)	Modern sounds	Individual presentation (My favorite bands)
9	Unit 7 (*Impact Intro*)	Food	Group presentation (At the restaurant)

tion, memorized what they wrote, and gave the presentation in front of the class. The other students watched and assessed each performance. During this period, however, there was little improvement in fluency, delivery, and enthusiasm in the way that students deliver their presentations and teachers began questioning the effectiveness of the speaking tests. Some teachers thought the speaking tests were too difficult for students who did not have a basic knowledge of English grammar. In addition, students' grades varied to a great extent, depending on which teacher they had.

When Sato first visited the school as a researcher and advisor in September, he strongly recommended that teachers hold regular meetings to discuss assessment criteria. In October, teachers finally began to meet weekly. In the meetings, teachers watched videotapes of the students' performances and discussed how best to assess them. Some teachers had relied on the assistant language teacher for assessment, but they all agreed the Japanese English teachers should also participate in assessing the speaking tests. In the following meetings, the teachers shared the problems they were having in the class and their ideas for improvement.

As the teachers collaborated toward the goal of developing coherent assessments and performance tests, the students' performance improved significantly. Students began to enjoy the presentations they had created. The students' communication skills (fluency, delivery, and enthusiasm) improved as they began to expand on their memorized scripts. One teacher, Ishikawa,[3] reported,

> *Students developed presentation skills over the year. They could perform with gestures and emotions. (second interview, March 2002)*

Mike, the assistant language teacher, commented on the speaking tests:

> *Students gained self-confidence. They still may be very, very shy. I think their confidence is growing. Certainly, they are learning new skills. They are becoming more and more interested in presentations. Once we did a group presentation, and there were some really original skits. (second interview, March 2002)*

In a meeting, the teachers discussed the ratio of each assessment component for Oral Communication. Although they had been relying on term examinations as the single assessment component, they decided to incorporate speaking tests and to have them count for as much as 40% of a student's final grade. Thus, the teachers now had three assessment components for Oral Communication: (a) term examination, 50%; (b) speaking tests, 40%; and (c) participation and assignments, 10%.

---

[3] All teacher and student names, except for authors', are pseudonyms.

From their initial experience, teachers learned the following:

- Giving nine speaking tests throughout the year is important because it takes time for students to get used to and to gain confidence in using English. Teachers, therefore, must be patient and try new ways of working.
- Continuous assessment through speaking tests can develop students' speaking and listening skills.
- It is important to discuss assessment criteria because it encourages teachers to observe more carefully the students' performances and stages of learning.
- Both teachers and students should participate in the assessment of speaking tests. Students can learn much from watching the performances of other students. Japanese English teachers need no longer rely on the assistant language teacher.
- A weekly meeting is important because it gives teachers the opportunity to share their problems and teaching ideas.

However, teachers stopped having weekly meetings in January as students became used to making oral presentations. Without the weekly meetings, the teachers stopped sharing their ideas as well as problems they were having in their classrooms. They seemed satisfied with the students' performance and thus believed there was no need for the meetings.

Student Learning: The Pleasure of Using English

At the end-of-year departmental meeting, teachers did not have enough time to discuss what they had learned, what kind of problems they had had, and how they could develop the Oral Communication class in the following year. Although they had conducted a student self-evaluation survey twice during the year, the results were not fully discussed. It was clear, however, that the students wanted the challenge of participating in more spontaneous and natural conversations, as their comments in their portfolios showed.

> **Mika:** *I enjoyed presentations but I don't have confidence in speaking with a native speaker. I want to be able to have a natural conversation in English. (third portfolio, February 2002)*

> **Takeshi:** *I want to be able to think in English so that I can speak more freely in a conversation. I hope we can have many interactive activities. (third portfolio, February 2002)*

The students evaluated their own speaking and listening skills in October and February, comparing them with those from the previous April. They responded to a questionnaire developed by Takahashi. The results showed the students believed their speaking and listening skills had improved through their oral presentations (see Tables B1 and B2 in Appendix B). For example, in terms of speaking skills (Table B1), the percentage of students who said "I can hardly speak" decreased from 19% to 1%. In terms of listening skills (Table B2), the number of students who said "I could hardly understand" decreased from 28% to 4%. Because the students' level of English was not high, teachers were afraid that pair activities and speaking tests would be too difficult for students and, thus, the students would not enjoy these activities. However, the surveys showed students liked the student-centered and communication-oriented classes better than the teacher-centered grammar translation class. As students made oral presentations, their communication skills gradually improved and they began to enjoy using English in class.

Unfortunately, most teachers did not seem to notice how much students wanted to continue to learn oral English. As their comments show, students had a strong desire to try more spontaneous and natural conversations. However, their teachers did not use the results from the student surveys when they evaluated their Oral Communication classes, nor did they attempt to share at meetings what they had experienced. Although teachers became aware of the improvement in students' oral skills, they did not consider working toward further improving students' communication skills. In addition, as the curriculum shows (see Table 2), there was no Oral Communication class in the second year. The new school year started without enough discussion and evaluation of the program. The next section describes how 2nd-year teachers struggled to revitalize a writing class.

THE SECOND YEAR: WRITING FOR 2ND-YEAR STUDENTS

The Process of Revitalization: Integrating Writing and Speaking

As there was no Oral Communication class for 2nd-year students, teachers had to teach a Writing class. Takahashi was again at a loss and asked Sato for advice. Sato recommended that three 2nd-year teachers try the approach used at his university. The approach, which integrates writing and speaking, had been successful at the university (Cholewinski & Sato, 2005). Brown (1994) maintains that the integration of language skills is the only plausible approach within the framework of communicative language teaching. He affirms that "by attending primarily to what learners can do with language, and only secondarily to the forms of language, we invite any or all of the four skills that are relevant into the classroom arena" and that "often one skill will reinforce another" (p. 219). Moreover, the student survey and the group interview conducted at the end of the first year clearly showed that the students wanted to continue to improve their oral communication skills.

Sato visited the school in early April 2002 and demonstrated how to teach writing and speaking in an integrated way. However, except for Takahashi, none of the teachers liked the approach. The other two teachers thought it was a speaking, not a writing, lesson. In particular, they resisted abandoning their familiar textbook, which included many translation exercises.[4] After a long discussion, the two teachers compromised and said they would use the textbook as a main tool and incorporate some free composition exercises. They said they might try the new approach after they observed how Takahashi's writing class went. Thus, in April 2002, the teachers implemented different writing classes for 2nd-year students. Mori, an experienced teacher, reflected on those days:

> *To be honest, I didn't like the approach. Although I participated in the demonstration and received explanation from Takahashi afterward, I was at a loss about how to teach. Because I am a teacher, I want to teach students with confidence in my class. Then we had a meeting among us. We had to compromise. I mean I had to be in the middle between Takahashi and Kawai. Otherwise, I thought we would go our own ways and get nowhere. So I made effort little by little and tried to cooperate with other teachers. (second interview, March 2003)*

As a consequence, two types of class were introduced. Kawai and Mori mainly taught according to the textbook, with some inclusion of free writing. Takahashi told her students to do all the exercises in the textbook as homework. In class, she attempted the new approach and had students express their ideas by writing on a range of topics, from Three Things About Me! to Asking About Japan.

The students in advanced classes covered 10 topics and the students in general classes covered 7 topics following the 8 steps listed below:

1. introducing three questions about a topic
2. practicing conversation strategies
3. writing assignment (homework): (a) what you want to say, (b) vocabulary you want to use for this topic, and (c) three new questions you will ask in the next conversation
4. peer correction of the composition
5. timed conversation, changing partners (3-minute timed conversation and 2 minutes of summarizing) × 3 times
6. recording: record the timed conversation on tape

---

[4] Although the new MEXT guidelines (2003) stipulate that "writing instruction is conducted more effectively by integrating writing activities with listening, speaking and reading activities" (p. 14), most teachers continued to ignore the guidelines and rely on the textbook with which they were familiar.

7. self-assessment (homework): (a) transcription of the recorded conversation, (b) self-assessment of the recorded conversation, and (c) setting a goal for the next conversation
8. writing assignment (homework): fun essay writing with pictures

For each topic, students were required to analyze their recorded conversation at home. After transcribing their recorded conversation, they answered the following self-assessment questions: (a) What were three things you said that you are proud of? (b) Find three mistakes you made and try to correct them. (c) What conversation strategies did you use? (d) What useful expressions did your partner say? (e) What advice can you give to your partner? and (f) What is your goal for the next conversation?

Takahashi gave a demonstration class in November and showed how much progress students had made since June. Other English teachers, two junior high school teachers, an inspector from the prefectural Board of Education, and Sato participated in the classroom observation. Students had 4-minute conversations and wrote a 15-sentence composition about a serious topic. After that, participants had a meeting at which divergent views were expressed. The inspector was impressed with the class and commented that this could be a model for communication-oriented English, which is the goal of the MEXT guidelines. However, toward the end of the meeting Kawai spoke up, and commented

I have been teaching the other half of the class that Takahashi taught today, relying on the textbook based on grammar translation method.

Then Kubo said

Why was our school assigned to do this project? How about higher level high schools? All they have to do is to prepare students for prestigious university entrance exams.

The inspector replied

The most important thing is to improve students' communication skills. We cannot ignore this goal. Teachers need to change their beliefs about English-language teaching.

After the demonstration lesson and meeting, other teachers (including those from other grades) attempted to use pair work in a positive way. For example, after practicing pair work, Mori tried recording conversations for the first time. Kawai also tried pair work for the first time and would sometimes ask Takahashi what the next topic would be and what kind of materials they would use. Little by little, Kawai and Mori began using innovative approaches. Kawai recalled what he did:

Well, I started to use a new approach, which would integrate writing and speaking in the second semester. I mainly used the textbook in the first semester because I was not sure of how to use new approaches. Anyway, when I saw students enjoying using English with their partners, I thought this might work well. Actually, I enjoyed teaching, too. Gradually, I got used to the new approaches and spent more time on free writing and speaking. (second interview, March 2003)

Takahashi's Episode 1: The Power of Portfolios

The following is Takahashi's first-person description of her writing class:

In the writing class for 2nd-year students, I asked the students to write a report assessing their portfolios at the end of the school year in March. When they looked over all the worksheets in their file, they noticed improvements. By reflecting on their learning history, students gained confidence.

However, slower learners seemed to make so little improvement that I often did not notice the improvement in class. For example, I was discouraged that the slower learners were unable to have 3-minute conversations, even in December, and to see them spending an entire period writing only 10 sentences. Thus, I didn't expect they could make improvements, and I began wondering whether this class was helping them learn. However, their semester reports showed that their speaking and writing skills did improve and that they had gained confidence in learning English. Some students wrote the following comments:

> **Hiromi:** *It was very difficult or almost impossible to have a 2-minute conversation even in October. I didn't know how to keep a conversation going. It's still difficult to ask new questions but I came to use conversation strategies more and more. (third portfolio, February 2003)*

> **Ichiro:** *I couldn't speak English at all in April, but now I can use the expression "How ya doin'?" to open a conversation, "How 'bout you?" to ask the same question, and "Nice talking with you!" to close a conversation. This is a big change for me. (third portfolio, February 2003)*

> **Kaori:** *I didn't know any conversation strategies. But I now use the shadowing strategy, and it is very helpful to keep a conversation going. (third portfolio, February 2003)*

For the speaking test in December, most students in the general class failed to have a 3-minute conversation. I gave a speaking test three times a year after I had covered a couple of topics. Students prepared for all topics but didn't know until the test started which topic they would have to talk about and who their partner would be. However, after writing their semester reports, the students gained confidence. I was surprised that for the speaking test in March, most students succeeded in having a 3-minute conversation.

Student Learning: The Pleasure of Communicating with Other Classmates

The 2nd-year students evaluated their own writing and speaking skills in October and February, comparing them with those from the previous April. (This included students in the other teachers' classes as well as students in Takahashi's classes.) These evaluations showed that students noticed their speaking and writing skills had improved by interacting during speaking and writing activities. For example, regarding writing skills activities (see Table B3, Appendix B), the percentage of students who said "I can hardly write what I want to say" decreased from 23% to 4% over 10 months, and the percentage who said "I can write what I want to say with grammatical mistakes" increased from 11% to 46%.

Regarding speaking skills, the survey asked students about timed, 2-minute conversations they had based on the writing assignments done as homework. They described what they wanted to say and the vocabulary they wanted to use and asked three questions. They were encouraged not to look at the writing assignment (the composition) when they had the timed conversation. The percentage of students who said "I can hardly speak" decreased from 32% to 5%. The percentage who said "I can speak without compositions" increased from 8% to 33% (see Table B4, Appendix B).

For 3-minute conversations (Table B5, Appendix B), the percentage of students who said "I can speak using compositions" decreased from 61% to 36%, and the percentage of those who said "I can speak without compositions" increased from 19% to 40%.

In summary, students felt they had made progress in speaking and writing skills through continual self-assessment and by setting a specific goal for the conversation. Students initially wrote only five to six sentences about a topic and had a conversation for 2 minutes at the most. By the end of the semester, students in advanced classes could write approximately 20 sentences about a topic and had 4- to 5-minute conversations. In general classes, students wrote 10–15 sentences and had 3-minute conversations without looking at their compositions.

AFTER THE FIRST PROJECT: TEACHING ON THEIR OWN

When the next school year started in April 2003, the teachers finally met to talk about what they were going to do and how they were going to teach. In a meeting, Takahashi proposed following Sato's advice that they continue to use the integrated approach and develop students' communication skills by using discussion and debate. Nonetheless, the teachers could not come to an agreement, mainly because some teachers thought it would be too difficult for their students. Another reason might have been that the teachers had never debated in English when they were students. Although the teachers finally agreed to use the book *Impact Topics* (Day & Yamanaka, 1999) instead of a MEXT-approved textbook, they disagreed about the speaking tests. Mori and Takahashi decided to try discussion and debate, whereas Kawai and Goto, a new teacher, preferred the more familiar individual presentations. The four 3rd-year teachers started to teach on their own and had little communication with other teachers.

Project 2 (2004 and 2005 School Years): Revitalizing the Curriculum Through Teacher Collaboration

INTRODUCTION

The second project started in April 2004. The high school was designated a model school because of its excellent English program and was assigned another 2-year project. This time, the prefectural Board of Education asked Sato to be an adviser. A report on the study was to be presented at a national conference for high school teachers of English in November 2005. First, there was a heated discussion among those in the English Department about whether they should accept the project. Many teachers were reluctant because they felt they were under pressure and that preparing for the conference presentation would take too much time. Then, four teachers, including Takahashi, volunteered and formed a team. Sato advised them to create a syllabus and have weekly meetings, which he attended. With the help of Sato, Takahashi made a syllabus and presented it at the meeting. The syllabus was modified and agreed on by the teachers. The next section reports what happened in 2004 when the four teachers began working together. The results were surprising.

THE FIRST YEAR: REVITALIZING 2ND-YEAR WRITING AS A TEAM

The Process of Revitalization: Sharing Ideas and Problems

The four teachers, including Takahashi, met several times before the school year started in April 2004, during which time they devised a plan. First, the teachers organized an orientation meeting for every class. They showed students a video created by recent graduates to introduce the new subject—

Writing. Before school, during the spring holidays in March, Takahashi asked two graduates to explain in Japanese what they had learned from her class and how they had prepared for it. Takahashi thought students would understand what these graduates said better than they would the teachers' explanations. In addition, teachers gave each student a syllabus written in Japanese. The syllabus included goals, topics to be covered, and assessment components as follows:

Goals
- Improve communication skills (focus on speaking and writing skills)
- Develop awareness about language learning

Objectives
- Enable students to have 3-minute conversations about daily topics
- Enable students to write 15 sentences about daily topics
- Enable students to be autonomous learners through peer editing, self-assessment, and portfolio assessment

Topics
- Three Things About Me!
- My Favorite Stories
- The Athens Olympics (Part 1)
- The Athens Olympics (Part 2)
- My Hometown
- The School Trip to Okinawa
- People I Admire

Assessment Components
- term examination (50%)
- speaking test (20%)
- fun essay (25%)
- portfolio (5%)

It was the first time teachers had given students a complete syllabus in an English class. Takahashi commented on it in her first interview:

Our new attempt is that we showed our students concrete goals of the class at the beginning of the year. Also, we explained the syllabus by using the video made by our graduates. I guess our students could have an overall picture about this class and were encouraged to see graduates as models. Moreover, they could recognize that all the students in the same grade will take the class using new approaches. (1st interview, September 2004)

The orientation meeting was successful in that all the teachers and students were put on the same track.

Next, based on Sato's request, teachers began holding weekly meetings. Sato asked Takahashi to arrange each teacher's timetable so that all four 2nd-year teachers could participate in the meeting. Because of their tight schedule, not all teachers willingly came to the meeting. Yet as time passed, the teachers began to appreciate having an opportunity to communicate with other teachers. At the meetings, the teachers shared their ideas and problems. In particular, around the beginning of the year, the three teachers who had just started to teach the new subject asked Takahashi and Sato many questions about how to teach and what to do next. Sato observed all four teachers' classes, videotaped part of each class, and showed the video to the teachers in the weekly meeting, reasoning that they could learn much better by watching other teachers' classes. One of them, Sugiura, made a comment in the meeting:

> *I really appreciate the opportunity to watch the video of other teachers' classes. I can learn a lot about how other teachers use the same activity in a bit different way. Every week I can learn something new in the meeting. (field notes, April 21, 2004)*

Sato also occasionally gave advice to teachers. For example, he advised teachers to create assessment criteria for the speaking test. Teachers sat together, watched a videotape of a few performances, and negotiated the criteria. This gave them the information they needed to develop rubrics. Table 4 shows the original rubric for the speaking tests, and Table 5 shows the modified version, which was created after a long discussion. At first, teachers had difficulty defining each criterion; however, they learned to develop their understanding and clarify the definition of each criterion in the end. For example, "Asking questions" in "Fluency" in Table 4 could be included in "Strategies," and "Spontaneity" in "Delivery" could be included in "Fluency." Also, the group decided that "Impression" was too subjective and thus deleted it when they modified the rubric (see Table 5). The revised version had a greater focus on criteria for communicative effectiveness and provided more detailed descriptors. In addition, allowing all students to achieve a mark other than zero in each category was less demoralizing for weaker students.

The weekly meeting offered many learning opportunities for teachers. As Sugiura commented, talking about teaching and teaching issues became the norm among these teachers. Moreover, they got together at other times when they felt a need, despite their busy schedules.

Finally, in addition to the required materials, teachers started to develop

Table 4. Rubric for the Speaking Test (July 2004)

Criteria	Total points	Description and rating
Fluency	8	• Asking questions (2, 1, 0) • Response rate (2, 1, 0) • Answer in more than two sentences (2, 1, 0) • Maintain a 2-minute conversation (2, 1, 0)
Accuracy	2	• Grammar (1, 0) • Pronunciation (1, 0)
Delivery	4	• Volume (2, 1, 0) • Spontaneity (not memorization) (2, 1, 0)
Strategies	4	• How ya doing? (1, 0) • Nice talking with you. (1, 0) • Shadowing (1, 0) • How about you? (1, 0)
Impression	2	• Impressive (2, 1, 0)

their own materials and to share them. For example, Kubo made a handout about the Athens Olympics, which included three quizzes. For the topic The School Trip to Okinawa, Sugiura created a handout to check the use of strategies. She was concerned that her students might not be able to use the conversation strategies she had taught, so she asked them to interview three students (using four questions) and circle the strategies they had used on a handout (see Figure 1).

For the topic People I Admire, Takahashi created a guessing game as a warm-up activity (see Figure 2).

In short, the teachers developed materials and shared them with other teachers. This allowed the teachers to learn from one another and to further develop the curriculum. Sugiura commented in her first interview:

I am glad that I could join this team. I think I could develop my teaching repertoire. Now I have many choices and can choose a suitable activity in the future. We shared our teaching experiences with one another. I really think we became open-minded and talked about many problems. In the past, we didn't share what we were doing. (1st interview, September 2004)

Takahashi's Episode 2: The Power of Peer Editing

The following is Takahashi's first-person description of how peer editing helped her students learn:

Table 5. Modified Version of the Rubric for the Speaking Test (December 2004)

Criteria	Total points	Description and rating
Fluency and content	10	(10) Be able to maintain 3-minute conversation fluently, with good content (7) Be able to maintain a 3-minute conversation with some silence, with adequate content (4) Be able to maintain a 3-minute conversation with some silence, with poor content (1) Be hardly able to maintain a 3-minute conversation with some long silences
Accuracy (grammar and pronunciation)	3	(3) Be able to communicate with accuracy (2) Be able to communicate with some errors (1) Communicate with many errors, using mainly key words
Delivery (volume and eye contact)	3	(3) Be able to speak with good volume and eye contact (2) Occasionally speak with adequate volume and eye contact (1) Be hardly able to speak with adequate volume and eye contact
Strategies (conversation strategies and follow-up questions)	4	(4) Be able to use many conversation strategies and follow-up questions (3) Be able to use some conversation strategies and follow-up questions (2) Use a few conversation strategies and follow-up questions (1) Be hardly able to use conversation strategies and follow-up questions

Figure 1. Conversation Strategies Handout

Communication Strategies
Me too./Me neither.
I see.
Oh, really?
Oh, yeah?

Questions
1. What did you eat in Okinawa?
2. What did you buy in Okinawa?
3. What was the most impressive place?
4. What else did you do?

Figure 2. People I Admire Guessing Game

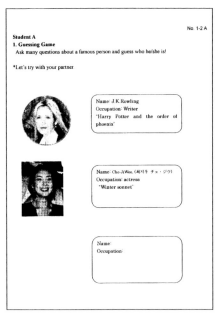
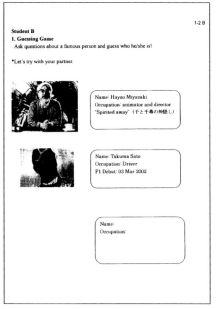

Sato advised us to try peer editing in a meeting. He demonstrated each step, and we started to try the technique in the classroom. I learned from my students that peer editing works well for slower learners, too. With the help of peers, students can deepen their ideas and are encouraged to rewrite their composition. What's more, they enjoy sharing their writings. For instance, after their 9-month study, students began writing and talk about a new topic, People I Admire, in January 2005. When a student in a general class, Hideki, finished writing about the topic, he had written only four sentences. To be honest, I was quite shocked to see his poor writing. Then it was time for peer editing. Students exchanged papers and began peer editing using the following four steps:

- *Step 1.* Read for 1 minute, and ask five questions to your partners about the topic. (Questions are given by teachers.)
- *Step 2.* Underline words and sentences and mark as ☆, more, or ?.
  ☆ = words and sentences you are impressed with
  more = words and sentences you want to know more about
  ? = words and sentences you don't understand
- *Step 3.* Write comments and questions about the content in your first language (Japanese).
- *Step 4.* Share the comments with your partner.

After the first peer editing, Hideki added three sentences to his composition. He tried to answer the questions from his peer (see Composition 1, Figure 3). Hideki and the others did two more peer-editing sessions with different students and were asked to rewrite their compositions at home. In the next class, I was surprised to find that Hideki's composition was longer (see Composition 2, Figure 4). He even brought to class a magazine that featured his fishing hero. After one more peer-editing and conversation activity with several different students, Hideki finished the final draft, which included pictures. He was very proud of the final product (Composition 3, Figure 4).

2–3. Takahashi's Episode 3: The Power of Conversation Strategies

The following is Takahashi's description of how conversation strategies helped her students develop their skills:

In Writing for 2nd-year students, students wrote and talked about a topic many times in class. Students had a 3- to 4-minute conversation with several different partners, an activity we called timed conversation. A final timed conversation was recorded on tape so that students could transcribe and analyze the conversation. To keep a conversation going, we introduced conversation strategies for every topic. Students practiced

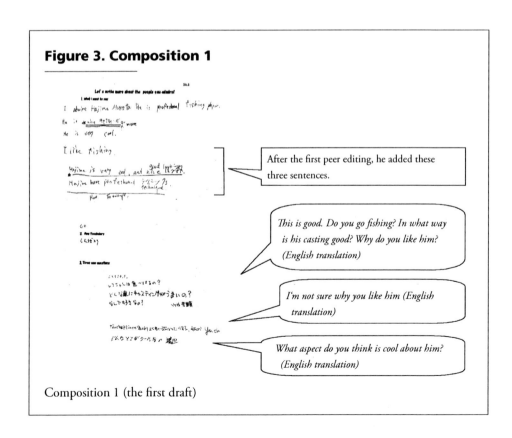

Figure 3. Composition 1

Composition 1 (the first draft)

Figure 4. Compositions 2 and 3

Composition 2 (the second draft)

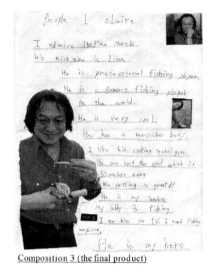

Composition 3 (the final product)

useful expressions such as "How 'bout you?", "Sounds great!", "Pardon me?", and "What does that mean?" They also practiced useful strategies such as how to shadow (echo) key words and ask follow-up questions. Some students were quiet and rarely had conversations with classmates in their daily life. They did not have communication skills, even in their first language. Therefore, I often wondered whether they could improve their communication skills through timed conversation. I was also worried they could never enjoy timed conversation or any interactive activities in class. However, I learned that even quiet students enjoy having conversations as they learn to use more and more strategies.

Another benefit of the timed English conversations was that they made students more open-minded. I will tell how one quiet student (Ami) came to enjoy timed conversations.

In everyday situations, Ami would speak with only a few friends at school. At the beginning of the course, I saw that she often had a tense face and spoke in a low voice. The class required Ami to converse with several different partners, a situation she had never encountered. I felt sorry for Ami and did not expect her to enjoy the class. However, as Ami learned more and more conversation strategies, she came to enjoy the timed conversations. When Ami learned how to keep a conversation going in English, she found she could relax more during a conversation. After the third speaking test in February, she said to me excitedly, "This

was a test, but I really enjoyed having a conversation. I feel so happy."
She also wrote the following comments in her portfolios:

> As I had timed conversations many times, I got used to having a
> conversation little by little. At first, I didn't know what to say, but I
> started to use "How 'bout you?" and shadowing during a conversa-
> tion. Then gradually I could understand what my partner said. (1st
> portfolio, July 2004)

> Before the summer vacation, I just said what I had memorized.
> However, as I came to use conversation strategies such as "Me, too!",
> "Sounds good!", and shadowing, conversations became more natural.
> I'd like to practice asking follow-up questions more, and I will make
> effort to say something even if I don't know the right expressions.
> (second portfolio, December 2004)

> In April, I was very nervous when I had timed conversations. Today
> I had a speaking test and I was surprised to notice how much I
> relaxed and enjoyed having a conversation. I was happy because
> I could enjoy talking. I explained to my partner what I didn't
> understand and asked her to explain more. It was wonderful! I can
> manage a conversation if I practice a lot. (3rd portfolio, February,
> 2005)

As Ami's transcription (see Figure 5) shows, she could maintain a
4-minute conversation by using conversation strategies (or communication
strategies). This was completely different from using a memorized conversation because Ami could negotiate the meaning with her partner. The next
section talks about how other students acquired these conversation strategies
and thus improved their communication skills. The results support Sato's
(2005) finding that developing learners' ability to use communication strategies leads to their overall acquisition of a second language.

Student Learning: Developing Confidence in Using English
Both teachers and students were unsure about what would happen in the
Writing class. Yet, by the end of April, teachers began to see some positive
results. Inagaki said in the meeting, "This approach is good because students
are busy working on activities, and they have no time to sleep in class" (field
notes, April 28, 2004).

As teachers became accustomed to this approach and began to see
students enthusiastically engaging in activities, their confidence increased.
Although there were ups and downs, students reflected on what they had
learned in February 2005 and reported in their portfolios that they felt they
had improved their writing and speaking skills.

Figure 5. Ami's Transcription and Fun Essay

Ami: Who do you admire?

Maki: I admire Tabuse Yuta. Do you know him? (*follow-up question*)

Ami: He is a basketball player.

---cut----

Maki: OK.OK Bur recently he…Tabuse laid off from Phoenix Suns.

Ami: Laid off? (*Shadowing: Asking for clarification*)

Maki: Ah…hmm..laid off….Now he can't play in the Phoenix Suns. So….

Ami: He leaves the team. (*using other words*)

Maki: Yes! Yes!

Ami: I see!

Maki: So he is …..now he is free. He is waiting offer from another team in NBA. He is very small.

Part of Ami's transcription

Ami's fun essay

Tomoko: *I wrote only five sentences in April, and it was difficult. Now I can write 10 sentences even if it takes a long time. And I now use a dictionary when I write! This is a big change for me! (3rd portfolio, February 2005)*

Satoshi: *We had a lot of timed conversations with different partners. After this conversation class, I managed to have a conversation for three minutes. It is important to have a lot of conversation practice. I also learned many expressions from my friends. (3rd portfolio, February 2005)*

Hiroko: *Conversations helped me write more about the topic, because I got more ideas during and after conversations. (3rd portfolio, February 2005)*

Student self-evaluation surveys conducted in October 2004 and February 2005 corroborated the results. In April, 58% (19% and 39%) of the students said they thought they could write fewer than five sentences about a topic and only 8% (6% and 2%) thought they could write 15 or more sentences. In contrast, in February, 8% (2% and 6%) reported they could write fewer than 5 sentences, and 57% (29% and 28%) reported they could write 15 or more sentences (see Table B6, Appendix B). Regarding speaking skills (Tables B7–9, Appendix B), in April 77% (32% and 45%) of students said they thought they could not maintain a 2-minute conversation without compositions. Only 2% thought they could speak for 2 minutes without looking at a written paper. In contrast, in February, 13% (2% and 11%) reported they could not maintain a 2-minute conversation without compositions, and 87% (34% and 30% and 23%) reported they could keep talking for 2 minutes without compositions. In February, 84% (40% and 32% and 12%) of students reported that they could have a 3-minute conversation without compositions. Of students in the advanced classes, 89% (48% and 23% and 18%) reported they could maintain a 4-minute conversation without compositions. In 2002, only 58% (40% and 15% and 3%, see Table B5) of students reported that they could achieve a 3-minute conversation without compositions. By 2004, there was a 26% increase in the number of students who could do so. In an interview, Takahashi commented why most students achieved the goal:

> *A good thing about this year is that we established goals and objectives and showed them to our students in April. Also we used the videos of speaking tests and written materials of our previous students two years ago. Our students were encouraged by the good models. Moreover, teachers collaborated more and held weekly meetings, which we could not do two years ago. As a result, students in all six classes worked toward the same goals. That made a difference, I think. (1st interview, September 2004)*

Another teacher, Inagaki, said that students in her class were impressed with the fun essays displayed on the wall that Takahashi's students had written.

> *When they wrote about the Olympic games, they wrote more than I had expected. Moreover, they were influenced by students in other classes. For example, some boys wrote using only a pencil at first. Then, after they saw other students' work displayed on the wall, they started to write with colored pens and add pictures. I was impressed with how all the classes were involved in this project. (1st interview, September 2004)*

In short, teacher collaboration resulted in better student outcomes. Compared with the first project, Takahashi felt that all six classes worked toward the same goals. Successful teaching experiences encouraged teachers. Kubo, a senior teacher, reflected on his experience in that year:

To be honest, I was really surprised to know this kind of teaching approach exists. I will retire in three more years. But, I really had a great experience this year. If I had studied English with this kind of approach as a high school student, I would have improved my communication skills. I had been teaching English based on a traditional approach for over 30 years. Therefore, it was an eye-opener for me. (second interview, March 2005)

The following section describes how three teachers continued to teach in 2005.

The Second Year: Challenging Discussion and Debate

Takahashi and two other teachers, Inagaki and Kubo, continued teaching the 3rd-year students and formed a team. With Sato's advice, they set goals to further improve students' communication skills. As they did the previous year, they developed a syllabus and showed it to students at the beginning of their Writing class. The syllabus was as follows:

Goals

- Improve communication skills (focus on speaking and writing skills)
- Develop awareness about language learning

Objectives

- Enable students to have 4-minute discussions about social topics
- Enable students to write a five-paragraph essay about social topics
- Enable students to think logically and express their opinions in a debate
- Enable students to be autonomous learners through peer editing, self-assessment, and portfolio assessment

Topics (from *Impact Topics*, Day & Yamanaka, 1999)

- I Can't Stop (Unit 4; discussion)
- My Pet Peeves (Unit 19; discussion)
- Smoking (Unit 3)
- Living Together Before Marriage (Unit 10; debate)
- English Should be a Second Official Language in Japan (Lesson 7: English and the Filipinos, from the textbook in English Reading class; debate)
- Cosmetic Surgery (from *Impact Issues,* Day & Yamanaka, 1998; debate)
- Cyber Love (Unit 8; debate)

Assessment Components

- term examination (40%)
- assignments (15%)
- speaking test (20%)
- fun essay (20%)
- portfolio (5%)

Furthermore, Sato advised teachers to use a video camera instead of a tape recorder so that students could see how they interacted with their partners. On recording days, students brought their own videotapes and watched them after recording for self-evaluation. As students became accustomed to discussions, they began learning how to debate in July, according to the syllabus. This was another challenge to teachers because they had never held a debate in class. Yet these teachers, with Sato's help, practiced debating, made a videotape, and showed it to their students in class. Takahashi tried a debate in her class (see Appendix A for sample handouts). Although the debates had not been very successful 2 years previously, they worked well this time. Takahashi talked about debates in her first interview in 2005:

> I tried a debate in my class. It was successful, and I have learned a lot about debate. When I tried it two years ago, it did not work. Since then I have learned what skills are necessary for debate. Following Sato's advice, we had our students practice summarizing what their partner said. Also, students were encouraged to use conversation strategies when they could not understand what their partner had said. I could understand that this kind of practice led students to successful debate. (1st interview, September 2005)

In November 2005, Takahashi presented the results of the two projects at a national conference for high school teachers of English, which more than 3,000 teachers and teacher educators attended. The other teachers helped Takahashi prepare for the presentation. Educators evaluated the projects very hightly, and the teachers gained confidence in curriculum revitalization at their school. Inagaki commented on the presentation,

> To be honest, before the conference, I did not clearly understand what we had been doing. I guess other grade level teachers did not understand, either. However, as we reflected on what we had done over five years, we could confirm the significance of the projects and some achievements we had made. (second interview, February 2006)

Conclusion

This chapter has described how teachers in an English department in a Japanese high school struggled with projects implemented by the prefectural government and overcame difficulties to revitalize their curriculum. The teachers were forced to work on curriculum revitalization based on top-down initiatives, and they often resisted and struggled with the projects. Yet, stimulated by the outside support of a university teacher, they began collaborating and striving to meet the same goals, particularly during the second project. The more they worked together, the more successful their teaching practices were. As the benefits of the teachers' efforts were confirmed by improved student outcomes, the teachers began to develop materials and share them with one another. They generated many teacher-learning opportunities within the context of their school as they worked on their curriculum revitalization as a team.

Throughout the first project, the teaching culture of the school was typical of the culture in other schools. Teachers resisted new approaches; lowered their expectations, especially in general classes; and avoided discussing teaching issues. As Kubo said, quoted earlier in our chapter, most teachers thought they could continue to teach based on traditional approaches, as done in other high schools. Moreover, they reported in their interviews that teachers of other subjects in their high school expected the English teachers to place more emphasis on examination-oriented English. Without sufficient communication and evaluation of the project, they might easily have gone back to their routine practices.

Yet, the teachers gradually began to take risks. They also changed their teaching practices and assessment strategies, communicated more about teaching, and moved away from the textbook. Through these activities, the teachers' beliefs about language teaching and learning evolved (see Sato & Kleinsasser, 1999), and this had the potential to affect the culture of the school (Sato & Kleinsasser, 2004). In particular, by changing how they performed assessments and developing coherent assessment criteria, teachers develop new and effective practices (see Sato & Takahashi, 2003). Falk (2001) affirms that "[i]nvolving teachers in scoring students' responses to large-scale standard-based performance tests offers rich opportunities to enhance teacher learning" (p. 127).

In the second 2-year project (2004 and 2005 school years), four teachers formed a team. They discussed goals and objectives and created a syllabus, which they gave their students at the beginning of the school year. Moreover, they spent 1 hour per week meeting together. The regular meeting became a place not only for asking questions about practices, but also for sharing their teaching ideas and materials. As Sugiura reported, the weekly meetings created learning opportunities within the school context that were grounded in their daily practices. As a consequence, all teachers and students began working toward the same goals. To the surprise of the teachers, the student self-evaluation survey indicated much better outcomes than 2 years previously. These teachers gained confidence in the curriculum revitalization they had been working on as they confirmed better student outcomes. The teacher learning influenced student learning, and vice versa (McLaughlin & Talbert, 2001; Sato & Takahashi, 2003).

Nonetheless, the teachers talked about the difficulties they faced. Above all, they stated time and again that they lacked time for communication. They discovered that one weekly meeting was not enough. For example, they could not afford time to talk about other English classes (English II or Reading), although they had agreed to improve these classes through the integration of language skills. Thus, horizontal articulation (between different English classes in the same grade) remains weak compared with vertical articulation. Fortunately, Sugiura became a leader for the three 2nd-year teachers and has continued to use the same approach in the Writing class, modifying some materials.

We conclude with a number of questions. How can these teachers continue to develop their curriculum after the project is over? How can a university teacher collaborate more with schoolteachers on curriculum development? How can teachers continue to communicate and collaborate with one another, discuss teaching issues, evaluate programs, and set up new goals? How can they involve other teachers in making a thorough 3-year curriculum? How can they generate more learning opportunities in their workplace and empower themselves to be lifelong learners? We believe the answers lie in continuing teacher development through reflective development of practice. As this chapter describes, the teachers transformed their workplace into a site for inquiry as they struggled, went through conflict, agreed and disagreed with one another, and tried new practices little by little (see Ball & Cohen, 1999). In other words, they began helping to transform their school from one with a weak teaching culture into one that is a learning organization or a "community of practice" (Murphey & Sato, 2005; Wenger, 1998) as they carried out their curriculum revitalization simultaneously with their own professional development.

Appendix A: Sample Handouts and Students' Work

ORAL COMMUNICATION (1ST-YEAR STUDENTS)
Unit 3: My Pastimes

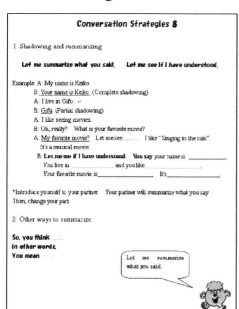

Worksheet Script for the Presentation

WRITING (3RD-YEAR STUDENTS)
Unit 3: Smoking

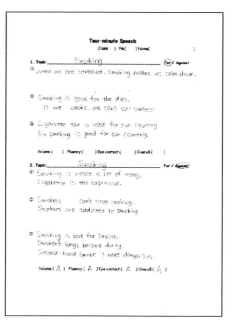

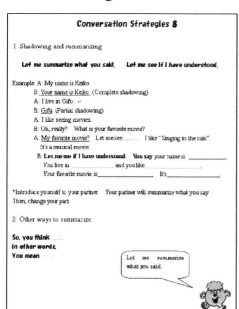

Curriculum Revitalization in a Japanese High School: Teacher–Teacher and Teacher–University Collaboration

WORKSHEET WRITING (THREE REASONS)

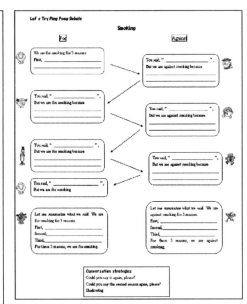

Worksheet

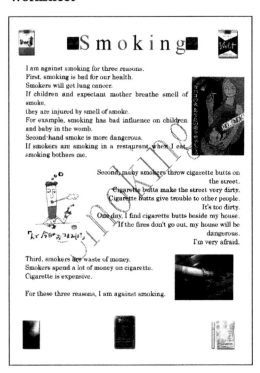

Appendix B: Student Evaluation Results

Table B1. Speaking Skills Evaluation, 2001 Data From 209 First-Year Students

Month	I can hardly speak (%)	I can speak a little using a script (%)	I can speak aloud without any script (%)	I can speak using gestures without any script (%)	I can speak with emotion without any script (%)
April	19	59	17	4	1
October	5	40	30	23	2
February	1	38	29	31	1

Table B2. Listening Skills Evaluation, 2001 Data From 209 First-Year Students

Month	I can hardly understand (%)	I can understand a little (%)	I can understand half of the class (%)	I can understand most of the class (%)	I can understand everything (%)
April	28	41	22	10	0
October	12	35	33	20	0
February	4	25	39	30	1

Table B3. Writing Skills Evaluation, 2002 Data From 197 Second-Year Students

Month	I can hardly write what I want to say (%)	I can write a little of what I want to say (%)	I can write half of what I want to say (%)	I can write most of what I want to say with grammatical mistakes (%)	I can write most of what I want to say without any grammatical mistakes (%)
April	23	45	21	11	0
October	7	28	27	36	2
February	4	21	28	46	1

Table B4. Speaking Skills Evaluation, 2-Minute Conversation, 2002 Data From 197 Second-Year Students

Month	I can hardly speak (%)	I can speak using compositions (%)	I can speak without any compositions (%)	I can speak aloud without any compositions (%)	I can speak with emotion without any compositions (%)
October	32	58	8	2	0
February	5	42	33	18	2

Table B5. Speaking Skills Evaluation, 3-Minute Conversation, 2002 Data From 197 Second-Year Students

Month	I can hardly speak (%)	I can speak using compositions (%)	I can speak without compositions (%)	I can speak aloud without any compositions (%)	I can speak with emotion without any compositions (%)
October	13	61	19	6	1
February	7	36	40	15	3

Table B6. Writing Skills Evaluation, 2004 Data From 193 Second-Year Students

Month	I can hardly write (%)	I can write 5 sentences about a topic (%)	I can write 10 sentences about a topic (%)	I can write 15 sentences about a topic (%)	I can write more than 15 sentences about a topic (%)
April	19	39	33	6	2
October	8	20	36	25	11
February	2	6	35	29	28

Table B7. Speaking Skills Evaluation, 2-Minute Conversation, 2004 Data From 193 Second-Year Students

Month	I can hardly speak (%)	I can speak using compositions (%)	I can speak without any compositions (%)	I can speak aloud without any compositions (%)	I can speak with emotion without any compositions (%)
April	32	45	20	2	0
October	5	33	50	11	0
February	2	11	34	30	23

Table B8. Speaking Skills Evaluation, 3-Minute Conversation, 2004 Data From 193 Second-Year Students

Month	I can hardly speak (%)	I can speak using compositions (%)	I can speak without any compositions (%)	I can speak aloud without any compositions (%)	I can speak with emotion without any compositions (%)
February	3	13	40	32	12

Table B9. Speaking Skills Evaluation, 4-Minute Conversation in the Advanced Class, 2004 Data From 38 Second-Year Students

Month	I can hardly speak (%)	I can speak using compositions (%)	I can speak without any compositions (%)	I can speak aloud without any compositions (%)	I can speak with emotion without any compositions (%)
February	0	11	48	23	18

Despacito por las Piedras— Slowly Among the Stones: Implementing Innovative Projects in Chile

11

PENNY KINNEAR, JANE HILL, MONIQUE PIGEON-ABOLINS,
MARIA ANDREA ARANCIBIA, KAREN CANDIA HORMAZABAL,
AND NAYARET TORO SOTO

In November 2004, 19 teachers arrived in Toronto to begin a month-long sojourn to improve their English language skills and learn more about English language teaching. They were one of four groups sent to various destinations as part of a program to improve English language education in Chile. The Toronto participants were immersed in a content-based program that combined the practice and theory of current English as a foreign language (EFL) teaching. This chapter primarily focuses on the efforts of three of those teachers.

In May 2006, education in Chile reached a crisis. Karen Candia Hormazabal, one of the chapter co-authors and teachers chronicled in this chapter, wrote in a personal communication,

I suppose you know by now that Chile has become a boiling pot. Students have spoken; they feel that changes must be made on Chilean policies about education (something that teachers already felt, anyway), and they started all this by formally submitting their demands.

Chilean police subdued the riots with tear gas and water cannons until President Michelle Bachelet intervened and acceded to demands for bus passes and free access to university examinations. Although public education is *free*, parents must pay for transportation, uniforms, book bags, books, notebooks, and pencils; these are costs that can be as much as 2% of families' salaries (Schiefelbein & Schiefelbein, 2000). In a country where 20% of the population lives below the poverty line and school-age children make up nearly 25% of the population, forcing families and students to divert money from already strained budgets to pay for free education adds to the volatile mix of educational promises and expectations in overcrowded classrooms.

The Chilean Context

Educational reform is not new to Chilean politics. Significant efforts had been made before the Pinochet years and after to extend education to all Chileans. (Augusto Pinochet was head of the military junta from 1973–1981 and president of Chile from 1974–1990). In 1991, the Chilean government began a series of program and policy initiatives, including ones to "provide systematic support for teachers and instructional leaders through reflection and evaluation techniques [and to] train teachers to design new methodological and curricular strategies to incorporate the students' reality" (Zona 2, 1995, as cited in Garcia-Huidobro, 2000).

English instruction and proficiency became a political as well as educational goal in 1999 when then Chilean President Ricardo Lagos stated, "As a country, we want to be a bridge and a platform for flows of international trade in the Asia-Pacific region" (Rohter, 2005, p. 2). The education minister, Sergio Bitar, addressed the implications of this economic policy for English language learning when he said, "We know our lives are linked more than ever to an international presence, and if you can't speak English, you can't sell and you can't learn" (Rohter, 2005, p. 2). With that, Chile strove to make opportunities formerly available only to the wealthy few available to all children. The government extended school hours, established teacher-training courses, and distributed thousands of new textbooks across the 12 regions that stretch from the Atacama Desert of the north to Antarctica. These texts have been thinly spread across the country and jealously guarded. One teacher ruefully described her overreaction to finding one of her brand-new books covered in adolescent drawings:

I got so angry that I asked for strict punishment for the student. He must pay [the full price of the book], and he was not allowed to come to the school for two days. Now that I think it over, I think I went a little crazy.[1]

[1] Teachers comments were collected during the 4-week course in Toronto from questionnaires filled out before and after the course and in discussions and observations during the July 2005 follow-up for the *pasantia* described in this chapter. We have edited the teachers' comments for spelling and grammar as we would our own, but we have retained expressions that may not be entirely the way a native speaker would phrase the thoughts so as not to lose the authenticity of the voices. All translations were checked by Maria Claire Bezies-Hadzis, certified translator from the University of Toronto, Ontario.

English teachers, government policy writers, and politicians believe that English is the key to the future, but many students and their parents remain unconvinced. Teachers confront the challenge of convincing students that time spent studying English is an investment in their futures in a setting in which employment opportunities that demand English fluency remain limited. South American residents can communicate almost anywhere on the continent in Spanish, so even international travel does not demand a foreign language.

In 2003, the Ministry of Education established a new department called English Opens Doors to improve the teaching and learning of English in Chile. The Web page (http://www.ingles.mineduc.cl) details the programs, which include training courses, English and methodology courses, city council level workshops, local networks, international training grants, and support for a foreign volunteer program in schools.

Ministry of Education policy decisions have determined that by 2007, students will take standardized tests in English reading and listening. English teachers appreciate the importance this gives to English language learning. However, these tests of student achievement and teachers' language proficiency have also been viewed as threats rather than as benchmarks through which improvements can be made. Secondary school teachers fear that the poor performance of students who were not adequately prepared in elementary school will reflect on the teachers. Elementary teachers who have struggled to learn enough English to teach numbers and colors are overwhelmed by the new expectations.

From this volatile constellation of support and challenges, 19 Chilean high school English teachers and one representative of the Ministry of Education arrived in Toronto, Ontario, in November 2004. The teachers had been selected to participate in one of the English Opens Doors training programs. They had competed against other teachers and been selected for the *pasantias* (i.e., a professional development program) on the basis of their "innovative projects" as determined by English Opens Doors, principals' recommendations, written tests, and telephone interviews in English. The teachers had made a commitment to implement their projects during the 2005 school year and to return to Santiago in July 2005 for the follow-up program. The innovative projects were meant to invigorate existing programs and practices without restructuring or rewriting the curriculum. Ideally, the teachers' new practices and new knowledge would serve as resources for other teachers within their school and geographical areas. Figure 1 illustrates the process.

In Toronto, the teachers were charged with improving their English language skills, learning new English language teaching strategies, and developing their innovative projects in 4 weeks. All the teachers were constrained

Figure 1. Project Flowchart

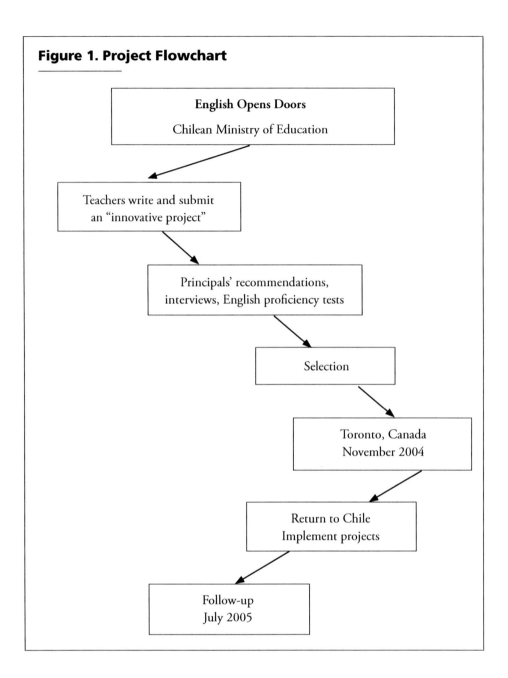

by the curricula of the schools, the backgrounds and motivations of the students, the physical resources, and sometimes by the lack of administrative and collegial support. The story of three of these teachers is highlighted in this chapter, although the voices of many others are also represented.

Schools in Chile

Much of the Chilean population of just over 16 million clusters in the metropolitan region around Santiago and the fifth region of Valparaiso on the coast (Chile is divided into 12 regions plus the capital of Santiago). Municipal, semiprivate, and private schools educate students. In the sample of 11,000 students who participated in the University of Cambridge ESOL Examinations, only 57% of 8th-grade and 45% of 12th-grade students attended municipal schools. Fewer than 10% of students attended private schools. The remainder attended "subsidized private" schools (*particulares subvencionados*). By 12th grade, 47% of students attend such schools and of those, 33% are identified as families of lower to middle socioeconomic levels (*Resultados nacionales del diagnostico de Ingles, aplicado en el año 2004–2005*, 2006). In the cities, children walk or take city transportation to school. In other regions, children travel to school by ferry or country buses. Many often board at the school. The competition between the private, semiprivate, and public schools encouraged by the government underlies the tension between students and their families and the government. The promise of free education has been compromised by the constant request from the *free* schools for money to use the Internet to complete assignments, buy school supplies in the technical schools, and so on.

A general educational reform initiated in 1999 made English an obligatory subject of study from the fifth grade rather than the seventh grade. The required three, 45-minute classes were increased to a minimum of five per week. The ministry allows schools to adopt special plans that begin English instruction in Grade 1. Semiprivate schools find this particularly attractive as they attempt to attract fee-paying pupils. These changes have exacerbated the unevenness in middle school English classes. By Grade 8, some students have had 8 years of English whereas others have had only 3.

Not only have students had different amounts of English tuition, they also have been taught by teachers with varying qualifications. According to a diagnostic English test conducted in 299 schools in 2005, only 55% of 8th-grade students were taught by certified English teachers. In contrast, in Grade 12, 88% of the teachers were certified. Many uncertified teachers have had training as translators or have taken courses in English language teaching institutes. However, 13% of the 8th-grade teachers and 3% of the 12th-grade teachers have had no English language study beyond the secondary requirements (*Resultados nacionales del diagnóstico de Inglés, aplicado en el año 2004–2005*, 2006). The length and the quality of a student's English language education depend on chance.

Learning Together in Toronto

The *pasantia* program put teachers together in an English-speaking environment away from classroom and school responsibilities. It provided an opportunity for the teachers to consider their own classroom practices, talk with other teachers, and reflect on what they might do to revitalize their own classroom curriculum and practice. The Chilean teachers, brought together for the first time in Toronto, learned about one another and one another's schools in the context of one of the most culturally and linguistically diverse cities in the world. According to the Toronto District School Board, more than 80 languages are represented, but somehow everyone manages to get along communicating in English in a wide variety of accents and proficiencies (Toronto District School Board, 2008). English, both written and oral, shaped the Chilean teachers' experiences in Toronto. Even their reflections on their own learning were mediated in English through the journal writing and instructors' English responses. This practice improved their confidence in their ability to effectively communicate and comprehend in English. It also changed their attitudes toward their own and their students' use of English in the classroom. Teachers reported to chapter co-author Jane Hill in her July 2005 visit how their different attitudes transformed their expectations of students and, subsequently, student behaviors and performances. Structural or curricular changes did not produce the differences; rather, they came about through a subtle interaction of teacher and student experiences. One teacher, Eliana Cuello Campos, reported

> *I am also motivated to make my students learn English, mainly, speak in English. They are trying with all the difficulties it means, but they are doing it and I know they will do it each time better. Now, they feel more confident at speech. It doesn't matter if they commit mistakes because now they are very conscious that they will learn from them.*

At the beginning of the 4-week intensive course, the instructors interviewed each teacher about his or her project. The course instructors and the teachers expected their projects to drive the specific content of the course. Given the broad range and scope of the projects, the instructors chose to engage in an examination of the elements of reflective classroom research, with particular reference to the teachers' innovative projects and to the constraints and possibilities of their contexts. They produced long-range plans and goals with detailed plans of the activities and materials they would use to begin their projects.

Effecting change in school structure, curriculum, and teacher and student behaviors depends on a complex constellation of interacting forces and conditions. At the beginning of the course, the Chilean teachers were asked to describe their classrooms and to think about their students' present and previous experiences as well as their community's history and current reality. Teachers were also asked to include the school's history, current structure, and expectations for teachers and students. They were asked what rules, stated and unstated, governed behavior and to describe the roles of students, teachers, families, and administrators. From this exercise, the group identified many issues they would deal with as they attempted any changes in classroom organization, student behaviors, or teaching practices.

The course followed a content-based approach to present both pedagogical theory and practice in English. The teachers reviewed current information on how languages are learned, explored methodologies, and read background information. They looked at adapting and supplementing course books; using art, film, music, and Internet resources; and facilitating cross-curricular initiatives. Language improvement was incorporated with a novel-reading project using literature circles, daily journal writing, and interviews with conversation partners—an editor, a writer, an actor, and an anthropologist led conversations, pairing a Chilean teacher with a Chinese teacher also studying in Canada. The participants found that working with authentic materials they scavenged in Toronto and visiting local high schools were particularly useful.

In the Classrooms

The three projects highlighted in this chapter were chosen because of the willingness of the three teachers to have their stories told, the diversity of their schools, and the range of their projects. In addition, all of the teachers are in or near Santiago, which made it possible for Hill to visit them in July 2005 during the follow-up phase of the program. Before and after the follow-up program, Hill spent a day in each of their schools and worked with the teachers to document their experiences and reflections.

Karen Candia Hormazabal, who teaches at the Liceo Tecnico Felisa Tolup Zeiman, San Fernando, hoped to upgrade the English in her classroom and more specifically the vocabulary particular to the vocations taught in her school. Nayaret Toro Soto, who teaches at the Liceo Politecnico Hannover, Santiago, wanted to improve her students' listening skills using the computer lab in her school. Maria Andrea Arancibia, who teaches at the Liceo Carmela Carvajal de Prat, Santiago, wanted to infuse her classroom with methodologies focused on communication rather than grammar drills.

DANCING IN ENGLISH IN SAN FERNANDO: KAREN CANDIA HORMAZABAL

According to Candia Hormazabal's principal, she is creative, imaginative, and "like a windmill." Her English is particularly fluent as she trained as a translator rather than a teacher. She teaches at an industrial/technical school for 850 girls located in San Fernando, 85 kilometers south of Santiago.

Ninety percent of the students come from rural areas. In March and April as the school year begins, the new students have difficulty concentrating on academic work. They must adjust to long hours on local buses and a new approach to learning as they begin career-focused programs in tailoring, culinary arts, tourism, social work, and assisting in Kindergarten. Candia Hormazabal, who is currently studying pedagogy to become certified, found two of the Toronto experiences particularly meaningful: a mask-making workshop and a demonstration using total physical response (TPR).

In Toronto, Frances Key of the Ontario Arts Council led a mask-making workshop. She demonstrated how following precise instructions using interesting materials provides a powerful means to acquire language. Candia Hormazabal was also intrigued by an exercise in which group members were introduced to some Chinese commands using TPR. She continued to read about TPR (Nunan, 2003) and now says, "That book you gave us is like a Bible to me."

Candia Hormazabal used these experiences to shape the changes in her classroom. She began with reluctant students by teaching body movement through dance, giving instructions such as "Turn left" and "Mark four times to the right with the tiptoe of the right foot." Candia Hormazabal said,

> *I came back from Toronto so fresh and excited that I'm sure I could transmit it. There is a group that doesn't feel really motivated because they don't trust themselves. They're not very confident. But in the Dancing in English classes, they started repeating and following orders, and the shy girls reacted very well to this experience. It seems that their shyness helps with their concentration level, because they were the first ones to learn the steps and the commands. The next step was to put one of the students in front of the group and there were many volunteers!*

Next they worked in teams to produce choreography booklets, such as the one partly illustrated in Appendix A. The students' work is intended to demonstrate the stage of language learning they have reached.

This example illustrates how Candia Hormazabal's response to an experiential lesson in learning Chinese resulted in innovation. Her interest in and understanding of TPR interacted with her perceptions and observations of her less motivated students and resulted not in the adoption of a TPR program, but rather in a Dancing in English project that produced confidence, concentration, and a choreography booklet in English. This kind of curriculum development recognizes the *localness* of curriculum as well as the role of broad nonprescriptive guidelines in producing curricular changes and teacher and student attitudinal changes.

Students in Candia Hormazabal's tailoring class searched the Internet with the key words *patterns* and *free*. These patterns required conversion from inches to centimeters—a skill likely necessary in a dressmaker's life. They loved working with a pattern for a ball gown from 1857 that could have been worn by the ladies of Valparaiso. They created the sewing instructions for Victorian underwear, adjusting the measurements for lacy drawers to current sizes. They moved on to make African bead necklaces and cell phone holders with cross-stitch embroidery and followed instructions for applying festive henna designs to their hands.

The 14-year-old tourism students study for careers in tourism in the wine district of Chile. Candia Hormazabal used her experience as a part-time tour guide while at university as the foundation for a bilingual field trip to Santiago. Many of the girls saw Santiago for the first time. Their journal entries were full of comments on the size of the airplanes they had seen at the airport and the weirdness of real bodies in tombs at the cathedral.

Candia Hormazabal used a template provided by the school to produce detailed courses of study for her students (see Appendix B). She was constrained by the requirement that four of the five evaluations required each term must be written tests; however, she was able to design quizzes that reflect the technological content included in her English teaching (see Appendix C).

Candia Hormazabal's experience clearly shows how her Canadian experience and her own learning and career history have interacted with a supportive administration, a seemingly constraining curricular template, and the interests and experiences of her students to create innovative classroom activities. As a result, her efforts have sparked interest among her students in the content of their courses and the English that mediates their understanding.

INAUGURATING DAILY COMPUTER USE IN A TECHNICAL SCHOOL IN MAIPU: NAYARET TORO SOTO

Nayaret Toro Soto teaches in a semiprivate technical school of 1,300 students in Maipu, a suburb of Santiago. Here, her students prepare for careers in electronics, accounting, telecommunications, and secretarial work. Boys outnumber girls by a ratio of 5:1. Through her observations, Hill sensed that the students' motivation to learn English to please the teacher was particularly strong in Toro Soto's classroom.

The proposed installation of a computer lab sparked Toro Soto's proposal to investigate ways of improving her students listening skills through computer-assisted language learning. In Toronto, an investigation of software programs designed for listening skills brought Toro Soto up against one of her school's constraints. The parents had raised money for the hardware, but software purchases also required substantial financial investments. The site license for the listening program cost $2,500 (U.S.), which was way beyond the school's reach. Toro Soto abandoned the idea of purchased software for listening as impractical and widened the focus of her project to include using the computers to practice listening, reading, writing, and speaking. She added to the English language goals "learner autonomy" and "collaboration." While in Toronto, Toro Soto explored a variety of English language Web pages. Some involved vocabulary and discrete grammar exercises, a kind of electronic drill book. Others, such as Web quests (an inquiry-oriented lesson format where most or all of the information comes from the Web), were more open-ended. Toro Soto determined that she would integrate computers into her language classroom routine.

Once back in Chile, Toro Soto and her colleagues dived into the project by spending one third of their English class time in the lab. The facilities include a spacious classroom with 23 computers connected to the Internet and a long table in the center to accommodate alternate activities for another 25 students. The true gift, one all teachers envy, is Cesar, a technician who can free Toro Soto from the worries of computer glitches.

Toro Soto and her two colleagues keep the room in constant use. Three-hour time blocks facilitate timetable planning for practical courses and for teachers who teach in more than one school, but also challenge the teachers of academic courses. Using computers helps provide the variety of activities essential in structuring 3-hour language classes for adolescents.

Toro Soto introduced her students to the three software programs the school had purchased. The software is very structured—the electronic drill books Toro Soto had explored in Toronto—but the technician can supervise students while she works intensively with students who do not have computers.

Internet activities are more complex. The possibilities and the amount of teacher time required to tailor a project to the specific needs of a group can overwhelm a teacher. The diversity of the programs offered in technical schools presents a further challenge. The creative programming Candia Hormazabal uses with her students in tourism and tailoring is not practical when specialties such as accounting or electronics lie outside the experience of most English teachers. Designing cross-curricular projects with content-area teachers requires time unavailable in the normal Chilean teachers' schedules.

In addition, although the Ministry of Education has provided free Internet service to all schools, most schools, like Toro Soto's, do not have high-speed connections. This results in frustratingly slow navigation of sites, especially when several students simultaneously access the Internet. Toro Soto has experimented with visits to the BBC Web site for news broadcasts and to www.Englishpage.com for students to generate their own lists of phrasal verbs. Her students have done projects on globalization and on endangered animals. The results have been mixed.

Toro Soto's situation illustrates the complexity of introducing new methodologies and technologies. It is difficult to separate the results of studying with the help of computers from the effects of other factors, such as student motivation or the classroom teacher's skill in using traditional methods. Student fascination with English language video games cannot guarantee English language learning, although the students' gaming abilities may improve!

Toro Soto's younger students love the novelty of the computer laboratory; however, her older students do not always take advantage of the facilities. When they say, "This is so boring," are they reflecting the mismatch of foreign language proficiency with cognitive development? Is *boring* a synonym for *too difficult*? Are they blessed with sharp critical skills?

For now, Toro Soto has chosen to focus on current events and environmental projects. She may be able to incorporate a Web quest approach to some of these. Toro Soto's classroom and project illustrate how seemingly unrelated factors interact to shape and be shaped by curricular and pedagogical decisions and how the actual outcomes may be less important than understanding the process. For Toro Soto, the institutional constraints include the necessity to use a computer lab, prohibitive software licensing fees, large blocks of uninterrupted time for classes, and crowded and overlapping teaching schedules in a school in which electronics, telecommunications, secretarial, and accounting dominate the curriculum content. In turn, these factors have interacted with Toro Soto's teaching personality, her interest in using technology, her skills in navigating and using software and Internet sites in English, and the effect she seems to have on her students' willingness to study English. Any analysis of the effectiveness of Toro Soto's project and implications for other schools considering an introduction of technology must consider these factors together.

Some generalizations can be made and factored into plans. These include the speed of the Internet connection, the students' and teachers' ability to efficiently use sites, the reliability and accessibility of technical support, and the availability of sufficient funding to support software and hardware purchases and maintenance. However, other aspects cannot be generalized or isolated; rather, the constellation of aspects must be examined. These include young students fascinated by and familiar with technology combined with simple English language drills and exercises presented via fancy computer programs and a schedule that allows a teacher to set half the class to work on the computers and half to work with the teacher.

LITERATURE CIRCLES IN PROVIDENCIA: MARIA ANDREA ARANCIBIA

Maria Andrea Arancibia teaches in a prestigious Santiago public school for girls. As she moves through the corridors and patios of her school, she sorts out a series of inquiries calmly and matter-of-factly. As part of an experienced and dynamic English department, she shares the five 7th-grade classes with a classmate from university who shares Arancibia's enthusiasm for improving the comprehension and communicative skills of their students. Their goal is to train all new students to expect English classes to be taught entirely in English so that the rest of the department can continue the practice.

Entrance examinations in this school ensure that the students are academically proficient in Spanish and mathematics. However, their English background varies. None of Arancibia's 7th-grade students had ever listened to a teacher who spoke only English in the classroom. Parents and students had to be assured there was no need to hire tutors. By the end of the second month, the parents had settled down, and the students felt confident they could understand classroom English.

Arancibia called her project Let's Communicate in English! She aimed to explore and apply new methodologies in the classroom focusing on communication rather than on grammar. Beyond that broad imperative, she had few explicit goals in mind. Arancibia flourished in the English environment in Toronto. She made connections between her own experience and what she wanted to accomplish in her classroom. Her broad goals perhaps allowed her to take advantage of the various language experiences in Toronto. By the time she left, Arancibia had decided she would use only English in the classroom and that she would begin with a survey in English and institute literature circles.

She started with a survey to find out what experiences her students had had with English classes and what topics interested them. She used this information as the basis for her plans. On her course questionnaire, Arancibia wrote, "I don't say we are studying the present continuous; I say we're doing a fashion show." She has 45 girls in every class; at the beginning, the students were a little confused and sometimes had to consult with each other to figure out what their teacher expected. But when Hill visited their classroom, she saw the students automatically reorient their chairs to get ready for the pair work they expected. Even the youngest could produce meaningful conversations when they were given situations. Information-gap activities no longer perplexed them. As Arancibia reported

Teaching the whole class in English at the beginning was a kind of shocking experience. The beginners tell me how worried they were

because they didn't understand anything, but now after these months applying the project they understand much more and they are able to communicate in English, according to their level of course. Determination is half the way.

Arancibia has had the greatest success with her literature circles (Daniels, 1994, 2002). Hill introduced this technique in Toronto because she felt that English teachers with a month free from their duties could enjoyably revive their English by reading. It also fit the program's goal of modeling the techniques and strategies introduced to the teachers. On the first day, Hill brought in a stack of adolescent novels and asked each of the teachers to choose one of the three titles.

With the formal literature circles, Hill also hoped to model a solution for situations in which teachers might not have sufficient copies of any one book for large classes. She thought that some of the participants might find a way to assign roles in discussion groups. But she was amazed to see Arancibia's students in *Segundo Medio* (Grade 10) faithfully following the prescribed method. She actually quizzed every single student in the class about her task in the group. One by one, they replied, "I'm the discussion director" or "I'm the literary luminary." Hill, almost in disbelief, prodded with, "What do you have to do?" The students all had answers.

The strategy of using literature circles in reading instruction has been widely adopted in North American schools, particularly in areas where resources are scarce and large numbers of students are English language learners. As a result, English as a second language teachers frequently prepare their students for this activity; however, the practice has yet to be widely used in EFL teaching.

In his early work, Harvey Daniels suggested beginning with specific roles with imposing titles. Arancibia did not simplify the flowery names but she did find that some of the roles that Daniels considered optional are essential for language learners, particularly that of Vocabulary Enricher (Daniels, 1994, 2002). In contrast, if one of Arancibia's groups is smaller than eight, she generally omits the roles Travel Tracer and the Literary Luminary. Table 1 summarizes Daniels' definitions of the roles in literature circles.

Arancibia began, as is recommended, by using the same book for all students. She chose an Oxford Bookworms edition of *The Monkey's Paw* (Jacobs, 2000), a book she had used in class before. She used the information Hill had given the group in Toronto and searched the Internet for more detailed explanations of the process. She prepared adaptations of Daniels' (1994) original activity planners (see Appendix D). Arancibia

Table 1. Daniels' (1994, 2002) Definitions of the Roles in Literature Circles

Role	Description
Discussion Director	Convenes the meeting, prepares and introduces discussion questions, encourages participation.
Word Wizard or Vocabulary Enricher	For each day's reading, finds 5–8 key words that may be unfamiliar to the group. Prepares an explanation for each.
Connector	Is in charge of helping students relate the literature to their personal experiences.
Literary Luminary	Chooses important sections of the text and prepares to read these aloud to the other group members.
Artful Artist/Illustrator	Responds to the text by preparing storyboards or other illustrations.
Investigator	Researches background such as time period, culture and setting.
Summarizer	Prepares a summary of the day's reading for the group.
Character Captain	Prepares character sketches or charts of both main and minor characters in the book.
Scene Setter/Travel Tracer	Compiles charts identifying and describing the settings and scenes of the reading.

appreciated how the variety of tasks gave students opportunities to choose an approach that best suits their own learning styles.

One of the challenges with the implementation of group work with large classes involves assessment and feedback. Arancibia adopted one of Hill's approaches, Process Observation, for monitoring progress and giving feedback to the students about their group discussion skills. Arancibia calls it the *Post-It Evaluation*. As the group works, Arancibia jots notes on slips of paper on her clipboard. She sticks these notes on her students' notebooks as they leave the room. Figure 2 provides a sample Post-It Evaluation.

When her class finished reading *The Monkey's Paw*, Arancibia gave the test from the teachers' guide she has used many times. She noticed the confidence with which the class tackled the test. Arancibia was accustomed to answering a great many questions during tests—this time she had none.

Although learning vocabulary and reinforcing sentence structure and syntax are the expected results of extensive reading, neither Hill nor Arancibia had anticipated the impact of this kind of work. With literature circles, Arancibia observed how her students improved their reading skills by discussing and sharing opinions and feelings about books in English. The care the students put into their work illustrates how much they valued this activity (see Appendix E for samples).

As with the other teachers who participated in the Canadian program, Arancibia experienced, reflected on, and made her own an activity that fitted her own teaching philosophy; school, classroom, and student constraints; and opportunities. Her experience of classes conducted entirely in English, her ability to effectively communicate in both social and academic contexts, and the opportunity to read and *study* a piece of English literature in English gave her confidence and practical means she could adapt to her own setting. In the end, her project yielded results beyond those she had expected.

Evaluating the Program in Follow-up Sessions

The training program set up by the Ministry of Education featured a meeting in Chile in July 2005, the midterm point in the Chilean school year. Foreign instructors from each of the four *pasantias* abroad were invited to participate in the meeting. Each of the foreign instructors was asked to meet with the participants from her particular program. Hill represented the Toronto program in Santiago. She asked each of the 19 teachers who had attended the Toronto course of study, including the three teachers featured in this chapter, to complete a survey form. From the answers to the open-ended questions on the effects of teacher participation in the program and their efforts to implement their initiatives, Hill found four major themes. The teachers wrote of the effects of confidence, support, time, and reflection.

Figure 2. Sample Post-It Evaluation

> Suzanna
>
> 1:09 - good eye contact while listening to Carmen
>
> 1:25 - listing Maria's vocabulary words
>
> 1:34 - looking out window
>
> 1:40 - back at work reading passage out loud.

CONFIDENCE

Almost all the Chilean teachers talked about how much more confident they felt about their own speaking and how they have incorporated the exclusive use of English into their classrooms. This confidence has many facets. Teachers risked using an English-only policy in their classrooms. They risked negative responses from colleagues, students, and parents. However, as they persevered, based on their own increased confidence in their ability to understand and to be understood, they described secondary effects, including a greater understanding of the role of mistakes as learning opportunities and more vocal participation from their students. Edith Ascencio Mendoza explained

> *If I as a teacher don't speak English, how can I expect my students to speak English? My students are much more motivated and enthusiastic because they are not in silence anymore; they are participating actively; the teacher is not the one who says or does everything in the class lesson.*

Wilma Melin Silva reflected

> *I think that teachers sometimes pay much more attention on mistakes and correctness than on right things. That makes students to be afraid of speaking or participating. Learning a language is related to emotions. I dare to do things that I wouldn't before. It has been a great experience, but I'm just starting with it. My piece of advice is to trust oneself.*

SUPPORT

The teachers also reported increased support from principals when parents complain that their children cannot understand. This may stem from the plan to have national tests of listening by 2007; it may also be influenced by the increased confidence principals observe in teachers conducting their classes in English.

Support has not been confined to administrative support. It has also come from colleagues impressed with the teachers' confidence, enthusiasm, and results. Support manifests itself in greater collaboration. In some schools, other English teachers are working with our participants to ensure that a whole grade level experiences the same program. Ana Maria Vasquez Santana reported

> *My colleagues just observed at first, and then the most daring ones have tried to develop some of my techniques. I would tell my colleagues don't forget to teach English through context, because I learned it's easier for students to get involved with English as a whole way of communicating.*

In most cases, teachers reported that colleagues recognized the new importance of English teaching. Schools have bilingual signs, staff room English lessons, parents' English classes, and situations in which "Some of my colleagues even greet me in English when I see them!"

Another manifestation of this respect and support stems from teacher participation in the local professional development meetings informally referred to as English Nets or nets. These have provided opportunities for teachers to share techniques and ideas. Edith Ascencio Mendoza commented on her presentation to her local net, "I felt so happy and motivated because my net asked me to report it a second time but now in English because they have realized the importance English has nowadays."

Fabiola Rodriguez Pavez initiated work in her school with a volunteer program from the Universidad Católica de Valparaiso. All of the 19 teachers in the Toronto *pasantia* have presented at net meetings in their regions, and many have ambitious plans for participating in mentoring programs, regional conferences, and videoconferencing with English language learners in other settings.

Any kind of institutional change incurs opposition as well as support. For some teachers, particularly those who have changed schools or who are the only English teacher in their school, the support and collaboration have not materialized. Some of the teachers have faced indifference or even outright opposition within their school. Others have had their practices criticized publicly. One teacher reported

> When I was reading fairy tales with my students, a teacher criticized me, saying that it was no use for reading comprehension because the students knew the story in Spanish. She said, in front of a group of teachers, that the methodology was useless. But I insisted, and I said that knowing the story in Spanish helped the students understand it in English. I proved it did, and they really learned because when retelling or writing the story, they had to know some English and they had to know even more when dramatizing the tale.

Despite the criticism, this teacher reported success and satisfaction with a project incorporating drama into teaching in his classroom.

TIME

Another impediment to collegial support and collaboration shows up in the teachers' comments about time. Although the 19 teachers who studied together in Toronto forged new friendships and collegial bonds, they have not all been able to maintain that mutual support as they have gone about implementing their ideas. Heavy teaching loads, long daily commutes, school computers being unavailable, e-mail servers being down, slow connections, or home computers monopolized by family teenagers all mitigate against regular communication. Angelica Saavedra Chamorro explained

> *I have to work 44 hours a week; 43 of them are in front of a class, and I really don't have time to prepare materials nor answer the journals or write to my colleagues. I feel so sorry to say that I am working alone.*

Where do teachers find the time to learn more about language teaching, maintain and develop their own language, reflect and practice different strategies and techniques, practice what they have learned, and talk with other English teachers? As Ruben Carez Larenas said, "We have to use a teaching practice not once but over and over again to see if it works and make the necessary changes and adaptations." Such efforts require time to reflect, revise, and practice again. The teachers would certainly agree with recent student demands for a shorter school day, "saying that a recently proposed eight-hour day is unreasonable" ("Chile Students Clash with Police," 2006).

REFLECTION

Throughout the 4-week program in Toronto, the teachers kept English journals, to which the three instructors responded. The teachers valued the opportunity to express their ideas, reflect on their experiences, and use their English. They all had expressed a desire to incorporate some kind of journal writing activity in their teaching practice when they returned to the classroom. They brought beautiful examples of student journals to the July 2005 meeting. They also brought stories of how hard it is to read even a portion of the students' writing when a teacher may meet more than 500 students a week. Toro Soto explained

> *I've started to use journals with some classes, and it has been a wonderful experience because, at the beginning, they didn't want to do it. But now they love it; every week they want me to read their journals to see how much they've advanced. One of my boys is really happy because he has realized that he can write. He wants to speak now. He wants to prove to himself he can speak this beautiful language.*

The value of reflective practice appeared as a fourth theme in the survey results. Reflection requires time and a catalyst. The month away from classroom and family responsibilities in an unfamiliar but relatively safe environment seems to have provided the necessary factors. Being students again prompted teachers to express a new respect and level of closeness toward their students. The use of journal writing with students provided evidence of the effects of the teachers' efforts.

This respect for students manifested itself in several ways. Some teachers wrote that their decision to speak only English in classes was based on a trust in their students' abilities. Another teacher wrote that she learned "to give respect and support to my slow students." One teacher wrote how her Toronto experience had helped her see that she held lower expectations for her Maipu [indigenous] students.

The teachers spoke of needing "to dare," to take risks, and to trust their instincts as teachers. Their focus seemed to have switched from teaching the mechanics of language to finding ways for students to use the language, from teaching about language to working with students to use language, and from teaching content to teaching students. In addition, the teachers' sense of renewal and enthusiasm seems to have infected their students. Carol Castro Ramos summed it up as follows:

I have realized that being respectful and teaching how to be respectful about each person might change students' behavior in the classroom. Little by little they are starting to understand almost everything, and communication has been developed through the semester wonderfully.

Successfully Picking a Way Through the Stones That Remain

Revitalizing the curriculum each day they enter the classroom challenges every teacher. Marta Mendez Madriaza reminded us of the realities of a classroom of adolescents when she complained, "You lose your time investigating who stole a cell phone, or why they did not clean the classroom or why they are drunk." Chilean teachers, even more than many teachers, have enormous demands on their time. Forty-five students cram into classrooms more suitable for 25 as schools struggle to switch from double-shift schools to full-day schools. Most teachers spend more than 40 hours a week in their classrooms with students, fill out thick ledgers after every class with details of the lesson taught and of student attendance and performance, and design every test in multiple versions to combat copying in the crowded classrooms. As women dominate language teaching in Chile and as 40% of women in Chile are single mothers (Jimenez, 2006), demands on the teachers' time do not stop at the school doors. Most teachers simply move from one realm of demands to another.

Being accepted for the 4-week program provided the 19 teachers the time to reflect, talk, study, use their language skills, and practice their teaching skills in a supportive community with other teachers who shared their challenges and frustrations. The practices with which they have had the most success are the ones they themselves practiced in Toronto for their own language development. The time together in Canada helped them develop a tolerance for error as a part of language learning. This willingness to plunge ahead, accepting mistake making in themselves and their students, is summed up in a Chilean proverb: *Quien no se arriesga, no cruza el río* (If you don't take a risk, you won't get across the river).

Part of what made these teachers' efforts successful comes from their willingness to take risks and the time they were able to be away from school and personal responsibilities. Although the program worked for this group of teachers, it also raises the following questions: Can *all* teachers take advantage of such a program? How many teachers will risk failure in the pursuit of learning? How many teachers can escape responsibilities for an entire month?

The path for Chilean teachers remains stone-filled. Few schools have access to the computer facilities provided for Toro Soto's classes. Arancibia's students are starting their third book in 3 months, but now that they have gained confidence in reading, they need a library stocked with appealing reading material in English. Candia Hormazabal is following government recommendations to adapt English instruction according to the specialty of the technical school. Her colleagues, like Eliana Soto Marin in Castro, are inventing authentic assessments with tourism students practicing, "On the left you will see a large white building on a plaza with a fountain. This is our Palace of Justice" and "Yes, you may get off to take a photograph. Please be back in just five minutes." But, will these innovative practices ensure or jeopardize student performance on the 2007 standardized examinations in listening and reading?

Marta Mendez Mandriaza poured over a book on motivation (Dörnyei, 2001), searching for ways to motivate her reluctant and resistant students. In the end, expertise, knowledge, facilities, and materials—even administrative and collegial support—will not sustain classroom innovation without the energy and heart that she flung into her classroom when she rapped her way through the vocabulary, grammar, and drills. Mendez Mandriaza won her difficult students over by teaching them how to use the stress and rhythm of rap music. What made these projects successful? Mendez Mandriaza captured the final element: "If you want to innovate you must be an actor, a dancer, a teacher, and many other things."

Appendix A: Choreography Book

THE BODY MOVES

Liliana Alarcón
Ornela Aránguiz
Dafne Paves
Paz Sereño

Movements of the Choreography

– Ten movements of right hips to the left marking with the feet

– The hand and the right foot to the right side
the hand and the left foot to the left side
the hand and the right foot to the right side
the hand and the left foot to the left side. (four times)

– Arm and right leg to the right side.
arm and left leg to the left side
arm and right leg to the right side
arm and left leg to the left side (four times)

– Circle with the arms and right leg to the front
circle with the arms and left leg behind
circle with the arms and right leg to the front
circle with the arms and left leg behind. (four times)

– Turn to the left

– The hand and the right foot to the right side
the hand and the left foot to the left side
the hand and the right foot to the right side
the hand and the left foot to the left side

Conclusion

With this activity we develop our dynamic capacity through the dance.
It is also a form easy to learn English since it is good us to direct groups and to carry out activities out doors, him which makes that the classes are more productive.

Appendix B: Curriculum Template

PLAN DE CLASES

Formación General

APRENDIZAJES ESPERADOS	CONTENIDOS DE APRENDIZAJES	ACTIVIDADES DE APRENDIZAJES	PROCEDIMIENTOS DE EVALUACIÓN	OBJETIVOS TRANSVERSALES
* Manejar conceptos relacionados con cantidades de dinero y equivalencias en otras monedas. * Resolver problemas sencillos que involucren dinero, en todas sus formas.	**I.- Money** *Vocabulary* - Currencies. - Numeros cardinales up to 999,999. - Definiciones de términos en inglés. - Aritmética basica *Grammar* - Present Simple - WH questions - Comparative and superlative adjectives.	- Se definen en ingles una serie de términos relacionados con dinero y con el uso del dinero. - Las alumnas ensayan sonido de los números, puliendo su pronunciación. - Escriben cantidades dictadas. Leen números y cantidades mayores en voz alta. - Resuelven problemas de planteo simples, relacionados con comercio ficticio de bienes y/o servicios.	- Asignación de tareas. - Prueba escrita.	
* Reconocer aspectos elementales de la geografia fisica, politica y humana de su país. * Ubicar geográficamente puntos importantes del país. * Describir y recomendar zonas turísticas.	**II.- My Country** *Vocabulary* - División político-administrativa del país. - Sistema de gobierno. - Población del país y distribución. - Ciudades importantes y razón de su importancia. - Zonas de interés turístico por región.	- Observan un mapa de Chile, y señalan la división en regiones y el nombre de cada una, así como su capital y población estimada por región. - Escuchan una breve descripción del sistema de gobierno, y de las autoridades por cada una de las divisiones del país. - Confeccionan un gráfico con la distribución de la población en Chile por sexo, edad y otras variables. Exponen sus resultados frente al curso. - Escuchan una serie de afirmaciones, y corrigen oralmente en caso de ser falsas. - Ubican en un mapa regiones, accidentes geográficos pertenecientes a cada región y su	- Asignación de tareas. - Presentación frente al curso, con vestimenta acorde. - Informe escrito. - Prueba escrita.	

		- ubicación dentro de la zona.	
	- Puntos cardinales.	- Ubican sectores de interés turístico con los puntos cardinales y describen usando adjetivos calificativos.	
	- Geografía básica.		
	- Estadística		
	Grammar		
	- *Present Simple-Present Continuous.*		
	- *Past Simple-Present Perfect*		
	- *Passive voice*		
	- *Reported speech*		
* Leer comprensivamente	**III.- Reading Workshop**	- De una novela dada, se analizan detalladamente los elementos básicos de la comunicación escrita.	- *Lectura en voz alta (sin nota)*
* Adquirir modelos de comunicación a través de la lectura comprensiva.	*Basic contents*	- Cada clase se lee un capitulo de la lectura. Se extraen palabras nuevas, las alumnas las definen en inglés; seleccionan extractos y analizan tiempo verbal y congruencia significativa de lo leido.	- *Prueba escrita*
	- *Vocabulario basico.*		- *Revision de "journals"*
	- *Tiempos verbales simples y perfectos.*		- *Revision de tareas en clase.*
* Entender, comentar y resumir una lectura.*	- *Estructuras y normas gramaticales.*	- De la lectura, analizan personajes, tiempo, hechos e hitos importantes y relación con la realidad.	
		- Las alumnas llevan una bitácora de lectura donde anotan la fecha de la lectura, un resumen breve de lo leido y un comentario.	

Appendix C: Quiz

Exercises.

"T" or "F". Justifique "F".

a) The tsp. and tbsp. are exact measures.
False.
Non exact measure.

b) 2 Kilos equal 0,920 p.
False.
~~Equal 2 pounds.~~

c) In ten Kilos, we have sixty pounds.
False.
~~Why, we have two Kilos.~~

d) Milk is measured in pounds.
False.
No, measured ounces, pints.

e) Sugar and flour are <u>mixed</u> and not <u>stirred</u>.
True.

f) The liquid ingredients are measured in litres, tables_
poons.
True.

June 1

g) Six tsp. are equal to thirty ml.
True. ✓

h) To "dip" is : "to put onto with a knife"
False.
Dip, is put into a liquid.

i) One "strip" is a : "thin and long piece".
True. ✓

II) Responde las sgtes. preguntas :

a) What foods are measured in pounds ? 2 examples:
Solid ingredients.
Ex : Potatoes, meat.

b) What foods are measured in litres ? 2 examples.
Liquid ingredients.
Ex : Milk, water. ✓

c) What is "spread" ?
Is put onto with a knife. ✓

d) What is "grated cheese" ?
~~In tiny cheese.~~

e) What is "pound meat" ?
Is ~~measured the pounds meat.~~

f) How many tablespoons are in a litre ?
Is sixty six tablespoons. ✓

g) How many teaspoons are in a cup ?
Is fifty teaspoons. ✓

Valeria Donoso R.
Roxana Morales l.
3° año B.

Appendix D: Activity Planner Sample

Adapted from Daniels (1994)

LICEO CARMELA CARVAJAL DE PRAT
ENGLISH DEPARTMENT /
Teacher: Andrea Arancibia

LITERATURE CIRCLES

ILLUSTRATOR/ARTFUL ARTIST

Name : Vania Gutierrez
Date : 5.04.05
Novel you're reading : The Monkey's Paw
Pages read to prepare for this discussion : 1 - 15

As the Illustrator/Artful Artist, it is your job is to draw some kind of picture related to the reading. It can be a sketch, cartoon, diagram, flow chart, or stick figure scene. You can draw a picture of something that is discussed specifically in your book, something that the reading reminded you of, or a picture that conveys any idea or feeling you got from the reading. Any kind of drawing or graphic is okay. You can label things with words if that helps. Make your drawing on this paper. If you need more room, use the back.

MEETING 1

MEETING 2

MEETING 3

Appendix E: Literature Circles Student Work

LICEO CARMELA CARVAJAL DE PRAT
ENGLISH DEPARTMENT/
Teacher: Andrea Arancibia

<u>LITERATURE CIRCLES</u>

<u>LITERARY LUMINARY</u>

Very good!!

Name : Fernando Malamala
Date : 5-04-05
Novel you're reading : The monkey's Paw
Pages read to prepare for this discussion : 1-15

As the Literary Luminary, it is your job to read aloud parts of the story to your group in order to help your group members remember some interesting, powerful, puzzling, or important sections of the text. You decide which passages or paragraphs are worth reading aloud, and justify your reasons for selecting them. Write the page numbers and paragraph numbers on this from along with the reason you chose each passage. You must choose a minimum of 3 passages.

Some reasons for choosing passages to share might include:

> Pivotal events
> Informative *informative*
> Descriptive *descriptivo*
> Surprising *sorpresivo*
> Scary *mixto*
> Thought-provoking
> Funny *divertido*
> Controversial *controversial*
> Confusing *confuso*
> Personally meaningful *x*

<u>Meeting 1</u>

Location	Reason for choosing the passage
Page: 6 and 9 Paragraph: 10 and 1 of page 9	Because I believe this paragraphs are very important for understand the content of the story. They are descriptive and informative about of the book

<u>Meeting 2</u> 1

Location	Reason for choosing the passage
Page: 10 Paragraph: 7 (line 21)	Because is informative and controversial about can happen in the story. This is the conflict of the text and is the negative of monkey's paw

Meeting 2:

Location	Reason for choosing the passage
Page: 17 Paragraph: 4	It's a informative paragraph, because to indicate the dreams of the protagonist, maybe it can to realize only with a monkey paw. This is ambition, and descriptive of situacion of the persons

Meeting 2:

Location	Reason for choosing the passage
Page: 19 and 20 Paragraph: 10	It's surprising and scary paragraph, because in all the story it not happen. It produce very suspicion at lecturer. Is a controversial part of the text; because before of it, all was laugh and with it was fight.

Meeting 3:

Location	Reason for choosing the passage
Page: 28 Paragraph: 11 and 12	They are very surprising and confusing paragraph because to unexpected an event. Then of this event, the story change because the principal character have a great problem.

Meeting 3:

Location	Reason for choosing the passage
Page: 31 Paragraph: 1, 2 and 3	They are personally meaningful paragraphs because the petition wish at the monkey's paw is fact, but change of their son, is terrible, and the lecturer remember mentioned at Tom Morris said. This part is apogee the story.

Meeting 3:

Location	Reason for choosing the passage

Reviving, Revising, or Revolutionising? Supplementing Coursebook Teaching With Internet-Based Instruction

12

JAROSŁAW KRAJKA

Choosing a coursebook can be challenging for today's language teachers. There seems to be a constant stream of new titles and accompanying materials, all convincingly marketed. It is the coursebook that to some extent imposes its curriculum on teachers based on the book's selection, ordering, and grading of content. Teachers generally choose coursebooks after a thorough evaluation, taking into account the needs of the class and the practical considerations of their contexts. Although teachers may take great care when selecting coursebooks, it is unlikely that any one coursebook or curriculum will meet the needs of all students in a particular class given the variation in the students' language proficiency levels, learning styles, levels of intelligence, backgrounds, and preferences.

Within this framework, Internet-based instruction can help teachers revitalize a curriculum by expanding on, replacing, or restructuring curriculum topics. Such Web-based language lessons have significant potential, in particular, for developing students' language proficiency as they use authentic language in truly engaging yet pedagogically sound tasks.

The Motivation for Innovation

My motivation for implementing Internet-based instruction began with my experience as an English teacher in upper secondary schools in Poland. I found that outdated textbooks, overcrowded classes, and a lack of exposure to the language hampered the students' opportunities to learn English and affected their motivation. Typical teaching problems in Poland centre on overcrowded classes and a lack of fully qualified teachers, especially at the lower levels of learning and in rural areas. In addition, the lack of a sufficient number of computer labs for classes other than information technology (IT) has been a serious problem in public schools that do not have many resources. The situation is slowly changing in the face of substantial governmental support, fewer schools because of changing demographics, and school administrators' increasing awareness of the benefits of Web-assisted teaching in subjects other than IT. Moreover, the problem of underqualified teachers, largely the result of a rapid shift from teaching Russian to teaching English and other Western languages after the fall of communism, has been largely ameliorated by in-service teacher training and postgraduate studies enforced by ministerial regulations. Although the situation is changing, the problems will likely persist for some time.

The Curricular Context

This section outlines the curricular framework in which teachers of English in Poland operate. Until the late 1980s, there was a single, centrally imposed curriculum for every school and every subject, with one corresponding coursebook that reflected a centralised view of society and state control over every aspect of life. Today, teachers have much greater independence in creating and implementing curricula, both publisher-created and teacher-created, although teachers must still conform to the general Core Curriculum published by the Ministry of National Education and Sport (2001), with subsequent revisions.

According to the requirements of the educational reform program implemented in 1999, every school must have a set of curricula for all subjects. Also, every teacher must have a curriculum ready for teaching his or her particular subject; the curriculum has to be suited to the students' needs and capabilities as well as the schools' logisitical considerations, such as the availability of equipment and the availability of a lab specialist.

Thus, teachers are fully autonomous in their choice of curricula and coursebooks provided they are accredited by the Ministry of National Education and Sport, an autonomy that is an important freedom guaranteed by law. If, after careful consideration, teachers believe existing curricula are not fully suitable for certain types of learners, the environment, or school policy, they are free to develop an authored curriculum to use at a single school if the curriculum fulfills the formal requirements of the ministerial Core Curriculum, receives a positive review from another language teacher or a teacher of higher development rank, and is approved by the school's teachers board.

The context for the curricular innovations described in this chapter is upper secondary schools in Poland. After the reform of national education in 1999, the traditional 8 year + 4 year model (primary + secondary) was divided into three stages: primary (6 years), lower secondary (3 years), and upper secondary (3 years). The end of each stage includes a mandatory nationwide standardised examination covering many subjects, including a foreign language at the second lower secondary and upper secondary stages.

Since 2005, the mandatory examination, known as the New Matura, has had an element of external objective assessment. Thus, improving the effectiveness of foreign language teaching and maintaining its quality have become important goals. Because of the maturity of learners at upper secondary level, their previous learning experiences, and their generally high levels of motivation, it is important for teachers to diversify instruction by incorporating different types of input and tasks and by adding student self-study to the traditional face-to-face model.

One aim of governmental programs is to provide computer resources to schools for use during all school subjects, not only IT. Thus, all secondary schools in Poland are supposed to be wired, enabling the Internet to be incorporated into the teaching process. However, even though the equipment is adequate at most schools, obtaining access to the Internet lab for non-IT lessons on a regular basis has been a key problem. Therefore, teachers of English are faced with the challenge of making school administrators aware of how Internet-based instruction can play an important role in the success of foreign language teaching. Similarly, ensuring smooth, mutually beneficial cooperation between the IT teacher (building the elements of students' computer literacy) and the English teacher (exploiting the IT competence to conduct language-oriented instruction) is of paramount importance.

To be of maximum benefit, Internet-based tasks should consist of a balance of the following objectives: (a) building language knowledge and skills, (b) building computer skills, (c) and building cognitive skills. Based on specific learner profiles, teachers must structure the tasks so that certain objectives have greater prominence. One example is the Web-based activity Treasure Hunts, in which the focus of activities can be shifted to suit the needs of a particular class (Luzon Marco, 2001) as follows:

- In a fully guided hunt activity, students are given several questions, each associated with a URL of a particular Web site. Students practise reading the Web site for the gist, scanning for specific information, or identifying and understanding key words. This activity focuses mainly on language skills.

- In a self-guided hunt activity, students are given questions and Web-site URLs but are not told specifically which site to access to answer the questions. In addition to focusing on language skills, this activity encourages the development of cognitive abilities, such as evaluating Web sites and finding information.
- In an open-hunt activity, students find their own sources for obtaining the required information. Although this type of hunt helps students develop high-level Web searching and evaluating skills, it requires teacher support and should be used cautiously so learners do not become overwhelmed by the complexity of the language material.

Thus, when structuring Internet-based programs, teachers should focus foremost on the needs and skills of learners, which teachers determine through a needs and skills analysis. Teachers must focus on providing instruction that can change by incorporating different tasks.

Revitalizing a Curriculum

THE INTERNET AND COURSEBOOKS: TWO TALES OF INTERNET-ASSISTED TEACHING

In this chapter, I present two classroom situations in which, for many reasons, the coursebook that was chosen was not satisfactory for the teacher or students, and other media had to be used to achieve teaching goals. These classroom situations are based in the practical reality of foreign language teaching in Poland, where formal instruction in English starts in grade 4 of primary school and lasts for 9 years, at which point students take the New Matura compulsory examination before leaving secondary school. After I describe both classroom settings and their associated lesson plans, I share my reflections on the two experiences in Internet-based lessons.

CLASSROOM SITUATION 1

The first classroom was in a public upper secondary school in a small town. I was working at the school as a replacement for a teacher on maternity leave. When I took over the classes, I inherited the respective coursebooks. Because of the difficult financial situations of the students' families, with most having three or more children, it was not possible to change the coursebook because the younger children in a family would use their older siblings' coursebooks. Thus, the coursebook used in the class, *Flying Start 2* (Abbs, Freebairn, & Mariani, 1994), was relatively old. Because the coursebook's content and recordings were outdated, it lacked the necessary connection to the students' reality. It had old-fashioned graphics, promoted celebrities who were no longer popular, and took an outdated approach to the presentation of language, all of which had a detrimental effect on students and failed to motivate them to work on the material. In addition, because the same coursebook had been in use in a given family for several years, all the tasks and exercises were completed. With these factors in mind, I had to seriously consider whether the coursebook would be effective in helping me attain my teaching goals. For example, a lesson in the coursebook focused on reading comprehension. For this lesson, students were required to read about a pop star (Michael Jackson), translate the text, learn new vocabulary, answer comprehension questions, and practise asking questions in the present simple and present continuous tenses using the information from the text. Finally, they had to conduct an interview in pairs, with one student being the reporter and the other Michael Jackson. In the interview, students were to use the vocabulary from the text and consolidate their knowledge of the two tenses. However, the *hero* of the lesson was no longer admired, and students perceived the photographs accompanying the text as ridiculous. Therefore, teaching this section of the coursebook would be difficult, particularly as learners did not have the motivation to engage with the materials.

I decided that one way to overcome this problem was to replace some coursebook lessons with Internet-based lessons, thus *reviving* a moribund curriculum. The resulting Internet-based plan (referred to here as Lesson 1; also see Appendix A) used the same lesson phases as the coursebook; that is, students would read a text, translate it, and learn new vocabulary. They would also answer reading comprehension questions, practise asking questions in the present simple and present continuous tenses using information from the text, and use the information acquired to practise the two tenses. The aim of the pre-Web stage of the Internet lesson was to activate students' background knowledge about the topic and elicit useful vocabulary and structures. The online part of the lesson allowed students to choose which texts to use. During this phase, students were asked to read for details, which they would share later with other students. The online instruction was followed by another period of offline group work during which learners created a description of the things they would like to see invented. The lesson culminated with students submitting their ideas for an invention to a Web site.

As the topic and the lack of variety and choice were the main factors demotivating the students, I changed the lesson topic to Inventors and decided to use two Web sites (http://www.enchantedlearning.com/inventors and http://www.ideafinder.com) to give students the freedom to choose which inventions to read about. By adding the elements of variety and choice, I hoped to foster the students' autonomy and empower them to become decision makers. By using current and authentic materials, I hoped

Reviving, Revising, or Revolutionising? Supplementing Coursebook Teaching With Internet-Based Instruction

271

to create strong, intrinsic student motivation. Appendix A shows the lesson plan and student tasks.

CLASSROOM SITUATION 2

The second classroom situation occurred when I was a regular, full-time teacher in an upper secondary school in a large city. The school had small classes, up to 15 students, and the Internet laboratory was available for English lessons. During my first year at the school, I found that using the textbook alone did not fill the teaching time available. My class at this school followed the *extended programme* of teaching English, which is used in Poland and can be characterized as follows:

- The amount of language instruction time was relatively long (5–6 hours a week).
- Instruction was delivered solely in language groups (up to 15 students) in which students were divided according to their proficiency level as determined by a placement test.
- The classes were at a higher starting level (at least intermediate) than classes at other schools.
- The classes at each language level were more homogeneous than at other schools.
- Students were more intrinsically motivated to learn the foreign language.
- Students were under pressure to take the advanced version of the New Matura secondary school examination.

Students in the school were extremely motivated to learn English and willing to take part in any innovative activity the teacher introduced. The coursebook, *Opportunities Pre-Intermediate* (Harris, Mower, & Sikorzyńska, 2000), was relatively new and interesting to the students. It had current materials and a good balance of grammar exercises and skills practise. However, the coursebook was developed for a standard 120-hour course (i.e., 3–4 hours a week in a typical school year), and the curriculum at the school provided for many more hours of English per week. A calculation showed the coursebook material would be covered in as few as 20 weeks. With this in mind, I decided to supplement the coursebook teaching by adding additional activities and lessons. I developed an Internet-based lesson plan (referred to here as Lesson 2) to expand the coursebook instruction, consolidate the material introduced during lessons, and prepare students for future lessons.

For example, a coursebook lesson focused on developing listening comprehension and featured several recordings on the topic of Campaigning for Human Rights. These elements were accompanied by pre-listening activities (e.g., "Match the descriptions with the pictures," "Make sure you understand the key words provided," and "Read the listening strategies"), listening activities (e.g., "Listen and decide whether the statements given are true or false" and "Listen and underline the stressed words"), and post-listening tasks (e.g., "Use the key words to make notes about the famous campaigners," "Form groups and discuss your opinions," and "Listen to another recording and match the people given with their causes"; Harris et al., 2000, pp. 22–23).

The Internet-based lesson I developed to expand on this coursebook lesson relied on the exploitation of authentic Internet materials in an interactive way. This allowed students to practise their writing skills at a high level while developing their reading and speaking skills. The main goal of the lesson was to reinforce the structures and vocabulary acquired during the regular coursebook lesson through the productive use of grammatical and lexical material in real-life tasks, such as sending a card or letter protesting a global issue. Through these activities, I hoped to establish the important link between classroom instruction and real-life target-language interaction. The activation of the students' language and background knowledge was followed by multistage online work, in which students read about and selected a cause they wanted to advocate or actions they wished to protest. In the productive stage of the lesson, students composed and sent a formal or informal letter using the interfaces given. To achieve success in the post-stage, students had to extract information; that is, which Web site they visited, the cause, the country, the person or institution addressed, and their personal feelings about the issue or cause. Group interviews in the post-Web group stage relied on the material students accessed through their online work.

The class was fairly heterogeneous, as the students had different levels of linguistic accuracy and fluency. Based on this, I developed a lesson plan to encompass three groups of learners: high proficiency, average proficiency, and low proficiency.

To provide instruction to all students at the same time while still meeting individual needs, I selected a common theme, Writing a Letter, and structured the lesson in a slightly different way for each level of learner. For example, students at the high level of proficiency would send a formal letter of complaint and students at the lower level sent an ecard inviting friends to join the fight for the cause.

I also provided different materials (e.g., from Amnesty International and Greenpeace) to meet the approximate language level of each group of students. In practical terms, the lesson was done in proficiency-based groups, with learners being given worksheets containing instructions and a list of URLs to use.

In summary, the lesson exploited the information gap created by

Reviving, Revising, or Revolutionising? Supplementing Coursebook Teaching With Internet-Based Instruction

273

introducing the element of variety and choice, which contributed significantly to the development of the students' communication skills. In addition, the lesson focused on technology and computer skills by teaching students how to effectively use interactive writing interfaces online. Most important, writing instruction was effectively combined with an increase in students' awareness of global issues. Appendix B shows the lesson plan and student tasks.

REFLECTIONS

Although developing each lesson plan was time-consuming, I did not feel overburdened. Because I had accessed the Web sites on previous occasions, my planning procedure focused on deciding what kinds of tasks could be accomplished using the Web sites rather than searching for and evaluating online resources. I spent more time designing the pre-Web and post-Web stages, making sure the activities were properly integrated with the coursebook lessons and that the vocabulary and structures were used in authentic language exchanges.

I knew it was important to use activities and materials that would keep the students engaged over the course of the lesson. This goal was achieved mainly because the Internet offers a variety of materials and students were allowed choices when working online. Another motivating element was that the students could personalise the lesson content by taking on personal causes and engaging in protests. The range of protest topics was extensive; for example, students protested against the killing of animals for furs or violent treatment of football fans by the police. The level of student involvement was high because they were given several opportunities to be creative, as the Idea Wish List in Lesson 1 (see Appendix A) shows. Students proposed inventions ranging from a homework transmitter to an opposite-sex affection sensor to an instant mess transformer.

Based on the students' range of abilities, I sought to create three learning paths for Lesson 2 based on the three levels of proficiency (see Appendix B). Although all three groups studied the same topic, the materials they used differed in the lexical density, amount of text to read, type of input learners were exposed to (verbal versus visual), and type of response students were to produce (a letter of protest versus an animated e-card). By including three learning paths for the online stage and using the same pre- and post-stages for the entire class, I was able to individualise the instruction while meeting the needs of the class.

The execution of the lesson went as expected, although I should have allowed more time for the online stage. In particular, writing tasks can take longer if students have poor typing skills and insufficient familiarity with filling in interactive forms online; this can cause students to become frustrated and decrease their motivation.

Both lessons show how Internet-based instruction and regular coursebook teaching are strongly connected. Web-based instruction relies on previously taught structures, vocabulary, or writing genres, whereas coursebook instruction is developed on the basis of the information obtained from the Internet (e.g., "Prepare a one-page poster about the cause you have protested against"). The online tasks served as a stimulus and model for student production, especially those in Lesson 2. Much of the resulting work showed the depth of the students' involvement, both emotional in terms of content and linguistic as related to lexical and grammatical sophistication. The students' enthusiasm was visible not only in their willingness to create letters and e-cards, but, more importantly, in the quality of their work. This experience proved that customizing instruction (e.g., using an animated e-card to make choices about input and output) is a key element in effective language learning.

Student feedback was generally positive and highlighted the contribution of the Internet-based lessons to general learning and language learning. As Joanna, a student in the first lesson, commented, "The lesson was interesting, something completely new, and I learnt a lot of new things. Right after coming back home, I visited the sites again and read more about the inventions."

A student in the second lesson, Magda, noted the connection between what she had been doing in class and the world outside the classroom: "I know the Internet, and I use it quite often, but I did not know that I can send a real letter of protest which can save somebody's life. Now I feel proud of myself."

Appendix C shows comments, both positive and noting areas for improvement, from other students.

Designing, Adapting, and Evaluating Internet-Based Teaching

CONCEPTUALIZING THE CURRICULUM

For the two lessons described above, I began the process of adapting the regular secondary school curriculum to include Internet-based instruction by considering the rationale for the decision. As I have said, the usual starting point for conceptualizing the process is to consider the coursebook on the one hand and student needs on the other. Once I decided to supplement the regular curriculum with an external method or medium, I had

Reviving, Revising, or Revolutionising? Supplementing Coursebook Teaching With Internet-Based Instruction

275

to consider the needs of a particular class in relation to the coursebook. I looked at the following:

- syllabus type (grammar-oriented, task-based, lexical)
- balance of skills (receptive versus productive, oral versus written)
- amount of space devoted to skills work versus that given to grammar development
- amount of grammar work versus vocabulary focus
- quality and quantity of textual input
- variety and interest of topics of texts and units
- types of tasks and forms of work

It was clear that in the first classroom situation, the coursebook was outdated; thus, the coursebook text did not have the desired effect of motivating the students. On the other hand, the coursebook in the second classroom situation did not provide enough language input.

After evaluating the curriculum and the coursebook using the criteria above, I tried to ascertain what modifications were needed to make the instruction more comprehensive. I considered the following techniques of materials adaptation:

- omit, replace, add, and adapt (Grant, 1987)
- add, rewrite, replace, reorder, or reduce (Harmer, 2001)
- select, adapt, replace, and supplement (Acklam, 1994)

Thus, the teacher could modify the lesson by changing the materials used for a task to make the task more appealing to students while leaving the structure of the lesson intact (i.e., reviving the lesson).

Alternatively, the teacher could modify tasks to better suit a particular classroom context (i.e., revising). Finally, the teacher could completely change the lesson plan by selecting external materials and devising language tasks to realise the same aims (i.e., revolutionising). I decided to maintain a close relationship between the coursebook and the Internet-based instruction. In Lesson 1, I used a combination of coursebook tasks and Internet materials (reviving). In Lesson 2, I expanded the coursebook's content with additional materials and tasks (revising) based on the students' cognitive maturity, greater level of motivation, and higher proficiency level.

The next important decision was what mode of instruction to use: Web-based face-to-face in a regular classroom (in other words, students are in the classroom using Web materials under their teacher's guidance), fully online in a self-study mode, or regular teaching supplemented with online instruction.

I made the decision after analysing the logistical considerations; that is, determining the availability of computer resources at the school and the level of access students had to the Internet away from school. To avoid excluding the students who lacked Internet access outside school, I took great care to ensure limited self-study access after lessons under the supervision of an IT teacher or through a school-based IT club.

The ratio of regular coursebook instruction to Internet-based teaching was another crucial consideration. A thoughtful decision to use Web-based tasks to replace obsolete parts of a coursebook or to restructure the tasks to make them more authentic or current requires making Web-based instruction an integral part of the curriculum as well as a separate curricular thread that replaces or expands on parts of the coursebook. In Lesson 1, I decided to use Web-based lessons at irregular intervals on a remedial basis, when the obsolete character of the coursebook made classwork difficult or ineffective. In Lesson 2, the need to expand the impact of instruction in the classroom required me to construct an entirely Web-based curriculum component, with one Web-based lesson per unit (each unit having approximately eight coursebook lessons).

The selection of activity formats for Web-based lessons is another important part of the process, contrary to what is seen in some materials (see Gitsaki & Taylor, 2000). Internet use in the classroom cannot be limited to searching Web sites, extracting detailed information, and sharing the information with other students. The curriculum must include standard communicative language activities (e.g., dialogues, role-plays, simulations, multiple choice) as well as Web-based activities, such as interpersonal exchanges (keypal exchanges, electronic appearances, ask-an-expert), information collection and analysis (treasure hunts, telefield trips), Web publishing and editing (collaborative writing, class Web publishing), and online problem-solving (simulations, games, online research modules). Lessons 1 and 2 mainly used information collection analysis (treasure hunts) in the online Web stage and various types of communication activities in the offline stage.

CREATING AN INTERNET-BASED CURRICULAR SUPPLEMENT

Teachers can develop a curricular supplement using the following basic steps:

- Create a student profile based on a needs analysis.
- Analyse coursebook structures, topics, functions, and lexis, and devise corresponding Web-based ones.
- Formulate aims and prioritize them to decide which basic curriculum aspects require Web-based supplementation.
- Order topics and tasks in a syllabus.

Reviving, Revising, or Revolutionising? Supplementing Coursebook Teaching With Internet-Based Instruction

277

- Find and evaluate relevant materials (e.g., texts, recordings, activities, and resources).
- Match the materials with structures, topics, functions, and lexis.
- Create classroom tasks and language exercises.
- Develop full lesson plans.
- Ask colleagues to beta test the Web-based lesson.

The stage of formulating aims is reflected in the procedures used based on carefully selected materials. The aims of the Internet-based instruction must relate to the curriculum and be deeply grounded in the teaching programme. They should cover many areas, including

- language (e.g., developing students' communicative skills or having them use a given structure in a natural context)
- instruction, which could be general (e.g., learning how to make a group project) or computer-related (e.g., searching the Web and evaluating search results)
- cognition (e.g., expanding students' knowledge of the world and the culture of English-speaking countries)

The next step is to decide on the subject and content of the lesson. For Lesson 1, I tried to match the subject of the lesson to the overall subject of the learning station (i.e., a unit or module) so that vocabulary and structures introduced earlier were reinforced by online work and acquired lexis would fit in with previously gained knowledge. In Lesson 2, I added new content and guided the lesson into new areas to sustain the students' interest and motivation to work. When choosing a language focus, one must decide whether to introduce new language structures or lexis or provide additional practise in those already acquired. The choice of skills for students to practise reflects the aims adopted, both in terms of language skills and computer skills. After making these decisions, teachers should have a clear plan for the design stage, in which they will devise activities and select if students will work together as a class, in small groups, or in pairs. At this stage, designing activities is more a matter of wishful thinking and includes the teachers' expectations of materials they have not yet found. The search for appropriate materials can be executed in a variety of ways and methods, especially through

- keyword searches using English-speaking portals such as www.yahoo.com, www.lycos.com, www.excite.com, or www.yahooligans.com (child-related content) or using search engines such as www.google.com, www.altavista.com, www.hotbot.com, www.webcrawler.com, or www.metacrawler.com

- full-question searches using natural language portals (Ask.com, http://www.ask.com, or Ask for Kids, http://www.askforkids.com)
- directory searches using popular standard portals (e.g., Yahoo!) or children-focused portals (e.g., Yahooligans or LycosZone)
- link searches using English as a foreign language (EFL) or English as a second language (ESL) portal sites such as Dave's ESL Café (http://www.eslcafe.com/search/index.html) or *The Internet TESL Journal* (http://iteslj.org/links)

For sites used in Lesson 1 (IdeaFinder and Enchanted Learning), I used the keyword search at Yahooligans! and later an analysis of Yahooligans! directory results to decide which sites to use for the planned tasks and activities. In contrast, for Lesson 2, I obtained resources from a specialist discussion list, TESLCA-L (Computer Technology and TESL, http://www.hunter.cuny.edu/~tesl-l/branch.html) on which an activity based on Amnesty International appeals for action was proposed.

When evaluating and selecting sites for an Internet-based lesson, teachers must make sure that they allow for a variety of activities and give choices to students. Teachers should use a Web site that offers flexibility, allowing them to design a variety of tasks for different stages of the lesson.

A Web site is flexible if it offers a diversity of materials of parallel structure, has a balance of visual and textual input, and is easy to navigate. The site should also provide variety and choice; it should reflect the students' needs and involve students in the decision-making process. The IdeaFinder Web site was ideal because it has many parallel texts that different students can use to follow the same task.

Language control is not necessarily a key factor in the choice of materials because, in principle, the teacher should grade the task rather than the text. Thus, I wanted to expose students to authentic Web sites to increase their contact with the authentic target language materials. Using materials that are above the students' level, comprehensible input—which according to Krashen promotes acquisition (Krashen's i + 1, 1982)—can enhance students' awareness of incompleteness of linguistic message and help them learn to make inferences and contextual guesses. However, the tasks must be tailored to the students' language and cognitive levels. In Lesson 2, I devised ways to make the Amnesty International and Greenpeace Web sites accessible to all students, including those of a lower proficiency, by exploiting their visual appeal and overall meaning more than textual aspects and comprehension of details.

ANTICIPATING AND SOLVING PROBLEMS

When I began to plan an Internet-based thread to the curriculum, I was aware that the administration of the schools expected me to anticipate possible lesson management problems and to prepare for them in advance. Teachers can use the following steps to maximize the chances for a successful Web-based lesson:

- Add optional language activities to engage students if the Web site is slow in loading.
- Determine which activities can be omitted if time runs short.
- Plan additional activities or enhanced responsibilities (e.g., help other students, prepare a report, create or update a class Web site) for students who finish tasks early.
- Find additional sites that will enable similar tasks, and preview the selected sites just before the lesson begins to make sure the sites still exist, their layout has not changed significantly, and that they will still enable students to accomplish the task.
- Prepare alternative low-tech solutions (e.g., handouts containing some of the content) in case of technical problems.

Teachers should continuously evaluate the materials they have chosen and revise them when necessary. The goal is to ensure the activities and sites are fully applicable and valid before the lesson begins. I always check the selected Web sites well beforehand and then check again 2–3 days before the actual lesson begins. I also save Web pages so they can be used through the local area network if the remote server breaks down. I try to choose Web sites (e.g., those of organisations, government agencies, and major commercial enterprises) that are likely to continue to exist on the Internet with their URL unchanged. I designed Lesson 1 so that it did not require the use of a particular feature (e.g., a specific picture) of a Web page. Lesson 1 addressed a general idea that could be studied using other resources.

Another consideration is that some teachers may not be confident of their IT skills. This can cause problems because an Internet-based lesson can involve occasional IT teaching. Other factors can make teachers wary of implementing Internet-based instruction in the curriculum. For example, teachers may not have adequate knowledge of the Web or effective troubleshooting strategies (e.g., how to handle access problems or pop-up ads). Problems can also arise when teachers do not properly preview materials. The solution depends on the context. For example, a frequent practise in Polish schools is for teachers to teach collaborative lessons, with the language teacher responsible for subject content and the IT teacher for the computer skills necessary to complete the lesson. For Lessons 1 and 2, I teamed with the IT teacher to give students' specific computer training that would also give them the skills they needed for lessons in regular classes.

In Web-based learning, control of content is of great importance. In contrast to the coursebook, which is more likely to provide correct and appropriate materials, the Internet has the potential to be unsafe and intimidating, providing information that can be falsely perceived by some students. The temptation to access inappropriate sexually-oriented or violence-promoting materials need not simply be eradicated; it must also be countered with a clear preventive programme. This requires teachers to exercise control before, during, and after the lesson.

Control before the lesson can be exercised through a "software approach" (Dudeney, 2000, p. 35) that is, by using dedicated censorware such as CyberPatrol (http://www.cyberpatrol.com) or Net Nanny (http://www.netnanny.com) to block access to sites containing specified words. Control during the lesson requires teachers to take an active role by walking around and monitoring what students are doing on the computer screen and, if possible, by using lab management software to view the students' screens. Control after the lesson should be based on monitoring the history feature of the Internet browser as well as the computer's hard disk to ascertain what sites the students accessed while performing the task, and more important, whether they used potentially unsafe or prohibited materials.

DEVELOPING TEACHER SKILLS

Today's dynamics and environment make it mandatory for language teachers to expand their IT and Web knowledge and skills. One way to do this is to engage in self-study teacher training using online ICT tutorials. The following list provides some sources for such training:

- ICT4LT, available at http://www.ict4lt.org
- Power to Learn—Teaching with Technology, available at http://www.powertolearn.com/articles/teaching_with_technology/
- *The Internet TESL Journal*, available at http://iteslj.org/links
- Teaching English with Technology, available at http://www.iatefl.org.pl/call/callnl.htm

Teachers can also receive IT and Web training by participating in online discussion groups, especially those of online communities of practise, such as Webheads in Action (http://groups.yahoo.com/group/evonline2002_webheads/). Another great source of teacher training opportunities in the area of computer-assisted language learning is Electronic Village Online workshops (http://www.geocities.com/ehansonsmi/evo2005/announce.html). The site offers workshops covering a wide range of technology-related topics (e.g., blogs, building a Web presence, using course management systems, and podcasting). The workshops usually last a few weeks, during which time participants read materials, exchange e-mails, share samples of their work, and take online quizzes. I benefited from all of these training venues, finding inspiration for Web-based tasks and identifying appropriate Web sites for educational use. I also used Internet lesson plans published in the *Teaching English with Technology* electronic journal to help me design my lessons plan.

Conclusion

Today, the widespread availability of electronic media makes contact with the target language much easier. Thus, language teachers must critically evaluate available curricula and coursebooks and reflect on how applicable they are in relation to the specific needs of their students. Teachers can use the Internet to construct Web-based face-to-face lessons that make individualised instruction easier to achieve. The future may bring more flexible approaches in which teachers can use a coursebook as a common platform in the traditional mode or as an online resource.

Based on the experiences I describe in this chapter, I discovered that the most important elements of the teaching process are a critical evaluation of existing materials and reflection on the extent to which the materials satisfy the requirements of the teaching context, the students, the parents, and the school's administration. Teachers who view the Internet as a reservoir of authentic materials that are available in a variety of modes and ways will be liberated from the constraints imposed by coursebooks, allowing them to truly individualise their language instruction.

Another important reason for using Web-based instruction in an EFL context is to enhance the teachers' language proficiency and language awareness. In many schools in Poland, nonnative teachers of English, sharing the same mother tongue as most of their students, have limited language competency; that is, they lack extensive vocabulary and appropriate language use. With the use of the Internet as a medium for classroom instruction, teachers expose students to authentic language use and to a wider range of language expressions than that available in a coursebook. Another factor that motivates teachers in Poland to use the Internet for English language teaching is the external requirement imposed on teachers by Polish educational regulations. Under the regulations, teachers who want to be promoted to the next rank of the teacher development system must demonstrate effective use of IT and Web tools in teaching their subject.

Turning to the students, Internet-based instruction (especially the use of computer-mediated communication tools in collaborative projects) gives a real communicative purpose to target language use, especially in homogeneous classes as in Poland, where virtually all students and teachers share the same native language. Web-based teaching can open the classroom to the world, encourage natural use of the target language, and provide opportunities for cooperation with other classes. By doing so, Web-based programs address the educational priorities of the European Union.[1] Authentic target language opportunities, when brought to mainly homogenous language classes through involvement in Web-based collaborative projects such as eTwinning Action (http://www.etwinning.net), can significantly influence the effectiveness of the language teaching process.

In addition to the important issues outlined in this chapter, goals imposed by the Ministry of National Education-formulated Core Curriculum in Poland influence any decision to adopt an Internet-enhanced curriculum. These goals require the teacher to, among other things,

- expose learners to authentic materials, if possible, of a multimedia kind
- give students the opportunity for target language use by enabling inter-school collaboration. The widespread implementation of the European Schoolnet portal (http://www.eun.org), with its partner finding opportunities was continued in the eTwinning Action of the eLearning Programme (http://www.etwinning.net), which was launched in 2005. The programme officially encourages teachers to start partnerships to achieve a variety of teaching goals.
- introduce elements of learner autonomy
- enable learners to use the target language as a tool to accomplish interdisciplinary projects
- develop attitudes of curiosity, openness, and tolerance toward other cultures

Based on the issues a secondary school foreign language programme must address, as specified by the Core Curriculum in Poland, an Internet-based component can help teachers and students

- successfully integrate all language skills
- use the language in authentic situations and different registers and modes
- develop a wider knowledge and appreciation of the target language culture
- effectively comprehend authentic media discourse
- search, select, and organize information in authentic utterances

---

[1] Pan-European class partnerships have been the focus of European Union authorities for some time.

- develop individualised learning skills, including the proper use of reference sources (e.g., dictionaries, encyclopaedias, and glossaries) and information resources (e.g., multimedia and the Internet)

A final and equally important reason to adopt Internet-based instruction is to provide students with many skills in various areas, not only in linguistic competence. The IT and Web skills involved in Internet-based learning, such as browsing the Web, evaluating Internet materials, skimming/scanning Web sites for information, composing different genres of text, and processing information to respond orally, will be very useful to students after they leave school.

The process of curriculum evaluation and improvement makes substantial demands on the teacher in terms of time, effort, familiarity with the Internet, and level of computer skills. The process also requires investment in these areas. In the long run, however, the investment in time and resources will pay off in greater teacher autonomy and awareness of the educational process.

In the future, although all teachers may not choose to construct a curriculum and develop teaching materials on their own, they will have the knowledge base to proceed with curriculum improvement through Internet-based instruction.

Appendix A: Internet Lesson 1—Inventions

I. Introduction

1. Learners were divided into groups. They were to put these things in the order from the most to the least useful: bubble gum, theory of relativity, printing press, Kellogg's Corn Flakes, Hula Hoop, tea, can opener

2. Then they matched the inventors to the inventions: Walter E. Diemer (bubble gum); Albert Einstein (theory of relativity); Johann Gutenberg (printing press); Will Keith Kellogg (Kellogg's Corn Flakes); Richard P. Knerr (Hula Hoop); Emperor Shen Nung (tea); Ezra Warner (can opener)

II. Internet Work

1. One part of the class used the Internet to check the answers in example 2 above using the following steps:

    *   went to IdeaFinder (http://www.ideafinder.com/history)
    *   clicked "Enter," and then "History facts and myths" on the left in the menu, "Inventor profile" (or went directly to http://www.enchantedlearning.com/inventors).

2. While browsing the Web sites, students completed the table below by inserting a few inventors' names and the years of their inventions:

	Invention 1	Invention 2	Invention 3	Invention 4
Inventions that help us expand our knowledge of the universe				
Inventions that help us live healthier and longer lives				
Inventions that help us communicate with one another				
Inventions that make our lives easier				
Inventions that entertain us				
Inventions that take us from one place to another				

They then went to http://www.worldalmanacforkids.com /explore/inventions.html and to see how many of their answers matched.

3. The class then

    *   went to http://www.ideafinder.com
    *   clicked on "Enter" and then "Idea showcase" on the left of the page and then "Idea wish list" (or go directly to http://www.ideafinder.com/showcase/wishlist.htm).

Students read the wishes and identified the three they believed to be the most necessary.

Wish 1	I wish…
Wish 2	I wish…
Wish 3	I wish…

4. Learners were asked to think about the things that they would really like to be invented. They worked in pairs and created a description

   I wish I had…
   It would be a thing that we could use to…
   It would help us do…

   They were asked to imagine that another student is a famous inventor and ask questions using the present simple and present continuous tenses to learn as much as possible about the life of the "famous inventor."

5. Students scrolled down the "Idea wish list" page (http://www .ideafinder.com/showcase/wishlist.htm) and clicked "If you didn't find it here, then tell us what consumer product you wish were available. You can enter a wish here." (or they went directly to http://www.ideafinder.com/forms/q-feedback.htm).
   They entered the wish in the box provided, and clicked "Agree and Submit." Students did not have to put in personal information if they did not wish to do so.

III. Homework

1. The teacher collected the Idea wish list from the whole class and displayed it on the board.

Appendix B: Internet-Based Lesson 2— Campaigning Online

I. Introduction

1. Students were asked what they remembered about Pankhurst, Havel, Mandela, and King and what causes they were fighting for or against.

    He/she was a...
    He/she lived in...
    He/she campaigned/fought for...
    Animal rights, freedom of speech, women's rights, racism, slavery

2. Students worked in pairs and brainstormed the causes, methods of action, and place of action of Amnesty International, Greenpeace, and the World Wildlife Fund.

3. Learners were asked to give some basic structures for writing a letter of complaint, similar to the ones below:

    *   I am writing to protest against...
    *   I am writing to express my dissatisfaction at...
    *   I would like to ask you to consider changing your policy and stopping...

4. The teacher asked students about their personal convictions and whether there were any causes they would like to fight for.

II. Internet Work

1. The lesson was flexible for use with more and less proficient classes; the language level of Web sites determined the difficulty level of tasks. The more proficient part of the class

    *   went to the Amnesty International Web site (http://www .amnesty.org),
    *   opened up "Appeals for Action" from "Quick Launch Bar" on the right at the top of the page (or went directly to http://www. amnesty.org/en/how-you-can-help)
    *   read short descriptions of causes and chose the one that was closest to the student's convictions (when necessary, they also read "Other Appeals" at bottom of the page)
    *   read the description of a selected cause and used a dictionary to look up key words

- took action to protest against the cause by
  — copying and pasting the letter provided
  — logging in to their e-mail accounts
  — sending the letter by e-mail or the regular postal service to the address provided
  — or read the letter provided and signed the petition under it by typing in the first name, family name, e-mail, selecting the country, and clicking "Sign Now"

The less proficient students:

- went to the Action Centre of the Greenpeace Web site (note: Web site is no longer available)
- clicked "more" for the cause they would like to read about
- clicked the link to send an e-card to their friends asking them to join the campaign
- typed in their name, e-mail address, selected the country, and introduced the personal message
- typed in the recipient's e-mail addresses and clicked "Send E-Card"

The lowest level students:

- went to the Action Centre of the Greenpeace Web site
- chose one of the e-cards (on the right hand side of the page) to send
- typed in their first and family name, country, and personal message, then clicked "Proceed to Step Two"
- entered the e-mail addresses of recipients and clicked "Send E-Card"

2. Students completed the following table with the information about the cause chosen:

	Student A	Student B
The Web site visited		
The cause		
The country		
The person/institution addressed		
My personal feelings about the cause		

III. GroupWork

1. Students interviewed their partner about their campaigns and completed the table above for Student B.

   - Which Web site did you visit?
   - What did you protest against/for?
   - What is the problem about?
   - Where/who did you write to?
   - What do you think about the cause?

IV. Homework

1. Learners prepared a one-page poster about the issue they wanted to protest against following these directions:

   - Create a title using a large font.
   - Include a picture.
   - Add some text of your own.
   - Write what people can do (write a letter) to help.
   - Give the address to which they can send their protests.

Appendix C: Sample Student Comments on the Two Lessons

Lesson 1 *(author's translations from Polish)*

"I liked the idea of using the Internet for an English lesson. I think it is a new and interesting way of learning. It was nice to learn about some of the inventions which are around us, especially my favourite—chewing gum."

—Ewa

"The lesson was interesting, something completely new, and I learnt a lot of new things. Right after coming back home I visited the sites again and read more about the inventions."

—Joanna

"I thought the Internet Web sites would be too difficult to understand, and I was surprised I could understand a lot. However, there were still some words I did not know."

—Bartek

Reviving, Revising, or Revolutionising? Supplementing Coursebook Teaching With Internet-Based Instruction

289

"The lesson was fine, but I think we did not have enough time to spend on all the activities. The teacher made us do the activities quicker, and I wanted to read the texts again. I think such Internet lessons should cover two classroom periods."

—Jan

Lesson 2 *(original comments in English)*

"I know the Internet and I use it quite often, but I did not know that I can send a real letter of protest which can save somebody's life. Now I feel proud of myself."

—Magda

"The teacher divided us into three groups of different levels. I was in the lowest, and I had to send an electronic card. I think it was unfair, as the best group did a much more interesting and important task."

—Piotr

"I liked the lesson, as I could read and talk about real people and their fight for human rights. Perhaps we could do such things more often, and for example listen to speeches of famous people as well."

—Iza

"Writing is not my favourite task, and I was glad I can work on writing a formal letter. However, I think that we should not write letters in class as we did not have enough time. The teacher should give letter writing as homework."

—Karolina

Learning English in China for Today: Revitalizing a Curriculum Through Task-Based Learning

13

RONGGAN ZHANG

English as a foreign language (EFL) has been taught in schools in China since 1902 (Curriculum and Teaching Materials Research Institute, 2001). Previously, most students of English learned the language for unspecified future needs. The world has changed, however, and in China today the English language is no longer confined to the classroom. Rather, English plays a part in EFL learners' daily lives, especially in large cities. Nevertheless, English use in the classroom is different from its use in the outside world. Classroom language activities have specific pedagogic goals and features, whereas language use outside the school is not mediated by instruction.

This chapter describes the reality of English use in China and examines how introducing tasks into the EFL classroom helped learners make use of the resources available to them to increase their English knowledge and skills. I first examine the changed EFL context in China and review the existing curriculum and teaching methods. I then outline how I introduced tasks into my teaching process as a way of addressing what I saw as deficiencies in the existing curriculum. Last, I discuss how the task-based supplement revitalized the curriculum.

Learning English for Today

In the field of education today, the concept that life within the classroom and life outside the classroom should not be separated is commonplace. A century ago, John Dewey stated his position on "education as a necessity of life" (1916, Ch. 1) and said "that the school must represent present life—life as real and vital to the child as that which he carries on in the home, in the neighborhood, or on the playground" (1897, Article II, para. 3). Researchers in China today (e.g., Guo, 2000; Lu, 2004) also advocate a return to real-life needs for classroom learners.

The Changed Scenario: The Motivation for Classroom Revitalization

In recent years, China has emerged as one of the largest and fastest-growing economies in the world, becoming ever more open and a dynamic participant in the global economy. With this has come considerable improvement in the average living standards. As Chinese society has changed with the economy and globalisation, the scenario for EFL learning has changed significantly from what it was even one or two decades ago. For example, consider the school at which I have worked as an EFL teacher for more than 12 years. The school has more than 200 staff members and 2,000 students. A decade ago, there were only two telephones for use by the entire school, and hardly anyone had heard of the Internet. Today, like many other schools in the city of Guangzhou, our school has a campus Web site. It also has four computer labs with more than 250 computers and one electronic reading room with 60 seats. All the labs, as well as all other classrooms, have access to the Internet. Outside the classroom, today's Chinese EFL learners have access to more English resources than ever before. In addition to the Internet, English newspapers, magazines, books, films, and television and radio programmes are widely available. English language classes and schools are flourishing, most of which make a profit from the "national obsession" ("Is English Skill That Important?," 2004, para. 1) with learning English. As the *Shanghai Star* ("English Patients," 2002, para. 27) notes, "Reports show that ESL has become a 10-billion-yuan business in China." This is most evident in large cities such as Guangzhou, which has one of the strongest economies in China. For example, within 3 kilometres of my school are two modern cinemas that show Hollywood films in English with Chinese captions. Guangzhou is close to Hong Kong, and many households have cable television and receive two Hong Kong channels in English.

Also noteworthy is that each year, more than 10 million visitors come to China, approximately 25% of whom visit Guangdong Province (National Bureau of Statistics of China, 2004). Thus, EFL learners, especially those in large cities such as the provincial capital of Guangzhou, are more likely to have contact with foreigners in public places, at school, and even at home. Every year, at least two international exchange programmes send students from my school to English-speaking countries or place foreign learners in students' homes in Guangzhou. Many foreigners work or live in China, and they often visit their Chinese colleagues or neighbours. Thus, many EFL learners must communicate with native English speakers face to face.

As the world economy becomes increasingly globalised and English assumes the position of a global language, products labelled in English or in both Chinese and English are easily found in stores in today's China. The use of some products, such as computer software and digital cameras, requires knowledge of the English language.

In summary, the English language in China today is no longer confined to the classroom. Rather, English has a high profile in the daily lives of EFL learners, especially those in large cities. The responses of grade 11 students to a September 2005 survey question about how the English language manifests itself in students' lives outside of school confirmed the importance of English in China today (see Overall section in Table 1 for the students' general responses).

Thus, EFL learners in China have many opportunities to learn English and to use the language in their daily lives. Even so, some EFL learners may not know about or take advantage of these resources or opportunities. For example, only 58.3% of grade 11 respondents to the survey were aware of the availability of English Web sites (see Table 1, question 10), even though the school provides easy access to the Internet. In contrast, responses to another questionnaire showed that 81.3% of students of the same age in the same school reported having access to the Internet at home or at school (Zhang, 2004). These surveys show that some students surf Chinese Web sites only and have no idea that the world of English is a click away. These students thus lose out on a potentially significant language learning resource.

The Existing Curriculum and Teaching Methods

My motivation for revitalizing the curriculum for my classes stemmed from a realization that the existing curriculum did not take advantage of the available resources and opportunities to help students use English in a context beyond the school. The main emphasis was on future needs rather than current ones. In 2001, the Ministry of Education (MOE) issued new English curriculum guidelines for compulsory education (including primary and junior high schools) and senior high schools (MOE, 2001) and in 2003, issued additional guidelines for senior high schools (MOE, 2003). The MOE documents state that foreign language education in primary and secondary schools is "to satisfy the school graduates' needs to obtain employment, to go to college, and to survive future living" (MOE, 2003, p. 1); that is, "to lay a solid foundation for their lifelong learning and development"

Table 1. Responses to Question 6, "In What Ways Does English Language Manifest Itself in Your Life Outside School?"

No.	Choice	Response Rate (%)			
		Controls	Group 1	Group 2	Overall
1.	Contacts with foreigners visiting your family	17.3	12.9	10.0	14.6
2.	Contacts with foreigners visiting your school	9.6	6.5	5.0	7.8
3.	Communication with foreign teachers	34.8	45.2	40.0	38.8
4.	Contacts with foreigners met in public places	23.1	16.1	10.0	18.4
5.	Communication with relatives abroad	13.5	9.7	0.0	9.7
6.	Communication with pen pals abroad	13.5	22.6	25.0	18.4
7.	Online English forum/communities	19.2	19.4	30.0	21.4
8.	Travelling/visiting relatives abroad	19.2	38.7	25.0	26.2
9.	International exchange programmes	11.5	6.5	10.0	9.7
10.	English Web sites	46.2	77.4	60.0	58.3
11.	English television	76.9	77.4	80.0	77.7
12.	English broadcasts	25.0	38.7	50.0	35.0
13.	English novels	32.7	58.1	45.0	42.7
14.	English newspapers	61.5	67.7	65.0	64.1
15.	English magazines	38.5	41.9	50.0	41.7
16.	English movies	86.5	87.1	90.0	87.4
17.	English songs	90.4	93.5	75.0	88.3
18.	English in advertisements	57.7	77.4	60.0	64.1
19.	English on merchandise	48.1	74.2	55.0	57.3
20.	IELTS/TOEFL	3.8	0.0	5.0	2.9
21.	Applying to a foreign school	3.8	0.0	5.0	2.9
22.	Open-ended choice (not tabulated)	5.8	3.2	5.0	4.9

Note. N for controls = 52; N for Group 1 = 31; N for Group 2 = 20; N for overall = 103

(MOE, 2001, p. 2), indicating a perspective of *learning English for tomorrow* and relatively less interest in *learning English for today*. A closer look at the guidelines, however, shows that one learning strategy goal is for students to use resources such as the Internet to learn English and that a general goal is to be able communicate with English-speaking persons about familiar topics.

Following these official guidelines, the English coursebooks are designed more to meet goals for learning English for future needs than for learning English to use today. As an example, *Senior English for China: Student's Book, 2A* (2004a), the most widely used English coursebook in senior high school, claims to "be close to modern life" (*Senior English for China: Teacher's Book, 2A,* 2004b, p. i) and "have fully taken learners' interest and needs into consideration" (p. v). Thus, the coursebook has information on the latest developments in science and technology as well as an introduction to U. S. country music. A closer look, however, shows that the text is more a simplified encyclopaedia in English than an EFL coursebook, providing the thickest English coursebook for senior high schools ever!

For example, the goal for the coursebook's unit on news media is not to learn to gather information from the English news media but to "talk about news and the media" (*Senior English for China: Student's Book*, 2004a, p. 9). This is illustrated in the writing activity for this goal: "Write a paragraph in which you compare two kinds of media, for example websites and newspapers" (p. 16). The coursebook seems designed to prepare EFL learners to form opinions about the news media but not to prepare them to surf English Web sites or watch and understand English language television. It does not seem to respond to the changed EFL scenario in the learners' daily lives.

Furthermore, education in China is still test-oriented, although in recent years authorities have been encouraging quality education aimed at all-round development (see e.g., Wang, 2004). Most notable is the influence of the Matriculation Tests on teaching and learning in senior high schools. Listening comprehension, for example, accounts for 20% of the Matriculation English Test (MET; National Education Examinations Authority of Ministry of Education, 2005). Thus, senior high school students must complete MET mock listening exercises at least once a week from the day they enter the school. The MET, however, does not seem to have a learning-for-today perspective. For example, it has no oral tests, although many senior high school students are placed in situations in which they communicate with foreigners. Also, the MET does not include items that test the students' ability to use the Internet for English resources, although the Internet is readily available to the students.

The previous sections have demonstrated that the existing English curriculum and teaching methods do not place much emphasis on learning for today, thus failing to respond to the greatly changed EFL context in China. As a post by "liutuo1234" on an online forum notes, the school "teaches and encourages elite English instead of practical one" ("Is English Skill That Important?," 2004, para. 1).

Using Tasks in the Classroom

In my experience, an EFL learner's attention must be directed to English language resources and opportunities for using English outside of school before he or she gains the ability to notice and take advantage of them independently. Learners need a reason to make use of these resources and opportunities; that is, they need a purpose and a situation in which to use English outside the classroom. One way to motivate EFL learners to use English is through tasks that "provide a vehicle for the presentation of appropriate target language samples to learners . . . and for the delivery of comprehension and production opportunities" (Long & Crookes, 1992, p. 43). Tasks give learners a purpose for using the target language in specific situations, which encourages them to make use of available English language resources or to take advantage of opportunities to use English in their daily lives. I believe tasks can be helpful in teaching English in China, where English language resources and opportunities to use English outside the classroom are now available to many learners.

ADDRESSING THE CHALLENGES

Introducing tasks into EFL teaching in a Chinese senior high school is not as simple as designing a task and presenting it to the class the next day. There are challenges.

One problem with task-based learning and teaching (TBLT) is finiteness (Long & Crookes, 1992), with tasks overlapping one another. Some tasks could or will involve others. For example, inviting a foreigner to dinner requires extending the invitation, giving directions to the restaurant, ordering food in the restaurant, and so on. Some of these sub-tasks can be broken down further; for example, ordering food could be divided into explaining the different dishes and asking the guest for ideas about the dishes. This can be challenging because introducing tasks into the classroom requires the teacher to decide where one task ends and the next begins.

Another problem involves the task cycle. Researchers have proposed different task cycles or frameworks for designing task-based lessons (e.g., Ellis, 2003; Lu & Zhang, 2005; Skehan, 1996, 1998; Willis, 1996). They all, as Ellis (2003) notes, have in common three principal phases: a pre-task, a during-task, and a post-task phase. Although only the during-task phase is obligatory, options in the pre-task or post-task phases also "serve a crucial role in ensuring that the task performance is maximally effective for language development" (Ellis, 2003, p. 243). In other words, the nonobligatory phases should not be left out. Take the post-task phase for example. Willis (1996), among others, suggests that the post-task phase should include some language-focus activities (e.g., language analysis and practice), which have long been considered essential in the "listener-oriented" and "teacher-controlled" (Jin & Cortazzi, 1998, pp.746–747) classrooms in China. It thus seems essential to include a full, rather than a partial, task cycle when introducing tasks into an EFL classroom in China. It is difficult, however, to predict how much time a full task cycle will take. Can the task be completed in 40 or 45 minutes, the normal duration of a class in China, or will it have to be spread over several lessons?

With limited available class time, the coursebook brings challenges, too. At my senior high school I, like many others, have to keep pace with my colleagues. I must finish teaching certain units and cover certain content in the coursebook by a set date, whatever teaching approach I use. In the teaching year I discuss in this chapter, I had six or seven 40-minute periods of class time (240 or 280 minutes) to cover one unit. One unit of the coursebook includes 11 sections in the student's book, *Senior English for China: Student's Book, 2A* (2004a). The sections are Goals, Warming Up, Listening, Speaking, Pre-reading, Reading, Post-reading, Language Study, Integrating Skills, Tips, and Checkpoint. The Workbook has six additional sections: Listening, Talking, Practising, Integrating Skills, a Project (for every three units), and Assessing. Altogether, these provide at least two listening, two speaking, three reading, and two writing activities. The teacher's book, *Senior English for China: Teacher's Book, 2A* (2004b), encourages creative use of the coursebook. Although theoretically teachers do not have to cover everything in the coursebook, in practice, there are few sections teachers can skip. It is a common understanding that China has a learning culture of respecting coursebooks as the authority, and teachers are expected to add something to rather than to skip anything in the book. So as I tried to introduce tasks into the classroom, I also had to cover what my department and my students expected me to teach in the class.

Well aware of all of the challenges, I introduced tasks into my classroom by designing a Task of the Unit. I designed a Task of the Unit (TU) according to the topic of the unit being taught in the coursebook (Zhang, 2003). Learners were given the option of working on the TU in groups or individually in or out of class. After the unit was taught in the classroom, students were asked to hand in a written report or give an oral report that discussed their TU outcomes. Each task began when a particular coursebook unit was introduced in class and ended when the unit was finished. When the unit changed, the TU also changed. Learners then had more than 1 week to work on the TU as the teacher worked through the unit in the class at the same speed as his or her colleagues. In class, subtasks involving different coursebook activities were introduced to help learners achieve their TU outcomes. Outside of class, learners were to use all available real-world English resources to reach their TU outcomes. In other words, the TU was not limited to 40 or 45 minutes of class time or to a small room in the school building. Rather, the TU expanded to the world beyond the classroom.

WORKING WITH A TASK OF THE UNIT

In this section, I use the TU for Unit 7 of the coursebook, Living with Disease, to illustrate how I used TUs to motivate students to learn English for use not only in the classroom but also in their daily lives. (Appendix A shows all the TUs used in the study.)

TU: Living with Disease

The Living with Disease unit was introduced to the class in the week preceding World AIDS Day (December 1, 2004). With this in mind, I designed a TU in which learners were to organise an activity for World AIDS Day 2004 on campus or in the community and then hand in a report. In the classroom, I organised several subtasks for the TU to help learners achieve the TU goals while completing the required coursebook activities.

First, I invited students to discuss the diseases that currently afflict human beings and to define frequently seen acronyms (e.g., HIV, AIDS, and SARS). I then asked them to discuss what people can do to help fight these diseases. I combined these exercises with two coursebook activities (*Senior English for China: Teacher's Book, 2A*, 2004b): a role-play speaking activity "in which the students have to decide which social problem is the most serious" (p. 151) and a listening activity about a "disease detective" from the Center for Disease Control and Prevention describing her job and the way in which she works (p. 151). At the end of this period, I showed the class a Web page from www.unaids.org about World AIDS Day 2004 and asked them to find a key piece of information; that is, that World AIDS Day 2004 was to be held on December 1. Then, I presented the TU to the class.

For the next 5 days, learners discussed what types of activities they could organise for World AIDS Day. They suggested four activities:

- Conduct a survey.
- Tell a real story about the fight against AIDS.
- Interview a doctor or expert about AIDS.
- Present facts about AIDS to others.

Along with these, students partook in the following coursebook activities:

- Take a quiz about HIV/AIDS.
- Role play a meeting during which a decision is made about whether a student with HIV will be allowed to stay in school.
- Listen to an interview with a doctor regarding HIV/AIDS.
- Read two stories, one about a 12-year-old girl fighting AIDS and the other about how a person found out she had cancer and how she learned to live with the disease.
- Read a passage describing the HIV/AIDS situation in sub-Saharan Africa.
- Write about what problems young people living with HIV/AIDS may have.

Sample TU Results

I chose this TU as an example mainly because it dealt with a situation of great importance in the learners' real lives and because it required learners to participate in a meaningful activity in the community. To quote the learners' words, they did some "valuable things" (personal communication, December 5, 2004) as they worked through the task. This TU took language learning beyond the classroom and my students seemed more motivated. The TU, as all the TUs, was effective in engaging learners and encouraging them to use available English resources and take opportunities to use English in their daily lives. In addition, this TU was designed so learners had to use English resources to achieve their TU outcomes; that is, a report in English about their World AIDS Day activities. For example, learners had to use the Internet to access English resources about World AIDS Day 2004 or to learn how to express ideas about AIDS in English to prepare an English version of their fliers.

In their reports on the activities they organised for World AIDS Day, most learners explicitly stated that they surfed the Internet for information about HIV/AIDS before they prepared their task outcomes. Their activities included handing out fliers and giving public speeches in the community, doing a survey on campus, interviewing doctors at local hospitals, and sending facts about HIV/AIDS to friends and strangers by e-mail and instant messaging. Appendix B shows one group's report of an interview with an expert on AIDS.

Can Tasks Help Students Learn English in China?

THE STUDY

I started to use TUs in my classes in the late 1990s. Then, from 2004 through 2005, I conducted a systematic 1-year study of learners' perceptions of TUs. In this section, I discuss the results of the study, focusing on whether TUs helped learners notice and use the English language resources in their environment and take advantage of opportunities to use English outside the classroom.

THE SCHOOL AND THE PARTICIPANTS

I conducted the study in the senior high school at which I teach. This prestigious provincial high school has approximately 2,000 students. Every year, approximately 88% of graduates are admitted to key (first-tier) universities in China, and an additional 11% proceed to other universities and colleges. As I noted earlier, the school enjoys advanced facilities and frequent exchanges with schools and organisations in English-speaking countries. My study involved more than 100 students from the two Grade 11 classes that I taught from September 2004 to January 2005, the first semester of year 2004–2005. In the second semester (February to July 2005), the classes were rearranged, and the participants were placed in different classes. I taught some of the classes following TBLT, and other teachers taught other classes using more traditional methods. After the second semester, I designed and administered a questionnaire.

The rearrangement of the classes was not done for my study but was the result of an administrative decision made to cope with a new system of college entrance examinations. The rearrangement, however, aided my research as it resulted in two groups of participants for my study. Group 1 included students I taught during the first, but not the second, semester. Group 2 was made up of students I taught for both semesters. Another group served as a control and was composed of students I did not teach during that school year. Students in Groups 1 and 2 are called *participants* in my discussion of the study and its results.

THE QUESTIONNAIRE

The questionnaire I developed had eight questions, seven multiple choice and one open-ended. Questions 1, 6, and 8 are most relevant to this discussion. I designed Question 1 and the open-ended question, Question 8, to determine whether the participants found TUs more relevant to their daily lives than the control group found their assignments to be relevant to their daily lives. Question 6 dealt with awareness of the ways the English language might manifest itself in the students' lives outside class.

I first wrote the questionnaire for the participant groups and based on that, prepared the questionnaire for the control group by changing the term *TUs* to *assignments* in Grade 11. I changed other text; for example, I changed the statement for Question 1 from "For me, TUs meant . . ." to "For me, assignments in Grade 11 meant . . . ." Both questionnaires were in Chinese, not in English, so that English proficiency or a lack of proficiency, which was not being evaluated, would not affect the results.

The participants and the control group completed the questionnaire together in their classrooms; I served as the organiser. A total of 51 participants and 125 control group students returned valid questionnaires; I included a random selection of 52 controls for analysis. Of the 51 participants, 31 were in Group 1 (students in my class for first semester only) and 20 were in Group 2 (students I taught the entire school year).

The participants completed the questionnaires in their first month of Grade 12, 7 months after the first semester of Grade 11, when TUs were used as part of the teaching process. This allowed an interval of 7 months and 2 months, respectively, for participants in Group 1 and Group 2 to reflect on the TUs and their EFL class.

THE RESULTS

In the next section, I examine the questionnaire results from two perspectives: the TUs' relevance to students' daily life and students' awareness of English resources and opportunities in the environment.

Relevance to Real Life

Question 1 was multiple choice with 22 choices, among which 4 choices (19–21) fell into the category, Relevance to Real Life. The question asked the 51 participants and the 52 controls what TUs or homework assignments in Grade 11 meant to them. Similar percentages of controls (17.3%) and participants (23.5%) chose choice 19, *using English in real life*. However, significantly less participants (5.9% and 3.9% respectively) than the controls (28.8% and 21.2% respectively) responded to choices 20 (*not using English in real life*) and 22 (*learning English irrelevant to real life*). For choice 21 (*learning English relevant to real life*), the difference also reached significance with 60.8% of the participants and 34.6% of the controls responding to the choice. The results from choices 20, 21, and 22 suggested that the participants were more likely to agree that TUs were relevant to their real life, while those in the control group tended to agree that their homework assignments were irrelevant to real life.

Question 8 was open-ended and asked students if they were teachers whether or not they would include TUs in their class. Thirty-six of the 51 participants (70.6%) provided reasons that fell into the category of Relevance to Real Life; that is, they related TUs to their real life. This lent support to the results for Question 1.

Awareness of English Resources and Opportunities Outside the School
Question 6 asked respondents to choose from 21 choices which English resources and opportunities they were aware of outside the school. (See Table 1 for complete results.) The results showed that significantly more participants than controls had noticed such English resources and opportunities as English Web sites, English broadcast, and English novels. Also noteworthy is that more participants than controls were aware of English merchandise, with the difference close to significance.

DISCUSSION

Based on my experience using TUs in the classroom and the results of my study, I believe TUs can help make up for deficiencies in the curriculum and teaching methods and thus revitalize the curriculum. I believe TUs can be particularly beneficial in two important areas: bridging the gap and developing awareness.

Bridging the Gap
I designed the TUs to encourage learners to use English in their lives outside the classroom. This led to, for example, learners surfing the Internet for English language resources to achieve their TU outcomes. In this sense, TUs had, to borrow a term from testing, the *face validity* (Davies et al., 1999) of providing a vehicle for learners to use English language resources and take advantage of opportunities to use English outside the class. These activities helped to address the deficiencies in the existing curriculum and teaching process.

As the results from the study show, the participants agreed that TUs were relevant to their real lives, whereas those in the control group perceived that their homework assignments were not relevant. Thus, the TUs seemed to have bridged the gap between the EFL classroom and the outside world, whereas traditional homework assignments did not. The TUs were not constrained by the classroom in terms of time or space.

Developing Awareness
The results also show that TUs made a difference in the participants' awareness of English resources, particularly of English Web sites, English broadcasts, and English novels. This suggests that TUs channeled learners' attention to certain English resources, which supports Skehan's (1998)

selective-channeling rationale for the use of tasks; that is, tasks channel learners' attention in particular ways "so that particular pedagogic outcomes are achieved" (p. 112).

It is noteworthy that in addition to English Web sites, participants were also more likely to notice English broadcasts and novels than those in the control group. English broadcasts and novels should have received much less attention than English Web sites as the participants often had to access and use these Web sites, and not English broadcasts or novels, to achieve their outcomes. This suggests that TUs not only helped the participants become more aware of certain task-directed English resources but also helped develop their awareness of other resources.

To sum up, I introduced tasks as TUs to my teaching, and this task-based supplement helped revitalize the curriculum in that it bridged the gap between the classroom and the outside world and helped develop greater sensibility to English language resources and opportunities for using English in real life.

Conclusion

This chapter highlights the changed EFL context in China and calls for learning English for today, which the current curriculum and teaching methodology do not emphasize as much as learning English for tomorrow. Working within the framework of the existing curriculum and coursebooks, I made efforts to introduce tasks using TUs in my classes to address what I saw as deficiencies in the existing curriculum and teaching process. By doing so, I was successful in encouraging learners to use English language resources and to take advantage of opportunities to use English in their daily lives. The TUs were thus helpful in revitalizing the curriculum—to be specific, in bridging the gap between the classroom and the world beyond and in developing learners' awareness of the existence of English language resources and opportunities to use the language.

Acknowledgments

I would like to thank all my students who worked with me on *Task of the Unit* through the years. I am also grateful for excellent advice from the editors. Additional thanks also go to Dr. Martin Wedell from the University of Leeds and Dr. Ziwen Lu from Central China Normal University for their support and advice.

Appendix A: Survey on the TUs for the 10 Units in the *Senior English for China* Coursebook

Unit	Title	Topic	Task of the Unit
1	Making a difference	Science and scientists	Write an article for the class magazine of the "Olympic Class"[a] introducing the great mind you admire most.
2	News media	News and the media	Write an article for the UNESCO forum of News Media Tomorrow to discuss what a good reader should be, or introduce a reliable new medium you design for tomorrow.
3	Art and architecture	Art and architecture	Work in study group and prepare a presentation to introduce (a) your favourite work of art or architecture or (b) your own design of art or architecture.
4	A garden of poems	Literature and poetry	A. Prepare an essay about the topic, "Is poetry dead?" for the school Festival of English Poetry. B. Introduce how you like poetry so as to apply for the membership to the school's English Poetry Club.
5	The British Isles	Geography	Make a detailed travel plan for a 4-week trip through the United Kingdom with your friends.
6	Life in the future	Life in the future	Produce one booklet introducing (a) your study group members' futures or (b) people's life in the future.
7	Living with disease	Medicine, health, and diseases	Organise an activity for World AIDS Day 2004 on December 1 at the school or in the community and present a report.
8	First aid	First aid and medicine	Prepare a booklet of first aid for different situations living with farmers in Dalian[b] for the U. S. students who are coming to our school for an exchange programme of field biology.
9	Saving the earth	Nature, ecology, and environment	Prepare a speech that you are to give at the next Earth Summit.
10	Frightening nature	Volcanoes, typhoons, hurricanes, etc.	Follow the news and other reports about last weekend's massive earthquake and the tsunami[c] that followed, and report to the class in the first English class after the New Year holiday.

[a] The Olympic Class is a special class of top students from all over the Guangdong Province, some of whom were gold medallists at the International Mathematical, Physics, and Chemistry Olympiads for high school students.
[b] Dalian is a village where the students went for home stay with the farmers for 2 weeks.
[c] An earthquake-tsunami killed more than 226,000 persons inhabiting an area near the Indian Ocean in the last week of 2004.

Appendix B: Learners' Report of Interview of an Expert on AIDS (original, no changes made)

AIDS Day report

On Dec. 1st, we went to Zhong Shan Hospital to interview a specialist to know more about AIDS. Before we went to the Hospital we had prepared some questions. For example, what does AIDS means, what is the situation in China, how does HIV spread, what does the AIDS patients have to suffer from, why is AIDS dangerous to society, why is AIDS difficult to defeated, how to protect ourselves from HIV, etc. We asked the specialist many questions and taken some notes. After the interview, we went to the Internet to search information about AIDS and write an essay about AIDS.

What does AIDS means?

AIDS, which is short for Acquired Immune Deficiency Syndrome, is a serious disease which can breaks down human's immune system.

The trend of HIV transmit

Since the first AIDS patient was find out 20 years ago, the population of the people who have been infected with HIV in the world is over 42,000,000 and the population of the people who have been died of AIDS is about 27,900,000. In 2002, 5,000,000 people contracted HIV. For the moment, 15,000 people contracted HIV and 8,000 people are die of AIDS everyday. The AIDS patients and the people who contracted HIV are about 15 to 24 years old in China. The population of people who have AIDS is growing rapidly. The research show that about 6,000,000 people have been got infected with AIDS. In 2003 the population of new AIDS patients is 2,580,000 and the population of people who contracted HIV is 318,000 in China. The specialist said if government does not make available measure to control the transmitting of the disease, the population of people who have AIDS will be over 10,000,000 in 2010. The population of people who have AIDS in Guang Dong, which takes the forth place in China, is about 30,000.

About HIV

HIV, which is tiny, cannot been seen through common microscope. HIV mainly attacks human's immune system. It makes people weak by breaking down the immune system. So people will easily get sick after they were infected with HIV. Actually, HIV is weak and it cannot be alive after leaving the immune system.

How do people transmit HIV?

People transmit HIV by having unprotected sex, giving or receiving infected blood transfusion or through birth. The specialist said drinking too much, taking drags or share the inject container is also dangerous.

Why was AIDS dangerous?

As soon as person is got infected with HIV, he or she will feel sick. The symptom is like catch a cold. The person will get a fever, headache, pain in the throat, or feeling tired. But the medicine does not work. In one or two weeks, the symptom will disappear. The later 1 to 6 month, the disease cannot be found out by exam the sample of the blood of the person, but there are many viruses in the blood and other body liquid. The virus can transmit through the blood and the body liquid. In the later 5 to 7 years even more than 10 years, the person who has got AIDS will not feel sick. They may just lose weigh fast, feel tired. This period is called lie low period. "It is dangerous, you know, if someone who do not go to hospital to do the body exam, he or she will not know he or she has got AIDS and they may infect other people." After this period, the person become defenceless and he or she will get terrible sick. He or she will get high temperature and lose weigh continuously, and many diseases will occur to him or her. The AIDS will suffer from pain. At last the AIDS patient will lose their life.

Why is AIDS difficult to defeat?

AIDS is difficult to control. People do not know much about AIDS in poor countries and they do not have a good habit. There are many people do not know they have been infected with HIV and they may go on infecting some people who are healthy.

AIDS can be treated, but it cannot be cured at present. "If the viruses go in to the brain, the immune system cannot defeat them. Available AIDS vaccine still cannot be produced. The AIDS vaccine must be make sure that it will not cause AIDS or other diseases. The viruses always change itself, so the vaccine cannot kill all kinds of them." Another reason is that many of the AIDS patients refused to try the vaccine. The treatment is expensive and many people cannot pay for the treatment.

What effect to society do AIDS bring?

Many people become infected with AIDS and many people died of AIDS. In Africa, 5,500 people die of AIDS everyday because of a lack of proper healthy care, prevention and education. AIDS almost destroys Africa. More and more children have been infected through birth and many of them lose their parents. That causes strong pressure to society.

What should we do?

Though AIDS cannot be defeated for the moment, we can protect ourselves from being infected with AIDS. First of all, we should change bad habits and keep ourselves clean. Second, we must refuse unprotected sex, taking drags. Knowing more about AIDS is also important. In fact, we do not have to be too worried about AIDS because medical studies show that the AIDS virus cannot be transmitted via the following route: air, glasses, cups, handshake, hug, touch the AIDS patients, study with them or work with them. We should be more care about the AIDS patients and be friendly with them.

References

Abbs, B., Freebairn, I., & Mariani, L. (1994). *Flying start 2: Student's book.* Harlow, England: Addison Wesley Longman.

Abedi, J. (2004). The No Child Left Behind Act and English language learners: Assessment and accountability issues. *Educational Researcher, 33*(1), 4–14.

Abraham, P., & Mackey, D. (1997). *Contact USA: A reading and vocabulary text.* Upper Saddle River, NJ: Prentice Hall Regents.

Acklam, R. (1994). The role of the coursebook. *Practical English Teaching, 14*(3), 12–14.

Ahmed, M. K. (1994). Speaking as cognitive regulation: A Vygotskian perspective on dialogic communication. In J. P. Lantolf & G. Appel (Eds.), *Vygotskian approaches to second language learning* (pp. 157–172). Norwood, NJ: Ablex Publishing.

Alberta Education. (1989). *Social studies K–9.* Retrieved June 16, 2005, from http://www.education.gov.ab.ca/k_12/curriculum/bySubject /social/jhsoc.pdf

Alberta Education. (2000a). *English language arts program of study.* Retrieved February 27, 2006, from http://www.education.gov .ab.ca/k%5F12/curriculum/bySubject/english/elak-9.pdf

Alberta Education. (2000b). *English language arts K–9.* Retrieved June 16, 2005, from http://www.education.gov.ab.ca/k%5F12 /curriculum/bySubject/english/elak-9.pdf

Al Deen, M. E. (2005, December 29). UAE ready to post no-deficit budget. *Gulf News.* Retrieved February 2, 2006, from http://archive.gulfnews .com/articles/05/12/29/10008118.html

Al Nowais, S. (2004, November 25). Education system to get overhaul. *Gulf News.* Retrieved November 15, 2004, from http://archive.gulfnews .com/articles/04/11/25/141170.html

American Heritage Dictionary of the English Language (3rd ed.). (1992). Boston: Houghton-Mifflin.

AOL. (2005). *All this technical wizardry.* Retrieved October 10, 2005, from http://members.aol.com/ethnblight/poetry/technophobe.txt#editframe

Atkinson, D. (2002). Toward a sociocognitive approach to second language acquisition. *Modern Language Journal, 86,* 525–545.

Badders, W., Lowell, J. B., Fu, V., Peck, D., Summers, C., & Valentino, C. (1996). *Science discovery works.* Boston: Houghton-Mifflin.

Ball, D. L., & Cohen, D. K. (1999). Developing practice, developing practitioners: Toward a practice-based theory of professional education. In L. Darling-Hammond & G. Sykes (Eds.), *Teaching as the learning profession: Handbooks of policy and practice.* San Francisco: Jossey-Bass.

Benjamin, R. (1999). Developing the United Arab Emirates workforce for 2015. In Emirates Center for Strategic Studies and Research (Ed.), *Education and the Arab World* (pp. 309–322). Abu Dhabi, UAE: Emirates Center for Strategic Studies and Research.

Bird, B., & Short, J. (1993). *The battle for survival.* Bothell, WA: The Wright Group.

Black, P., Harrison, C., Lee, C., Marshall, B., & Wiliam, D. (2003). *Assessment for learning.* New York: Open University Press.

Black, P., & Wiliam, D. (1998). Assessment and classroom learning. *Assessment in Education, 5,* 7–74.

Block, D. (2003). *The social turn in second language acquisition.* Washington, DC: Georgetown University Press.

Bogart, J. (1991). *Sarah saw a blue macaw* [Illustrated by S. Daigneault]. Richmond Hill, OH: Scholastic-TAB.

Braidich, S. (2001). *What is a mountain?* New York: Rosen Publishing Group.

Britzman, D.P. (1991). *Practice makes practice: A critical study of learning to teach.* Albany, NY: State University of New York Press.

Brown, H. D. (1994). *Teaching by principles: An interactive approach to language pedagogy.* Englewood Cliffs, NJ: Prentice Hall Regents.

Brown, J. D. (2001). *Using surveys in language programs.* Cambridge: Cambridge University Press.

Bunnag, S. (2000, February 28). Students see system on creative thinking going the wrong way. *Bangkok Post,* p. 2.

Butterworth, C. (2001). *The whale's year.* Barrington, IL: Rigby.

Cameron, L. (2001). *Teaching languages to young learners.* Cambridge: Cambridge University Press.

Cefrey, H. (2002). *Tundra.* Barrington, IL: Rigby.

Chile students clash with police. (2006, May 30). *BBC News.* Retrieved May 30, 2006, from http://news.bbc.co.uk/go/pr/fr/-/2/hi/americas /5032012.stm

Cholewinski, G. M., & Sato, K. (2005). Building a collaborative school culture through curriculum development. In T. Murphey & K. Sato (Eds.), *Communities of supportive professionals* (pp. 35–46). Alexandria, VA: TESOL.

Clair, N. (1998). Teacher study groups: Persistent problems in a promising approach. *TESOL Quarterly, 32,* 465–492.

Clandinin, J. D., & Connelly, M. (1998). Asking questions about telling stories. In C. Kridel (Ed.), *Writing educational biography: Explorations in qualitative research* (pp. 245–254). New York: Garland Publications.

Clarke, M. (2006). Beyond antagonism? The discursive construction of 'new' teachers in the United Arab Emirates. *Teaching Education, 17,* 225–237.

Cochran-Smith, M. (2002). Inquiry and outcomes: Learning to teach in the age of accountability. *Teacher Education and Practice, 15,* 12–34.

Cochran-Smith, M. (2004). *Walking the road: Race, diversity, and social justice in teacher education.* New York: Teachers College Press.

Collier, V. (1995a). *Promoting academic success for ESL students: Understanding second language acquisition for school.* New York: Bastos Educational Books.

Collier, V. (1995b). Acquiring a second language for school. *Directions in Language and Education 1*(4). Washington, DC: National Clearinghouse for Education. Available at www.ncela.gwu.edu/pubs/directions/04.htm

Collier, V. P. (1987). Age and rate of acquisition of second language for academic purposes. *TESOL Quarterly, 21,* 617–641.

Collier, V., & Thomas, W. (1989). How quickly can immigrants become proficient in school English? *Journal of Educational Issues of Language Minority Students, 5,* 26–38.

Compton-Lilly, C. (2003). *Reading families: The literate life of urban children.* New York: Teacher's College Press.

Copenhaver, J. F. (2001). Running out of time: Rushed read-alouds in a primary classroom. *Language Arts, 79*(2), 148–158.

Cummins, J. (1979). Cognitive-academic language proficiency, linguistic interdependence, optimal age and some other matters. *Working Papers in Bilingualism, 19,* 197–205.

Cummins, J. (1981). Age on arrival and immigrant second language learning in Canada: A reassessment. *Applied Linguistics, 1,* 132–149.

Cummins, J. (2000). *Negotiating identities: Education for empowerment in a diverse society* (2nd ed.). Los Angeles: California Association for Bilingual Education.

Cummins, J. (2001). Instructional conditions for trilingual development. *International Journal of Bilingual Education and Bilingualism, 4,* 61–75.

Curriculum and Teaching Materials Research Institute. (2001). *A compilation curriculum standards/course guidelines in the 20th century of China: Volume of foreign language (English).* Beijing: People's Education Press.

Dadds, M. (2001). The politics of pedagogy. *Teachers and Teaching: Theory and Practice, 7,* 43–58.

Daniels, H. (1994, 2002). *Literature circles: Voice and choice in the student-centered classroom.* York, ME: Stenhouse.

Dauber, S. L., & Epstein, J. L. (1993). Parents' attitudes and practices of involvement in inner-city elementary and middle schools. In N. F. Chavkin (Ed.), *Families and schools in a pluralistic society* (pp. 53–71). New York: State University of New York Press.

Davies, A., Brown, A., Elder, A., Hill, K., Lumley, T., & McNamara, T. (1999). *Dictionary of language testing.* Cambridge: Cambridge University Press.

Day, C. (2000). Stories of change and professional development: The costs of commitment. In C. Day, A. Fernandez, T. E. Hauge, & J. Møller (Eds.). (2000). *The life and work of teachers: International perspectives in changing times* (pp. 109–29). London and New York: Falmer Press.

Day, R., & Yamanaka, J. (1998). *Impact issues.* Hong Kong: Longman Asia.

Day, R., & Yamanaka, J. (1999). *Impact topics.* Hong Kong: Longman Asia.

De La Cruz, Y. (1999). Reversing the trend: Latino families in real partnerships with schools. *Teaching Children Mathematics, 5*(5), 21–24.

Delgado-Gaitan, C. (1990). *Literacy for empowerment: The role of parents in children's education.* East Sussex, U.K.: The Falmer Press.

Deman, B., Frank, M., Jones, R., Krockover, G., McLeod, J., & Valenta, C. (2000). *Harcourt science text.* Orlando, FL: Harcourt School Publishers.

Dewey, J. (1897). My pedagogic creed. *The School Journal, 54,* 77–80. Retrieved October 27, 2005, from http://www.infed.org/archives/e-texts/e-dew-pc.htm

Dewey, J. (1916). *Democracy and education: An introduction to the philosophy of education.* The Macmillan Company. ILT Digital Classics (1994). Retrieved October 27, 2005, from http://www.ilt.columbia.edu/publications/dewey.html

Dewey, J. (1933, 1998). *How we think: A restatement of the relation of reflective thinking to the educative process.* New York: Houghton-Mifflin.

Díaz-Rico, L. T., & Leed, K. Z. (2002). *The cross-cultural language and academic development handbook: A complete K-12 reference guide.* Boston: Allyn & Bacon.

Donato, R. (2000). Sociocultural contributions to understanding the foreign and second language classroom. In J. Lantolf (Ed.), *Sociocultural theory and second language learning* (pp. 27–50). Oxford: Oxford University Press.

Dörnyei, Z. (2001). *Motivational strategies in the language classroom.* Cambridge: Cambridge University Press.

Dudeney, G. (2000). *The Internet and the language classroom.* Cambridge: Cambridge University Press.

Echevarria, J., & Short, D. (2004). *Making content comprehensible to English learners: The SIOP model* (2nd ed.). Boston: Allyn & Bacon.

Echevarria, J., Vogt, M., & Short, D. (2000). *Making content comprehensible for English language learners: The SIOP model.* Needham Heights, MA: Allyn and Bacon.

Edelsky, C., Altwerger, B., & Flores, B. (1991). *Whole language: What's the difference?* Portsmouth, NH: Heinemann.

Ehnebuske, J. M. (1998). In the comfort of their own home: Engaging families in mathematics. *Teaching Children Mathematics, 4*(6), 338–343.

Ellis, G., & Sinclair, B. (1989). *Learning to learn English: A course in learner training.* Cambridge: Cambridge University Press.

Ellis, R. (2003). *Task-based language learning and teaching.* Oxford: Oxford University Press.

Ellis, R., & Sano, F. (1997). *Impact intro.* Hong Kong: Longman Asia.

English patients. (October 24, 2002). *Shanghai Star.* Retrieved Oct. 25, 2005, from http://app1.chinadaily.com.cn/star/2002/1024/fe20-1.html

ESL in 2006: 17,613 students and counting. (2006). Retrieved November 16, 2006, from https://staffroom.cbe.ab.ca/cbeintranet/front+page/news/01+12+2006+-+esl.htm

Falk, B. (2001). Professional learning through assessment. In A. Lieberman & L. Miller (Eds.), *Teachers caught in the action: Professional development that matters* (pp. 118–140). New York: Teacher College Press.

Ferris, D., & Hedgecock, J. (2005). *Teaching ESL composition: Purpose, process, and practice* (2nd ed.). Mahwah, NJ: Lawrence Erlbaum.

Fillmore, L. W. (1990). Latino families and the schools. *California Perspectives, 1,* 30–37.

Flor Ada, A., & Zubizarreta, R. (2001). Parent narratives: The cultural bridge between Latino parents and their children. In M. de la Luz &

J. J. Halcon (Eds.), *The best for our children: Critical perspectives on literacy for Latino students* (pp. 229–244). New York: Teachers College Press.

Florio-Ruane, S. (2001). *Teacher education and the cultural imagination.* Mahwah, NJ: Lawrence Erlbaum Associates.

Foster, J., & Loven, R. (1992). The need and direction for parent involvement in the 90's: Undergraduate perspectives and expectations. *Action in Teacher Education, 14*(3), 13–18.

Fountas, I., & Pinnell, G. (1996). *Guided reading: Good first teaching for all children.* Portsmouth, NH: Heinemann.

Freeman, D. & Freeman, Y. (1988). Sheltered English instruction: ERIC Clearinghouse on Languages and Linguistics. Washington DC: ERIC Identifier: ED301070.

Freeman, D., & Freeman, Y. (2000). *Teaching reading in multilingual classrooms.* Portsmouth, NH: Heinemann.

Freeman, D., & Freeman, Y. (2002). *Closing the achievement gap: How to reach limited-formal-schooling and long-term English learners.* Portsmouth, NH: Heinemann.

Freeman, D., & Hawkins, M. (2004). Collaborative reflection as critical practice in teacher education. In M. Hawkins & S. Irujo (Eds.), *Collaborative conversations among language teacher educators* (pp. 1–15). Alexandria, VA: TESOL.

Freeman, Y., & Freeman, D. (1992). *Whole language for second language learners.* Portsmouth, NH: Heinemann.

Freeman, Y. S., & Freeman, D. E. (1998). *ESL/EFL teaching: Principles for success.* Portsmouth, NH: Heinemann.

Fullan, M. (2001). *The new meaning of educational change* (3rd ed.). New York: Teachers' College Press.

Fullan, M. G., with Stiegelbauer, S. (1991). *The new meaning of educational change.* London: Cassell Educational Ltd.

Gabriel, J. (2005). *How to thrive as a teacher leader.* Alexandria, VA: Association for Supervision and Curriculum Development.

Garcia-Huidobro, J. E. (2000). Educational policies and equity in Chile. In F. Reimers (Ed.), *Unequal schools, unequal chances: The challenges to equal opportunity in the Americas* (pp. 160–178). Cambridge, MA: Harvard University Press.

Gardner, D. (1999). The evaluation of self-access centres. In B. Morrison (Ed.), *Experiments and evaluation in self-access language learning* (pp. 111–122). Hong Kong: HASALD.

Gardner, D., & Miller, L. (1999). *Establishing self-access: From theory to practice.* Cambridge: Cambridge University Press.

Geisel, T. S. (1990). *Oh! the places you'll go!* New York: Random House.

Gestwicki, C. (2004). *Home, school, and community relations.* Clifton Park, NY: Delmar Learning.

Gibbons, P. (2002). *Scaffolding language, scaffolding learning: Teaching second language learners in the mainstream classroom.* Portsmouth, NH: Heinemann.

Gibbons, W. (2001). *Life in the rain forest.* New York: Rosen Publishing Group.

Gipps, C. (1994). *Beyond testing: Towards a theory of educational assessment.* London: Falmer Press.

Gitsaki, R., & Taylor, C. (2000). *Internet English.* New York: Oxford University Press.

Gonzalez, N., Moll, L. C., & Amanti, C. (2005). *Funds of knowledge: Theorizing practices in households, communities, and classrooms.* Mahwah, NJ: Lawrence Erlbaum Associates.

Gordimer, N. (1999). Once upon a time. In A. Barlow-Kedves, C. Collins, I. Mills, R. Pearson, W. Mathieu, & S. Tywoniuk (Eds.), *Sightlines 9* (pp. 39–43). Scarborough, ON: Prentice Hall Literature.

Grant, N. (1987). *Making the most of your textbook.* Harlow, England: Pearson Education.

Graves, K. (2000). *Designing language courses.* Boston: Heinle and Heinle.

Gray, J. (2002). The global coursebook in English language teaching. In D. Block & D. Cameron (Eds.), *Globalization and English language teaching* (pp. 151–167). London: Routledge.

Guo, Y. (2000). Curriculum design and reconstruction of learner's life. *Educational Science Research, Year 2000, 5,* 48–54.

Haas, M. (2000). *Thematic, communicative language teaching in the K-8 classroom.* Retrieved January 7, 2006, from http://www.cal.org /resources/digest/0004thematic.html

Halliwell, S. (1992). *Teaching English in the primary classroom.* Harlow, England: Longman.

Harmer, J. (2001). *The practice of English language teaching.* Harlow, England: Pearson Education.

Harris, M., Mower, D., & Sikorzyńska, A. (2000). *Opportunities pre-intermediate.* Harlow, England: Pearson Education.

Harrisonburg City Public Schools. (2007). LEP Student Enrollment Statistics 2006–07. Available from http://staff.harrisonburg.k12.va.us /~dbenavides/EnrollmentStatistics0607.html

Harvey, S., & Goudvis, A. (2000). *Strategies that work.* Portland, ME: Stenhouse.

Hawkins, M. (2004). Researching English language and literacy development in schools. *Educational Researcher, 33*(3), 14–25.

Hawkins, M. R., & Legler, L. L. (2004). Reflections on the impact of teacher-researcher collaboration. *TESOL Quarterly, 38,* 339–343.

Heath, S. B. (1982). What no bedtime story means: Narrative skills at home and school. *Language in Society, 11*(2), 49–76.

Herrera, M., & Zanatta, T. (2000). *New parade.* London: Pearson Education.

Hoobler, D., & Hoobler, T. (2003). *We are Americans—Voices of the immigrant experience.* New York: Scholastic, Inc.

Hoover-Dempsey, K. V., & Sandler, H. M. (1997). Why do parents become involved in their children's education. *Review of Educational Research, 67*(1), 3–42.

Hyland, K. (2003). *Second language writing.* New York: Cambridge. *IDEA proficiency tests.* (1993). Brea, CA: Ballard & Tighe.

Is English skill that important? (March 24, 2004). *Chinaview.* Retrieved October 25, 2005, from http://news3.xinhuanet.com/english/2004-03/24/content_1382422.htm

Jacobs, W. W. (2000). *The monkey's paw.* Oxford, England: Oxford University Press.

Janardhan, N. (2002, September 10). Reform grinds to a halt. *Asian Times.* Retrieved May 30, 2006, from http://www.atimes.com/atimes/Middle_East/DI10Ak02.html

Jimbo, H. (2001). *Hello there! Oral communication B.* Tokyo: Tokyoshoseki.

Jimenez, M. (2006, January 14). Her victory will be a revolution. *The Globe and Mail.*

Jin L., & Cortazzi, M. (1998). Dimensions of dialogue: Large classes in China. *International Journal of Educational Research 29,* 739–761.

Johnson, K.E. (2006). The sociocultural turn and its challenges for second language teacher education. *TESOL Quarterly, 40,* 235–57.

Johnson, M. (2004). *A philosophy of second language acquisition.* Binghamton, NY: Vail Ballou Press.

Johnson, M. J., & Janisch, C. (1998). Connecting literacy with social studies content. *Social Studies and the Young Learner, 10,* 6–9.

Kachru, B. (1985). Standards, codification and sociolinguistic realism: The English language in the outer circle. In R. Quirk and H. Widdowson (Eds.), *English in the world: Teaching and learning the language and literatures* (pp. 11–30). Cambridge: Cambridge University Press.

Kachru, B. (1997). World Englishes and English-using communities. *Annual Review of Applied Linguistics, 17,* 66–87.

Kalman, B., & Smithyman, K. (2004). *The native nations of North America series: Nations of the Northwest coast.* New York: Crabtree.

Kazim, A. (2000). *The United Arab Emirates A.D. 600 to the present: A sociodiscursive transformation in the Arabian Gulf.* Dubai, United Arab Emirates: Gulf Book Center.

Keithahn, E. L. (1988). *Alaskan igloo tales.* Anchorage, AK: Alaska Northwest.

Kelly, A.V. (1999). *The curriculum: Theory and practice* (4th ed.). London: Paul Chapman.

Kleinsasser, R. C. (1993). A tale of two technical cultures: Foreign language teaching. *Teaching and Teacher Education, 9,* 373–383.

Kłos, M., & Sikorzyńska, A. (2002). *Program nauczania języka angielskiego w lyceum* (Curriculum of teaching English in secondary school). Warsaw, Poland: Pearson Education Longman. Retrieved February, 21, 2006, from http://www.longman.pl/pub/PN/Liceum_i_Technikum _Wariant_A_i_B.pdf (in Polish)

Krashen, S. (1982). *Principles and practice in second language acquisition.* New York: Pergamon Press.

Krashen, S. (2004). The case for narrow reading. *Language Magazine, 3,* 17–19.

Lang, T. (2005). *Crossing borders: Stories of immigrants.* Parsippany, NJ: Pearson Education.

Lauber, P. (1995). *Who eats what? Food chains and food webs* [Illustrated by H. Keller]. New York: Harper Collins.

Lewis, C., & Ketter, J. (2004). Learning as social interaction: Interdiscursivity in a teacher and researcher study group. In R. Rogers (Ed.), *An introduction to critical discourse analysis in education* (pp. 117–146). Mahwah, NJ: Lawrence Erlbaum Associates.

Lewis, M. (1993). *The lexical approach.* London: Language Teaching Publications.

Lewis, M. (1997). *Implementing the lexical approach.* London: Language Teaching Publications.

Lewis, M. (Ed.). (2000). *Teaching collocation: Further developments in the lexical approach.* London: Language Teaching Publications.

Lipson, M., Valencia, S., Wixon, K., & Peters, C. (1993). Integration and thematic teaching: Integration to improve teaching and learning. *Language Arts, 70,* 252–263.

Long, M. (1985). Input and second language acquisition theory. In S. M. Gass & C. G. Madden (Eds.), *Input in second language acquisition* (pp. 377–393). Cambridge, MA: Newbury House.

Long, M., & Porter, P. (1985). Group work, interlanguage, talk, and second language acquisition. *TESOL Quarterly, 19,* 305–325.

Long, M. H., & Crookes, G. (1992). Three approaches to task-based syllabus design. *TESOL Quarterly, 26,* 27–55.

Loughran, S. B. (2005). Thematic teaching in action. *Kappa Delta Pi Record, 41*(3), 112–117.

Loughrey, B., Hughes, A., Bax, S., Magness, C., & Aziz, H. (1999). *English language teaching in the UAE: Evaluation report.* Roehampton, England: University of Surrey.

Lu, Z. (2004). *Pedagogy of English for primary schools.* Beijing: China Electric Power Press.

Lu, Z., & Zhang, R. (2005). *Principles and practice of real-use-task-oriented language teaching for schools in China.* Beijing: China Electric Power Press.

Luzon Marco, M. J. (2001). Information collection and analysis activities: The treasure hunt. *Teaching English with Technology, 1*(4). Retrieved February, 21, 2006, from http://www.iatefl.org.pl/call/j_esp4.htm

Mahoney, J. (Trainer). (September 2003). *Primary Years Programme training guide.* Wilton Manors, FL: Wilton Manors Elementary.

McLaughlin M. W., & Talbert, J. E. (2001). *Professional communities and the work of high school teaching.* Chicago: The University of Chicago Press.

Mediamark Research Inc. (2003). *American teens say quality of life and relationships are important.* Retrieved October 10, 2005, from www .mediamark.com/mri/docs/pr_2-3-03teenmark.htm

MEXT (Ministry of Education, Culture, Sports, Science and Technology). (2003). *The course of study for foreign languages.* Retrieved October 19, 2005, from www.mext.go.jp/english/shotou/030301.htm

Miller, L. (2000). 'What have you just learnt?': Preparing learners in the classroom for self-access language learning. *Modern English Teacher, 9,* 7–13.

Ministry of Education. (2001). *English curriculum standards for compulsory education and senior high schools.* Beijing: Beijing Normal University Press.

Ministry of Education [Bangkok]. (2001). *Handbook for the management of learning and teaching for foreign languages.* Bangkok: Ministry of Education.

Ministry of Education. (2003). *English Curriculum Standards for Senior High Schools.* Beijing: Beijing Normal University Press.

Ministry of National Education and Sport. (2002). *Podstawa programowa kształcenia ogólnego* (Core Curriculum of Mainstream Education). The Decree of the Minister of National Education and Sport from the 26th

February 2002 on the Core Curriculum of Mainstream Education. Retrieved February, 21, 2006, from http://bip.men.gov.pl/akty_pr _1997_2006/rozp_155.php (in Polish)

Mograby, A. (1999). Human development in the United Arab Emirates. In Emirates Center for Strategic Studies and Research (Ed.), *Education and the Arab world* (pp. 279–307). Abu Dhabi, United Arab Emirates: Emirates Center for Strategic Studies and Research.

Moore, N., & Reinders, H. (2003). Teaching for self-study: In the self-access centre. *Modern English Teacher, 12,* 48–50.

Murphey, T., & Sato, K. (Eds.). (2005). *Communities of supportive professionals.* Alexandria, VA: TESOL.

Naidoo, B. (1986). *Journey to Jo'burg.* New York: Harper Collins.

Nation, P. (1990). *Teaching and learning vocabulary.* New York: Newbury House.

National Bureau of Statistics of China. (2004). *China statistical yearbook, 2004.* Beijing: China Statistics Press.

National Education Examinations Authority of Ministry of Education. (2005). *Test handbook for 2005 matriculation Chinese, mathematics, English (French, German, Spanish), and general tests.* Beijing: Higher Education Press.

No Child Left Behind Act. PUBLIC LAW 107-110. (2002, January 8). Retrieved on November 17, 2007, from http://www.ed.gov/policy/elsec /leg/esea02/107-110.pdf

Nunan, D. (Ed.). (2003). *Practical English language teaching.* New York: McGraw-Hill.

Nunan, D. (2004). *Task-based language teaching.* Retrieved January 7, 2006, from http://assets.cambridge.org/ 052184/0171/sample/0521840171ws .pdf

Office of the National Education Commission. (1999). *National Education Act of B.E. 2542 (1999).* Bangkok: Office of the National Education Commission.

Oliver, B. (1995). *Habitat* ("Have to have a habitat"). Retrieved October, 15, 2005, from http://www.mrhabitat.net/songbook.html#habitat

Pennsylvania Department of Education. (2005). ESL Resource Documents: 22 Pa. Code §4.26. Available from http://www.pde.state.pa.us/esl/cwp /view.asp?a=3&Q=74490&eslNav=|4974|

Pennycook, A. (1994). *The cultural politics of English as an international language.* Harlow, England: Longman.

Pennycook, A. (1995). English in the world/The world in English. In J. Tollefson (Ed.), *Power and inequality in language education* (pp. 34–58). Cambridge: Cambridge University Press.

Peregoy S., & Boyle, O. (2004). *Reading, writing, and learning in ESL: A resource book for K–12 teachers* (4th ed.). Boston: Pearson Education.

Peressini, D. D. (1998). The portrayal of parents in the school mathematics reform literature: Locating the context for parental involvement. *Journal for Research in Mathematics Education, 29*(5), 555–582.

Phillipson, R. (2004). English in globalization: Three approaches. *Journal of Language, Identity and Education, 3,* 73–84.

Pica, T., Holliday, L., Lewis, N., & Morgenthaler, L. (1989). Comprehensible output as an outcome of linguistic demands on the learner. *Studies in Second Language Acquisition, 11,* 63–90.

Rea-Dickens, P., & Germaine, K. (1998). *Managing evaluation and innovation in language teaching: Building bridges.* Harlow, England: Longman.

Resultados nacionales del diagnóstico de Inglés, aplicado en el año 2004–2005. (2006). Ministerior de Educación, Santiago, Chile. Retrieved January 2006, from www.mineduc.cl

Richards, J. (2001). *Curriculum development in language teaching.* Cambridge: Cambridge University Press.

Robertson, R. (1995). Glocalization: Time-space and homogeneity-heterogeneity. In M. Featherstone, S. Lash, & R. Robertson (Eds.), *Global modernities* (pp. 25–44). London: Sage Publications.

Rohter, L. (2004, December 31). Letter from South America: Market-friendly Chile sees a future in English. *International Herald Tribune,* Paris edition, p. 2.

Roessingh, H. (1999). Adjunct support for high school ESL learners in mainstream English classes: Ensuring their success. *TESL Canada Journal, 17*(1), 72–85.

Roessingh, H. (2005). *Learning by design.* Retrieved June 16, 2005, from http://www.learningbydesign.ucalgary.ca

Roessingh, H., & Johnson, C. (2004). Teacher-prepared materials: A principled approach. *TESL Canada Journal, 21*(1), 44–63.

Roessingh, H., & Kover, P. (2003). Variability of ESL learners' acquisition of cognitive academic language proficiency: What can we learn from achievement measures? *TESL Canada Journal, 21*(1), 1–21.

Rosenmund, M. (2000). Approaches to international comparative research on curricula and curriculum-making processes. *Journal of Curriculum Studies, 32,* 599–607.

Rost, M. (2002). *Teaching and researching listening.* London: Pearson Education.

Routman, R. (2002). Teacher talk. *Educational Leadership, 59,* 32–35

Rujiketgumjorn, S. (2000). Self-access and second language acquisition. *The English Teacher, 3,* 73–86.

Salama, S. (2005, November 18). Education standards deplored. *Gulf News.* Retrieved November 22, 2005, from http://archive.gulfnews.com /articles/05/11/18/193203.html

Sato, K. (2002). Practical understandings of CLT and teacher development. In S. J. Savignon (Ed.), *Interpreting communicative language teaching: Contexts and concerns in Teacher Education* (pp. 41–81). New Haven, CT: Yale University Press.

Sato, K. (2003). Starting a local teacher study group. In T. Murphey (Ed.), *Extending professional contributions* (pp. 97–104). Alexandria, VA: TESOL.

Sato, K. (2005, October). *Teaching and learning communication strategies: From a sociocultural perspective.* Paper presented at the Second Language Acquisition Research Forum 2005 Conference, New York.

Sato, K., & Kleinsasser, R. C. (1999). Communicative language teaching (CLT): Practical understandings. *The Modern Language Journal, 83,* 494–517.

Sato, K., & Kleinsasser, R. C. (2004). Beliefs, practices, and interactions of teachers in Japanese high school English department. *Teaching and Teacher Education, 20,* 797–816.

Sato, K., & Takahashi, K. (2003). Teacher and student learning in the workplace: The impact of performance tests. In M. Swanson & K. Hill (Eds.), *JALT 2002 Conference Proceedings* (pp. 325–336). Tokyo: JALT.

Savignon, S. J., & Sysoyev, P. V. (2002). Sociocultural strategies for a dialogue of cultures. *Modern Language Journal, 86,* 508–524.

Schiefelbein, E., & Schiefelbein, P. (2000). Education and poverty in Chile: Affirmative action in the 1990s. In F. Reimers (Ed.), *Unequal schools, unequal chances: The challenges to equal opportunity in the Americas* (pp. 182–201). Cambridge, MA: Harvard University Press.

Seeq. (2005). *Embrace.* Retrieved October 10, 2005, from www.web-wired .com/klutch/art/embrace.htm

Senior English for China: Student's book, 2A. (2004a). Beijing: People's Education Press.

Senior English for China: Teacher's book, 2A. (2004b). Beijing: People's Education Press.

Sheerin, S. (1991). Self-access. *Language Teaching, 24,* 143–157.

Shihab, M. (2001). Economic development in the UAE. In I. Abed & P. Helleyer (Eds.), *United Arab Emirates: A new perspective* (pp. 249–259). London: Trident Press.

Short, D., & Echevarria, J. (1999). *The sheltered instruction observation protocol: A tool for teacher–researcher collaboration and professional development.* Santa Cruz, CA & Washington, DC: Center for Research on

Education Diversity & Excellence. Available from www.cal.org/crede /pubs/edpractice/EPR3.htm

Short, D., & Echevarria, J. (2005). Teacher skills to support English language learners. *Educational Leadership, 62,* 8–13.

Shulman, L. (1986). Paradigms and research programs in the study of teaching: A contemporary perspective. In Wittrock, M. C. (Ed.), *Handbook of research on teaching* (3rd ed.; pp. 3–36). New York: Macmillan.

Sinclair, J. (1991). *Corpus, concordance, collocation.* Oxford: Oxford University Press.

Skehan, P. (1996). A framework for the implementation of task-based instruction. *Applied Linguistics, 17,* 38–62.

Skehan, P. (1998). *A cognitive approach to language learning.* Oxford: Oxford University Press.

Soeder, P. (1998). *Discover American Indian ways.* Niwot, CO: Roberts Rinehart.

Syed, Z. (2003). The sociocultural context of English language teaching in the Gulf. *TESOL Quarterly, 37,* 337–341.

Taha-Thomure, H. (2003, October 29). Need to revamp Arab schools. *Gulf News.* Retrieved November 1, 2003, from http://archive .gulfnews.com/articles/03/10/31/101692.html

TESOL. (1997). *ESL standards for pre-K–12 students.* Alexandria, VA: TESOL.

Tharp, R., & Gallimore, R. (1988). *Rousing minds to life: Teaching, learning and schooling in social context.* Cambridge: Cambridge University Press.

Thomas, W., & Collier, V. (1997). *School effectiveness for language minority students* (Resource Collection Series, No. 9, December 1997). Washington, DC: National Clearinghouse on Bilingual Education.

Thomas, W., & Collier, V. (2002). *A national study of school effectiveness for language minority students' long-term academic achievement. Final report.* Santa Cruz, CA: Center for Research on Education, Diversity and Excellence.

Thomas, W., & Collier, V. (2003). The multiple benefits of dual language. *Educational Leadership, 61,* 61–64.

Toohey, K., & Waterstone, B. (2004). Negotiating expertise in an action research community. In B. Norton & K. Toohey (Eds.), *Critical pedagogies and language learning* (pp. 291–310). Cambridge: Cambridge University Press.

Toronto District School Board. (2008). *Facts and figures.* Retrieved on January 28, 2008, from http://www.tdsb.on.ca

UAE Ministry of Education and Youth. (1992) *English language document for basic and secondary education* (pp. 40–44). Abu Dhabi, UAE: Ministry of Education and Youth.

UAE Ministry of Education and Youth. (1998). *English for the Emirates: Teacher's book, Grade 3.* Abu Dhabi, UAE: Ministry of Education and Youth.

Valdes, G. (1996). *Con respeto: Bridging the distances between culturally diverse families and schools.* New York: Teachers College Press.

Van Lier, L. (2000). From input to affordance: Social interactive learning from an ecological perspective. In J. Lantolf (Ed.), *Sociocultural theory and second language learning* (pp. 245–259). Oxford: Oxford University Press.

Vieira, L. (1997). *Grand Canyon: A trail through time.* New York: Walker & Company.

Vogt, M. (1997). *Cross-curricular thematic instruction.* Retrieved November 1, 2005, from http://www.eduplace.com/rdg/res/vogt.html

Vygotsky, L. S. (1978). *Mind in society: The development of higher psychological processes.* Cambridge, MA: Harvard University Press.

Walker, B., Maynak, J., & Cassidy, J. J., Jr. (Eds.). (1995). *Through Indian eyes: The untold story of Native American peoples.* Pleasantville, NY: Readers Digest.

Wang, Z. (2004, October). *An antidote to modern test-oriented education: Toward a constructive postmodern education.* Paper presented at the 2004 Forum for Integrated Education and Educational Reform, sponsored by the Council for Global Integrative Education, Santa Cruz, CA. Retrieved March 28, 2006, from http://chiron.valdosta.edu/whuitt/CGIE/wang.pdf

Watson-Gegeo, K. A. (2004). Mind, language, and epistemology: Toward a language socialization paradigm for SLA. *Modern Language Journal, 88,* 331–350.

Watson Todd, R. (2001, September 9). Why has education reform failed? *Bangkok Post,* p. P3.

Watson Todd, R. (2005). Lessons learnt from the SEARs project. *Journal of English Studies, 2,* 5–15.

Wenger, E. (1998). *Communities of practice: Learning, meaning, and identity.* Cambridge: Cambridge University Press.

Wiggins, G. (1998). *Educative assessment.* San Francisco: Jossey Bass.

Willis, J. (1996). *A framework for task-based Learning.* Harlow, England: Longman.

Wiriyachitra, A. (2002). English language teaching and learning in Thailand in this decade. *Thai TESOL Focus, 15,* 4–9.

Wright, W. (2005). *Evolution of federal policy and implications of no child left behind for language minority students* (EPSL-501-101-LPRU). Tempe, AZ: Arizona State University, Language Policy Research Unit, College of Education. Retrieved on April 21, 2005, from http://www.asu.edu /educ/epsl/EPRU/documents/EPSL-0501-101-LPRU.pdf

Writefix. (2003). *Writing argument and opinion essays.* Retrieved October 10, 2005, from www.writefix.com

Yeung, L., & Hyland, F. (1999). Bridging the gap: Utilising self-access as a course component. *RELC Journal, 30,* 158–174.

Zhang, R. (2003). Task-based homework assignments for senior high school EFL learners. *Journal of Basic English Education, Year 2003, 4,* 19–23.

Zhang, R. (2004, May). *What contexts does a TESOL teacher of a branch school have to work with?* Paper presented at the Fourth International Conference on ELT in China, Beijing.

About the Editors
and Contributors

Maria Andrea Arancibia teaches at the Liceo Carmela Carvajal de Prat in Santiago, Chile. She has participated in a Ministry of Education video on teaching methodology.

Eileen N. Whelan Ariza received her doctorate in Multilingual/Multicultural Education from the University of Massachusetts, Amherst, in the United States and a masters in TESOL and Spanish as a second language from the School for International Training in Brattleboro, Vermont. After living and working in many countries, and teaching for several years at Harvard University's EIL program, Ariza settled in Florida, where she is an associate professor of TESOL at Florida Atlantic University and trains preservice and inservice teachers for ESOL preparation.

Deanna Benavides is an ESL specialist with Harrisonburg City Public Schools in Harrisonburg, Virginia.

Lynn Cade has been an elementary school teacher for more than 20 years, the past 10 at Beech Street Community School in Manchester, New Hampshire, in the United States. She enjoys collaborating with, mentoring, and learning from students, student teachers, colleagues, and teacher educators.

Matthew Clarke works in the Faculty of Education at the University of Hong Kong. Formerly, he was Dean of Education at the Higher Colleges of Technology (HCT) in the United Arab Emirates (UAE). He came to the UAE in 1999 from the University of Melbourne to lead the development of the HCT's BEd in English Language Teaching in Schools. He has also taught in primary schools and in English language teaching centers in the United Kingdom and Australia.

Barbara Fagan is an ESL education consultant working with Harrisonburg City Public Schools in Harrisonburg, Virginia, in the United States. She is also an ESL adjunct instructor at James Madison University in Harrisonburg, Virginia.

Kay Gallagher is head of Education Studies at Emirates College for Advanced Education in Abu Dhabi in the United Arab Emirates (UAE). She previously led the Education Department at Abu Dhabi Women's College, part of the Higher Colleges of Technology (HCT) in the UAE, where student teachers study for the Melbourne University certified, HCT BEd degree in English Language Teaching in Schools, thus becoming the country's first professionally qualified cohort of native teachers of English for young learners.

Kathleen Graves is a professor of second language teacher education at the School for International Training, in the United States. She is the editor of *Teachers as Course Developers* (Cambridge University Press) and author of *Designing Language Courses: A Guide for Teachers* (Heinle & Heinle). In addition to curriculum development, her professional interests include helping teachers create learning communities in their classrooms and collaborative professional communities with fellow teachers.

Margaret Hawkins is an associate professor in the Department of Curriculum and Instruction at the University of Wisconsin, Madison, in the United States, where she directs the ESL and bilingual programs. Current projects include collaborative research on the language and literacy development of young English learners in schools and supporting and researching school-based initiatives on home–school relations.

David Hayes is graduate program director, Department of Applied Linguistics, Brock University, Canada. His primary research interests are in systemic educational change and the lives and careers of nonnative-speaking teachers of English working in their own state educational systems. He has extensive experience with curriculum development and teacher education programs in South and Southeast Asia.

Jane Hill is a second-language consultant and an author of professional materials. She has been a department head and teacher of English as a second language for the Toronto District School Board in Toronto, Ontario, Canada.

Karen Candia Hormazabal teaches at the Liceo Tecnico Felisa Tolup Zeiman in San Fernando, Chile.

Carla Johnson is an ESL specialist at a public school in Calgary, Alberta, Canada, and is pursuing her PhD in TESL.

Caroline Johnson taught multiage first and second grade in Madison, Wisconsin, in the United States, serving as both the classroom and ESL teacher for her students. She is currently teaching first grade at the American School of Tampico, in Tampico, Mexico. Her interests include teaching English language learners and early reading and math intervention.

Kelly Jones teaches a multiage first- and second-grade class in Madison, Wisconsin, in the United States, serving as both the classroom and ESL teacher for her students. She is currently participating in an early intervention math study of first-grade students and recently worked on a committee designed to align district science standards with curriculum.

Sonthida Keyuravong is an associate professor in applied linguistics at King Mongkut's University of Technology Thonburi in Thailand. She is interested in self-access learning, and her most recent project has been the establishment of self-access centers in community colleges across Thailand.

Penny Kinnear is an assistant professor in the Professional Writing Program at the University of Toronto in Mississauga, Ontario, Canada.

Jarosław Krajka is a former teacher of English, both at the primary and secondary levels, in the public and private sector in the Lublin region of Poland. He has a PhD in computer-assisted language learning. His interest in computer-assisted language learning, specifically Internet-based classroom teaching, culminated in a doctoral dissertation, "The Internet as a Coursebook in EFL," which he completed in 2002. He is an assistant professor at the Warsaw School of Social Psychology in Poland, where he teaches classes in the methodology of teaching English.

Lynn Legler is a kindergarten teacher in the Madison Metropolitan School District in Madison, Wisconsin, in the United States. Her professional experiences include facilitating action research initiatives and speaking to local and national groups and organizations about language learning in classrooms. In 2003, she was awarded the Wisconsin Kohl Foundation Fellowship, which honors excellence in education.

Janet L. Pierce is an ESL teacher in the Franklin Regional School District outside Pittsburgh, Pennsylvania, in the United States and is a doctoral student at Indiana University of Pennsylvania.

Monique Pigeon-Abolins was a department head and teacher of French as a second language for the Toronto District School Board in Toronto, Ontario, Canada. Monique passed away shortly before the completion of the chapter that she co-authored. Her contributions to the course described in chapter 11 and the writing of the chapter continue to be appreciated.

Diane S. Pressman received her bachelors degree in elementary education, masters in educational leadership, and doctorate in curriculum and instruction from Florida Atlantic University. Her professional experiences include 27 years teaching grades K–6 and 3 years as an elementary principal. She currently teaches at Stirling Elementary School in Broward County School District. She remains active in school and district initiatives and works with university students pursuing careers in education.

Kazuyoshi Sato teaches at the Nagoya University of Foreign Studies in Japan. He holds a doctorate in applied linguistics from the University of Queensland, Australia, and has written several papers on communicative language teaching and teacher education. His research interests include teacher development, language learning strategies, and curriculum development.

Judy Sharkey is an associate professor of education at the University of New Hampshire in the United States. She teaches graduate courses in education, ESOL curriculum and methods, and teacher research. She enjoys learning from the students and classroom teachers who invite her into their learning communities.

Kullakan Suthidara works on the design of e-learning materials. She graduated with a master of arts in applied linguistics (resource-based English language learning) from King Mongkut's University of Technology Thonburi in Thailand. She is interested in Thai education reform, specifically its encouragement of self-study and lifelong learning.

Keiko Takahashi is a teacher at Gifu Prefectural High School in Japan. She holds a masters in education from Tsukuba University in Japan. Her research interests include communicative writing, extensive reading, and curriculum development.

Richard Watson Todd is an associate professor in applied linguistics at King Mongkut's University of Technology Thonburi in Thailand. He holds a PhD from the University of Liverpool and is the author of several books and articles on a wide range of topics.

Nayaret Toro Soto teaches at the Liceo Politécnico Hannover, Santiago, Chile.

Suzanne Webster is the ESL program coordinator at a charter school in Calgary, Alberta, Canada. She has an MEd in TESL and has taught in both EFL and ESL contexts.

Ronggan Zhang is senior lecturer at the Affiliated High School of South China Normal University and has been involved in introducing tasks into Chinese EFL classrooms since 1999. He has published papers and co-authored a book on task-based language learning and teaching. His interests include language testing and second language acquisition.

Index

Page numbers followed by an *n, f,* or *t* indicate notes, figures, or tables.

A

Ask.com, 279

Askforkids.com, 279

Assessment. *See also* Testing

> ecological perspective and, 189–190*f,* 200
>
> International Baccalaureate Primary Years Programme and, 144*f*
>
> literacy instruction and, 163
>
> Oral Communication class and, 215, 217, 230
>
> SEARs and, 36, 43*f*
>
> thematic matrices and, 55, 58*f,* 61*f,* 62*f*
>
> in United Arab Emirates, 23–24

Attitudes

> International Baccalaureate Primary Years Programme and, 145
>
> parental, 160
>
> SEARs and, 36, 48

Authenticity, 80–81, 283

Autonomous learning, 283. *See also* Student English Access Rooms

AYP. *See* Adequate yearly progress

B

Background information, 189–190*f*

Balance, 129, 276

Beech Street Community School, 182. *See also* Ecological perspective

Beyond the Science Kit, 175

Biographies Unit Excerpt, 117–121*f*

Biomes Unit, 187, 189–190*f,* 193*f,* 203. *See also* Ecological perspective

Blueplanetbiomes.org/world_biomes, 203

Boats, Balloons, and Classroom Video, 175

C

Calgary, 77. *See also* Cross-curricular integration

CALL. *See* Computer-assisted language learning

Canada, 1, 3, 7, 77, 239, 240*n,* 243–245. *See also* Cross-curricular integration; Professional development

Caring, 129

Censorware, 281

Centralised curriculum, 5–8, 15

Conferences, 153, 158–159. *See also* Family participation

Confidence, 46–47, 211, 226–229, 254

Connector, as literature circle role, 252*t*

Constant striving, 6

Contact USA: A Reading and Vocabulary Textbook, 58

Content areas

    English instruction and. *See* Cross-curricular integration

    English Opens Doors and, 245

    Intensive English program and, 104–112, 105*f*, 112–115

Contextual guessing, 96

Conversation strategies, 222*f*, 224–226

Creative thinking, 15

Cross-curricular integration

    adaptation to, 82–83

    conclusions regarding, 85–92

    curricular context of, 77–79

    defined, 79

    humanities unit demonstrating, 83–85, 85–89*f*, 90*f*, 100

    Internet-based instruction and, 283

    introduction to, 77

    materials for lesson 6 and, 97–98

    modified materials for lesson 3 and, 92–97

    motivation for change and, 79–82

Crossing Borders: Stories of Immigrants, 58

Cultural considerations

    Chile and, 240–242

    curriculum and, 246

    ecological perspective and, 184

    family participation and, 151–153, 161, 163, 164–165

    Internet-based instruction and, 283

    Oral Communication class and, 231

    thematic matrices and, 70. *See also* Thematic matrices

    United Arab Emirates and, 26–28

Curriculum

    centralisation of, 5–8, 15

    Chile and, 242–243

    cultural considerations and, 246

D

H

I

The Monkey's Paw, 251, 252

Mrhabitat.net/songbook.html#habitat, 203

N

Nakhao School, 34, 35*t*, 42–45, 43*f*, 44*f*. *See also* Student English Access Rooms

National Education Act, 32

The Native Nations of North America Series: Nations of the Northwest Coast, 58, 66

Needs assessment, 43*f*

Net Nanny, 281

New Beginnings, 61*f*, 62*f*, 63–65*f*

New Hampshire, 180. *See also* Ecological perspective

New Parade, 17, 19–26, 20*t*, 21*f*, 26–28, 29–30

NNES. *See* Nonnative-English-speaking students

No Child Left Behind Act, 102, 180, 202

Nonnative-English-speaking students, 53, 101, 127. *See also* Intensive English Program; International Baccalaureate Primary Years Programme; Thematic matrices

Number Jugglers: Math Card Games, 174

O

Observation, 24, 200

Opportunities Pre-Intermediate, 272

Oral Communication class

    Ami's Transcription and Fun Essay, 227*f*

    challenging discussion/debate in, 229–230

    Composition 1, 224*f*

    Compositions 2 and 3, 225*f*

    conclusions regarding, 231–232

    curriculum revitalization and, 210*t*

    curriculum revitalization (Project 1) and, 208–218

    curriculum revitalization (Project 2) and, 218–229

    introduction to, 205

    Modified Version of the Rubric for the Speaking Test, 222*t*

    Overview of Projects, 206*t*

P

Proficiency
    assessment of, 200
    vs. communication skills, 181
Pronunciation, Oral Communication class and, 222*t*
PYP. *See* International Baccalaureate Primary Years Programme

Q

Quality of Life Unit, 83–85, 90*f*, 92–100, 93–94*t*, 94–95*t*
Questionnaires, 36, 300–301

R

Read-alouds, 166–167, 194–197
Reading A to Z Web, 183
Reading development
    family participation and, 166–167, 172–173
    Intensive English Program and, 111–112*f*, 122*f*
Reading Families: The Literate Life of Urban Children, 167
Readinga-z.com, 203
Real-life application of learning. *See* Task-based learning
Record keeping, 24, 43*f*, 83
Recycling, cross-curricular integration and, 82, 84
Reflection. *See also* Evaluation
    International Baccalaureate Primary Years Programme and, 129
    Internet-based instruction and, 274–275
    professional development and, 256–257
    significance of, 6–7
Renewal, 6
Resistance, in United Arab Emirates, 22–24
Resources
    ecological perspective and, 203
    evaluation of, 254–255
    for humanities unit, 100
    International Baccalaureate Primary Years Programme and, 137–138
    Internet-based instruction and, 284
    SEARs and, 35*t*, 39*n*

S

T

Time considerations *(continued)*

    SEARs and, 46–47

    teachers and, 257

    thematic matrices and, 63–65*f*

Timetables, SEARs and, 41*f*

Title I, 183

Toronto, 239, 240*n*, 243–245. *See also* Professional development

Total physical response, 246

Training. *See* Professional development

Travel tracer, as literature circle role, 252*t*

TU. *See* Task of the Unit

Tundra, 186

U

Also Available From TESOL

CALL Environments: Research, Practice, and Critical Issues, 2nd ed.
Joy Egbert and E. Hanson-Smith, Editors

Content-Based Instruction in Primary and Secondary School Settings
Dorit Kaufman and JoAnn Crandall, Editors

Developing a New Curriculum for Adult Learners
Michael Carroll, Editor

ESOL Tests and Testing
Stephen Stoynoff and Carol A. Chapelle

Helping English Language Learners Succeed in Pre-K–12 Elementary Schools
Jan Lacina, Linda New Levine, and Patience Sowa

Helping English Language Learners Succeed in Middle and High Schools
F. Pawan and G. Sietman, Editors

Learning Languages through Technology
Elizabeth Hanson-Smith and Sara Rilling, Editors

Language Teacher Research in Asia
Thomas S. C. Farrell, Editor

Language Teacher Research in Europe
Simon Borg, Editor

Language Teacher Research in the Americas
Hedy McGarrell, Editor

Language Teacher Research in the Middle East
Christine Coombe and Lisa Barlow, Editors

Language Teacher Research in Australia and New Zealand
Jill Burton and Anne Burns, Editors

Literature in Language Teaching and Learning
Amos Paran, Editor

More Than a Native Speaker: An Introduction to Teaching English Abroad
revised edition
Don Snow

Perspectives on Community College ESL Series
Craig Machado, Series Editor
Volume 1: Pedagogy, Programs, Curricula, and Assessment
Marilynn Spaventa, Editor
Volume 2: Students, Mission, and Advocacy
Amy Blumenthal, Editor

PreK–12 English Language Proficiency Standards
Teachers of English to Speakers of Other Languages, Inc.

*Planning and Teaching Creatively within a Required Curriculum for
School-Age Learners*
Penny McKay, Editor

Revitalizing an Established Program for Adult Learners
Alison Rice, Editor

Teaching English as a Foreign Language in Primary School
Mary Lou McCloskey, Janet Orr, and Marlene Dolitsky, Editors

For more information, contact
Teachers of English to Speakers of Other Languages, Inc.
Publications Order Line: Toll Free 1-888-891-0041 (United States)
Local Phone: 240-243-2245 (metro Washington, DC area)
Outside U.S.: +1 (U.S. Country Code) 240-243-2245

ORDER ONLINE at www.tesol.org/

T E S O L